CLARKSON POTTER/PUBLISHERS

NEW YORK

THE ROADS TO ROME

Jarrett Wrisley
and Paolo Vitaletti

PHOTOGRAPHS BY JASON LANG

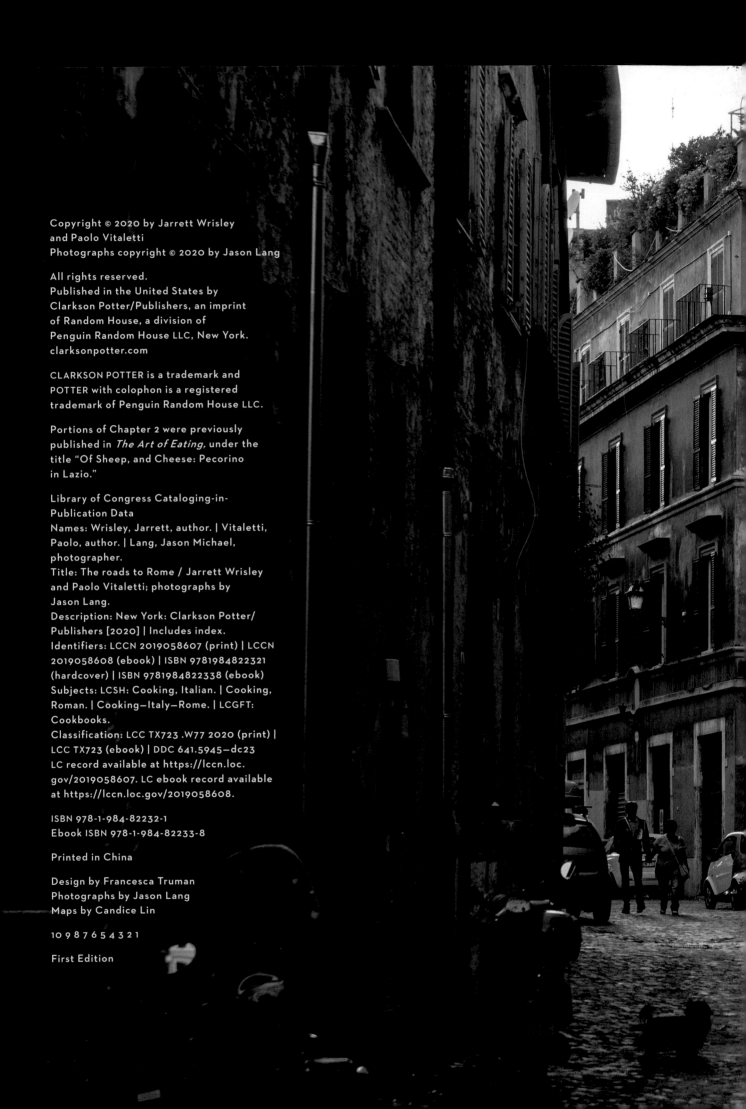

Published in the United States by
Clarkson Potter/Publishers, an imprint
of Random House, a division of
Penguin Random House LLC, New York.
clarksonpotter.com

CLARKSON POTTER is a trademark and
POTTER with colophon is a registered
trademark of Penguin Random House LLC.

Portions of Chapter 2 were previously
published in *The Art of Eating,* under the
title "Of Sheep, and Cheese: Pecorino
in Lazio."

Library of Congress Cataloging-in-
Publication Data
Names: Wrisley, Jarrett, author. | Vitaletti,
Paolo, author. | Lang, Jason Michael,
photographer.
Title: The roads to Rome / Jarrett Wrisley
and Paolo Vitaletti; photographs by
Jason Lang.
Description: New York: Clarkson Potter/
Publishers [2020] | Includes index.
Identifiers: LCCN 2019058607 (print) | LCCN
2019058608 (ebook) | ISBN 9781984822321
(hardcover) | ISBN 9781984822338 (ebook)
Subjects: LCSH: Cooking, Italian. | Cooking,
Roman. | Cooking—Italy—Rome. | LCGFT:
Cookbooks.
Classification: LCC TX723 .W77 2020 (print) |
LCC TX723 (ebook) | DDC 641.5945—dc23
LC record available at https://lccn.loc.
gov/2019058607. LC ebook record available
at https://lccn.loc.gov/2019058608.

ISBN 978-1-984-82232-1
Ebook ISBN 978-1-984-82233-8

Printed in China

Design by Francesca Truman
Photographs by Jason Lang
Maps by Candice Lin

10 9 8 7 6 5 4 3 2 1

First Edition

For our mothers

CONTENTS

INTRODUCTION

There were white puffs of pecorino on top of the sauce, sharp and sheeplike, and chewy tubes of rigatoni beneath, cut from old bronze dies. I was eating with my friend, business partner, and chef, Paolo Vitaletti, inside a basement restaurant built into Monte Testaccio, in Rome. We could see the room's crumbling walls, preserved behind a panel of glass, suggesting a catacomb more than a dining room. Those walls were made from the clay amphora, discarded and compacted over millennia, that had carried wines and olive oil from the fields of Lazio and beyond to Rome in ancient days. The provisions would arrive on boats along the Tiber or by carts on a road called the Via Appia. We were effectively eating inside a cave—a living relic of Rome's culinary past. A cave carved into Rome's grass-covered mountain of trash.

Seven years ago, Paolo and I opened a Roman restaurant in Bangkok, where we both live. Before we did, we thought it best to experience Roman and Italian food firsthand—and that subterranean restaurant happened to be where Paolo and I began our dig to unearth Rome's most celebrated recipes. After years of food criticism and magazine writing, I had a working familiarity with Italian cuisine. But I'd never had a guide quite like Paolo, who grew up among the butcher shops and bakeries of Testaccio, and later, in the nearby suburb of Falcognana. Paolo is the

sort who looks affectionately at a fine ham; when he speaks of his mother's cooking, he becomes visibly wistful. He has a constant longing to eat his own cuisine, and to share his knowledge of it. Through his guidance, and my own realization of the breadth and beauty of Italian products, not to mention the quiet reverie of eating them, something rather simple—a trip to Rome, a few meals at the best trattorias—became a bit more complicated. I had always liked to know where food comes from, but a meal in Rome opens so many windows into the past. Just as the architecture—the monuments and ruins—speaks of great empires and eras of despair, so too, does the food. This connection of history, taste, and memory was fascinating to me. I was hooked.

And so before we opened our restaurant, Appia, Paolo and I set out to unwind and tease out our understanding of this cuisine, like so many strands of pasta wrapped around a fork. When you ask a Roman why they eat this thing or that, answers come naturally. "Ham should be from Norcia," they might say, casually, or, "We've always eaten fried artichokes, because of the Jewish ghetto here." This is perfectly fine if you're Roman, but I'm not. So we needed to dig a little deeper. Paolo and I set off to research the food of Rome and the surrounding countryside together. To forge bonds with farmers and cheesemakers, and to cook in village kitchens. At first, for our restaurant. But as we traveled, it became clear that the journey we were on was something we wanted to share, beyond the walls of our restaurant.

That's what started this long affair in Italy. Of traveling down the roads that led out from Rome, and into the countryside. Of farmers and shepherds and ancient mountain paths. Of sleeping in caves, and stealing peas for supper. Of sheep, and of meat.

Of understanding.

A month after our first trip—which led us to Norcia, a town hours to the northeast that is the home of Rome's butchery tradition, and then later on to Tuscany and Emilia-Romagna—we sat in a coffee shop, agonizing over the name of our restaurant. For months, we'd been making porchetta, stuffing and sewing up pork bellies and loins, piercing the pig's thick skin and pulling the butcher's string tight. Afternoons were spent kneading pasta dough and cooking ragù over a lazy flame, preparing to open a Roman trattoria whose name still evaded us. "I was an ambitious chef," Paolo says, "and after fourteen years in five-star hotel kitchens, I finally had a chance to cook the kind of food that moved me—the food I grew up on. We

had to get this one right." Together, we wanted to create a distinct, regional, and uncompromising Italian restaurant.

I kept a notebook full of names. Porcello. Posto. Taverna. Finocchio. Fatto. Every time I thought I had a great one, Paolo told me it didn't sound right. Each time Paolo thought he'd nailed it, I told him it was too difficult to pronounce.

"What about . . . Appia?" he said.

The name is derived from the Via Appia, the ancient Roman highway that connected Rome to the South, and to the Adriatic Sea, and it ran behind Paolo's old house. He squinted his eyes, picturing the word in print, seeing if it fit. I loved its symmetry.

—

A few years ago, I was sitting behind the bar at Appia with Paolo. It was a gentle night, the kind of night in a restaurant where you can relax at the bar while keeping one eye on the room, or take off early and watch a movie with your wife, or maybe walk through a menu change. But instead, I poured two glasses of wine, and our conversation, and our mindset, began to drift back toward Italy.

As Paolo spoke, he sliced pieces of ham. Occasionally, he'd pass me one.

It had become clear—to Paolo, at least—that in our trips through Italy, we had a book on our hands, and that we needed to pursue it.

It was his stubborn persistence, rather than my own, that pushed us forward at first. I wanted to learn more so that I could understand the specific mechanisms of Italian cooking as comfortably as I had Chinese or Thai. I hadn't written professionally in a few years, save for several short magazine pieces. The idea of sitting behind a keyboard, chasing down adjectives, or combing the corners of my memory for similes, was anxiety inducing. (It still is.)

The greatest trick a writer employs is connecting one idea to the next, I explained to Paolo. And when you're out of practice, the storytelling process takes time. The transitions from one idea to another—once as effortless as a chef chopping an onion—suddenly become clumsy. We needed a strong structure, I argued. If not, this book wouldn't make it past the first draft.

"Let's drive down the Appia," he said. "All the way to Brindisi. We'll eat anchovies and the best semolina pasta, and burrata, and tomatoes . . . and meet some people we need to meet. The roads, Jarrett. The roads. We've been in Rome so many times. Let's explore."

That night I returned home and started to read a few of my favorite food writers. I paced around my small office, stacked with books and notes about cooking across the Mediterranean. I cracked open an ancient Roman cookery book, and another about shepherds and cheese. And though I'm not sure where I saw it, I came across an illustrated map of the Via Appia Antica.

It snaked south through the flats of Lazio, where beside it there were crude illustrations of sheep. And then, south of Naples it dipped past the ancient ruins of Paestum, where poorly drawn buffalo stood by the roadside. There were anchovies splashing in the Amalfi waters, and tomatoes growing just over the coast, near the outline of Vesuvius. All things we use in our food, and all along an ancient highway we'd named our restaurant for. That road fed the old empire through its expansion eastward, and through many centuries helped shape a cuisine. It was both a way forward, and a route to retrace the past. It was a means to explain the food we served, and it is, ultimately, the story of this book.

Roman food is mostly very rustic and simple. It is a product of the countryside, from the regions of Lazio, Campania, Umbria, and Abruzzo. It is a cuisine which has sprung from ancient traditions of shepherding and farming. It is mozzarella,

salted codfish, anchovies, and artichokes. It is lamb, and pecorino cheese, semolina, ricotta, and guanciale. Platters of salumi, hand-cut fettuccine with a piquant ragù, and nose-to-tail mains. Meat that is to be cut with a sharp knife, rather than surrender to the pressures of a fork.

Looking at that dinky little map I found somewhere on the internet, I finally saw it: *The Roads to Rome*. A journey along the trails that fed the capital of an empire, that forever shaped the cuisine of the city. What would we see, traveling these roads? What would we taste? The only way, it dawned on me, to begin to understand the food of Rome is to try to understand the food all along the roads to Rome. And so the roads themselves became our guide. They wound through mountain towns and seaside ports. These roads, still intact after the fall of the empire, remained conduits for trade. And so we would go down them, too.

I called Paolo and Jason Lang, our friend and photographer, the following day, and we began to formulate a return to Italy. I printed out that map of the Via Appia Antica, and plotted points along its course that would lead us to food staples along the way. We'd already been working with a few of the producers for years; but now we would go see them, and cook with them, and connect our story with their past.

That last trip—before we shot the recipe photos for this book—all seemed to come into focus in a little Chinese restaurant near my house in Bangkok. I laid the map on the table, and we all riffed on how the Appia's influence wound its way through Roman cooking, and how it had been there all along—too close to our noses to see, perhaps.

We left lunch with a lightness. That feeling one gets before a long journey; the promise that lies in traveling down a road one wants to know.

The book you hold in your hands is organized by the routes in the surrounding regions that historically brought cooks and products to Rome. Over the course of five years, we started in the city, then traveled

north into the mountains, up to Tuscany, Umbria, and Abruzzo, and then southward through Campania and Puglia, to the sea. In a classic Roman trattoria you'll eat hams from Umbria, salumi and cheese from Lazio, burrata from Puglia, and anchovies from Campania. So we went to those places. In these pages there are dozens of recipes that one might find in restaurants in Rome, which have been brought there over generations by restaurant chefs and grandmothers alike. Interspersed with these recipes—created by Paolo both in the restaurant and while on the road—are stories of farmers, cheesemakers, shepherds, and butchers.

We'll creep through the coops of Tuscan eggman Paolo Parisi, whose chickens are fed on sheep's milk, their eggs flown in pillows to Michelin-starred restaurants around the world. We open hams and great wheels of cheese with Claudio Volpetti, the last of an old guard of passionate, engaged shopkeepers whose eye for quality led us on our own quest for edible treasures.

The recipes in *The Roads to Rome* focus on the classics you'd eat in a home kitchen or at a traditional trattoria in or around Rome. But we went to their source. We'll show you how Paolo's mother carefully kneads her pasta, the way she has each afternoon for fifty-five years, sensing for doneness in the dough as it resists her fingertips. We'll show you how only a few ingredients—salted pork, cured sheep cheese, black pepper, and eggs—can coalesce into a perfect carbonara, with a little patience. If you want to know why vignarola—a dish of fava beans, artichokes, white wine, and peas—is so sacred to those in Lazio, you might walk with us through the fields, stealing peas and beans from a lazy farmer before they rot, then return home to cook them. We logged thousands of miles chasing history, as the trunk of our car filled with cheeses and meats and pastas and oils. It has been such a great privilege to explore this vast universe of Italian food traditions, and to meet the people who create it, and to bring those stories to you.

Because food, like great stories, is better off shared.

One

THE ROADS
NORTH AND EAST:
UMBRIA,
EMILIA-ROMAGNA,
AND TUSCANY

OUR STUDY, at first, was simply about the food of Rome, before the roads led us elsewhere. There was no road map. Just a desire to learn, and a hungry sort of wanderlust.

I still remember our first night in Rome clear as yesterday, as Paolo and I searched for a place to park. After circling the neighborhood of Testaccio, we wedged our Fiat into a crooked slot in the median, as one does there. It was late, and there was a chill in the air. Many restaurants were closed, and a few gruffly turned us away. We ended up at a restaurant called Flavio al Velavevodetto.

A plate of cold cuts and bread came first. There were salamis, thick with cubes of fat, and lardo, cured from the backs of pigs, and pickles. Then *insalata di nervetti*, a salad made from the tendons of a cow. We ordered three pastas. ("Just to try!" Paolo said.) There was a platter of *abbacchio*, pieces of the baby lamb cooked *scotaditto* style—seared on the flattop grill—with the sweetbreads and some intestine, and just a sprinkling of salt, a drizzle of olive oil, and rosemary. There was also *coratella*—the lungs, liver, heart, and kidneys of a calf. I cannot remember if we ate dessert, as I had reached that state of fullness where pain and pleasure seem to meet.

And then there was grappa. The waiter placed a bottle of the unforgiving white spirit on the table, and I poured our first glass. It's a *digestivo*—a sip of something hard and hot, meant to help your body digest. We'd eaten so much, they didn't charge us for it. So we drank another glass. Then we had an espresso, followed by another grappa. I hoped the alcohol might penetrate the fortified wall of starch, meat, and cheese in my stomach. As the chef turned off the lights to the kitchen, and the waiters looked at us grumpily, the bottle of grappa was nearly gone. While the liquor did its work, we hatched a plan.

We decided that we would drive north and east, out of Rome. Paolo wanted to show me the region his father was from, where the meats and many cheeses we had just eaten were produced. We called a cab, too tipsy to whip around Rome's narrow streets in our ragged Fiat. The next day, we gingerly returned to the illegal parking spot. There was no ticket in the window. Paolo smiled, we popped the purple car off the curb, and hit the road.

Paolo's father, Guido Vitaletti, was from Le Marche, the region far to the east of Rome, across the Apennine mountain range. As a young man, he slowly made his way westward, to the city, stopping in towns like Norcia and Amatrice. These places not only loomed large in Paolo's mind, but, I would learn, were also essential to the art of butchery, animal husbandry, and the development of Rome's cuisine. And so we went to them to eat, and to understand where the Roman culture of meat had come from. We followed the Via Salaria upward and eastward, through Tivoli, Rieti, and then the hilltop town of Amatrice. We ended up in Umbria. We stayed in the town of Norcia for several days, tasting hams and salamis, and cooking dinner on cold nights on a woodstove. There, we walked through forests of dangling hams that age in small factories, and also met independent, artisanal butchers whose salamis drape from the cobwebbed archways of caves.

After a long drive over mountain passes, we found ourselves in Visso, exploring the tiny production of one of Italy's most famed artisanal butchers, who produces ciausculo, a raw, sweet, spreadable sausage made safe with salt, the unique climate, and a few centuries of experience.

On the way back from Visso, we passed the town of Castelluccio, where the *lenticchie*, or lentils, spill down the sides of rounded mountains in an otherworldly valley. They bloom purple and yellow, like a technicolor quilt. The lentils are delicate, tiny, and very tender and precious to Italians. The recipes from this area—stews of lentils and beans, chicken liver crostini, rabbit cooked in the hunter style—are rich and rustic.

From Umbria, we took a detour to a special restaurant—Amerigo dal 1934—which in many ways inspired our own restaurant. We ended up in Bologna one dreary night, before heading back south, to Tuscany, to meet with Paolo Parisi, who makes some of Italy's finest ham and strangest eggs. We came for a day to see his chickens; we ended up staying nearly a week. This chapter will describe in detail the products from these places, and how to cook the rich, soulful food of this part of Italy—a place that had, over centuries, changed the food of Rome and, today, can change one's perceptions of its origins.

On Norcia, and Butcher Shops, and Salumi

Our drive from Rome northeast to Norcia began with a small detour to the Castelli Romani—the "Roman Castles"—several small towns that are perched on the steep Alban Hills. The most famous, Castel Gandolfo, has been the pope's summer residence for the past five hundred years. Climb up the stairs and you're greeted with an astonishing sight: the sapphire volcanic crater of Lake Albano, the surrounding towns, and the isolated palazzo that hugs the walls of the crater. This string of small towns once supplied Rome with much of its wine and freshwater fish. The Via Appia runs right below the center of Castel Gandolfo, straight to the center of Rome.

We continued past Castel Gandolfo, in search of sandwiches.

A few minutes later we arrived in the town of Ariccia, which claims porchetta—the whole, crisp-skinned, deboned, fennel-and-garlic-stuffed pig—as its own. We ate focaccia stuffed with it and stared out over the plain toward the sea. Then we stopped at a *fraschetta*, a place that is more like a permanent picnic than a restaurant, for a few jugs of fizzy orange wine, some cold cuts, and cheese. A man played the accordion, and Romans drank too much and sang songs. It was utterly charming—a rare glimpse of Roman life that seemed untouched by the mass tourism of the city's center.

After lunch, we angled north, toward Florence and the old Via Cassia, before veering east onto the SS4, heading toward Norcia. Since the times of ancient Rome, this route—the Via Salaria—had been used to transport salt, first by the Sabines, a thousand years before Christ, from the flats near the city's main port of Ostia—up and over the Apennine mountains, which began to appear on the horizon as we headed east.

The landscape changed with every hour we drove. The pignoli—the grand, broccoli-like stone pines of the flats—lead to the Alban Hills, where olives and grapes hang off the hillsides. We dropped back down into the pines, before rising up again into more rugged, temperate central Lazio. Then it all became alpine. Two hours into our trip, the temperature had dropped twenty degrees. Every coffee shop on the side of the SS4 was also a butcher shop; they had started as *poste*, or trading posts—places for travelers to eat, sleep, and then continue on their journey.

I had been curious about Norcia for years. Rome is a city of cured pork; of hams and salumi and especially guanciale, the jowl of the pig that is shaped like a slimmer American football, cured in salt and pepper, and hung from the rafters of *norcineria*. The butcher shops in Rome mostly bear this name—which means "of Norcia"—though the town lies about a hundred miles to the northeast, in Perugia. The great Roman pastas—carbonara, amatriciana, and gricia—all begin with cubes of this cured pork. So it is difficult to separate the trade of the *norcino*, the pork butchers of Norcia, from the classic dishes of Rome. One exists because of the other.

Norcia sits along the Via Salaria, in a cool, dry mountain valley thick with wild boars called *cinghiale*, and meadows perfect for pasturing sheep. Transhumance—the seasonal moving of sheep from north to south, and back, across vast stretches of the country—has occurred here for millennia. The paths have been worn bare over the centuries by shepherds who wound through mountain passes and grassy valleys, where roads were later cut. Beasts can roam and eat freely here. Norcia's unique location provides a rare combination of grass and space, and an ideal temperature to age cheeses and meats after slaughter. Add to that the salt that traversed the Via Salaria, and this tiny town became a center of butchery and curing.

We arrived at Norcia as the sun was disappearing behind the rolling hills to the west. Though it was late April, the air was brisk. Norcia is a fortified city, with steep mountains behind it, to the north and east. Once you enter through the thick, twenty-foot-high walls, a leathery scent fills the streets. It's the smell of pork, slowly curing in shop after shop. The toothy heads of wild boar hang on the butcher shop walls and glare at passersby.

We lit a small fire at a house we'd rented and Paolo and I walked out to the compact square. (Buildings in Norcia cannot exceed three stories, due to a papal decree from 1859, to save structures from the frequent earthquakes there.) The Cathedral of Saint Benedict, beautifully simple, built in smooth marble, caught the last rays of the sun. Water trickled from public fountains, beside large, head-high iron rings, where horses would have been tied. (Sadly, the cathedral was a victim of an earthquake that struck six months after our visit, on October 30, 2016.)

That evening, the temperature dropped close to freezing. We stoked the fire again in the woodstove, and cooked an impromptu stew of local lentils, beans, and *cicerchie*, a pulse I'd never seen before, with thick slices of guanciale, a little carrot and celery, and fennel-laced sausages. It was a perfect expression of place— of things cured and dried and stored for the winter months. We washed it down with cups of Sagrantino di Montefalco—a warming, almost viscous red wine with a rough tannic structure that complemented the sturdy stew. It is not a kind wine in its youth, but it suits the climate and the rustic food here.

The following morning, a Sunday, we wandered through thickets of aging hams—literally thousands—at Lanzi, one of Norcia's commercial producers of salumi. Two old men sat in a parking lot, smoking and sipping coffee. One of them was the owner, Signor Lanzi, who allowed us to enter his sprawling warehouse of hams, unattended. We began in an industrial-sized elevator full of meat hooks that brought us (and pigs) to the second floor. Hundreds of young hams sat in a cold room covered in salt. There were rooms where they are left to age for eighteen months. Paolo wandered, wide-eyed, smiling at the maturing hunks of pork. It was important for us to see this, to see the pride and the industriousness as well as the tradition in this food; I later learned from a supplier that we had been slicing Lanzi's hams, behind our counter in Bangkok, for nearly two years.

Outside the factory is a small store where customers arrived to buy strings of sausages, pancetta, and baskets of ricotta. Signor Lanzi, who has the air of a man who came from little but now has a lot, sat and smiled.

On Monday morning, we drove out of Norcia. We took a roundabout route, cresting a steep mountain pass near the hilltop town of Castelluccio. The landscape here is severe; steep, treeless peaks slide down into a flat, open valley. This is where Italy's most prized lentils are grown. They're delicate with thin skins that surrender quickly while cooking. Castelluccio sits on a pyramid of earth in a dramatic valley that fills with flowers in late spring, as the lentils take root.

We marveled at that mountain village, and looped around through another mountainous traverse, then drove downward into a deep ravine where Visso lies. It's a medieval place. Sober limestone buildings and archways snake around the village. A cold, rushing stream creates a natural border between the town and the surrounding mountains of Umbria and Le Marche, to the east. Paolo's father was born just over the ridge.

In a cave, lit by the blue light of a bug zapper, butcher Giorgio Calabro showed us salumi. Meats were haphazardly strung from the ceiling. A few flies buzzed around, but otherwise it was quiet. Because spring was just beginning here, up in the cold mountains, the butcher hadn't begun his slaughter.

When we left the caves, it was 3 p.m. and nearly dark. A few children ran around the gloomy square, eating gelato in the cold. We filled our car with sheep ham, and a slightly aged sausage called *ciauscolo*, seasoned with pepper and garlic. Rarely aged more than a month, it's more pâté than sausage. Both of us were transfixed by Calabro's operation—how his means of production hasn't wavered for generations.

Night falls early in Visso. And so we wound back through the tunnels that split the steep mountains, back to Norcia. We ate lentils, and fettuccine with wild boar ragù, and later, tried to keep warm beneath the covers.

PORCHETTA, LIKE IN ROME
CRISP-SKINNED ROLLED PORK ROAST

serves at least 10 as a main course

Filling

1/2 POUND PORK LIVER

1 LARGE WHITE ONION, JULIENNED

1/4 CUP OLIVE OIL

1 BAY LEAF

3 SAGE LEAVES

SALT AND PEPPER

1 CUP DRY WHITE WINE

Roast

8 POUNDS PORK BELLY WITH THE LOIN ATTACHED, SKIN-ON *(see note)*

KOSHER SALT

8 GARLIC CLOVES, SLICED VERY THIN

1 TABLESPOON GROUND BLACK PEPPER

1 1/2 TABLESPOONS FENNEL SEED POWDER OR 1 TEASPOON FENNEL POLLEN

2 TABLESPOONS CHOPPED FRESH DILL

2 TABLESPOONS CHOPPED FRESH ROSEMARY

> ## *Note*
> This cut of pork belly may be special-ordered at a good butcher. If they are familiar with Italian cooking, you can tell them you want to make a porchetta. Barring that, get a 6-pound piece of skin-on pork belly, and 2 pounds of pork loin. Also note that you will need a few feet of butcher's twine for this.

In Ariccia, where we stopped on our drive to Norcia, the sight of a whole hog porchetta is something to behold. A whole, deboned pig, head on, is rolled around a dusting of garlic, salt, pepper, and fennel. It's sewn back up, and roasted until the skin crisps up and bubbles. Over the course of the day, it's sliced from back to front, slowly disappearing in the butcher's case. But each piece is different, depending on which part of the beast it came from. The version presented here, made from a loin and belly, is more consistent. We also add a bit of liver.

The oven you use will have a great effect on the result and the cooking time. You can cook it outdoors on a spit, over fire, in a conventional oven, in a rotisserie, or in a convection oven. At the restaurant, we use a big rotisserie, which helps the roast drip fat without creating smoke, and it spins in hot, dry air, aiding the crisping process. If you're making this in your oven at home, fill a drip pan with some water and place it underneath the roast to catch dripping fat and avoid scorching (and a very smoky kitchen). If you have a convection setting, please use it. It will help.

While the results on your first try will likely be delicious, it does take time to really master a porchetta. But once you do, you've basically got a restaurant on your hands. Which isn't always a good thing.

MAKE THE FILLING: First, clean the pork liver, removing veins, fat, and blood. Cut it into 1/2-inch cubes.

Place the onion in a heavy frying pan with the oil, bay leaf, and sage leaves, and place over medium heat. Cook down the onion, stirring, until the volume is reduced by half, and continue cooking until it starts to caramelize, about 15 minutes.

Add the liver, and some salt and pepper, and continue to cook until the liver is beginning to caramelize.

When the liver is cooked and brown, add the white wine and deglaze and let it cook for another 5 minutes, until the wine is well reduced and syrupy. Remove the bay leaf.

Put the mixture in a food processor or blender and blend to a paste. Taste for seasoning. Place in a container, and let it cool in the fridge.

MAKE THE ROAST: Place the open porchetta in front of you. If the loin is attached, make sure the loin side is closest to you. Cut a seam in the loin, about 1 to 2 inches deep, and season the inside with salt and pepper. If you have two pieces—one loin and one belly—do the same, but leave the loin separate from the belly for now.

Now, on the belly end of the piece of pork, using a sharp knife, separate the first layer of fat, just beneath the skin, from the skin. Do this about halfway through the belly, making sure not to pierce the skin and cut that fat away. This creates some space to roll and tie the porchetta tightly.

Season the meat well, on all sides, with salt. Smear the pork liver mixture on the belly, with your hands, and also inside the seam of the loin. You want to coat the inside of the belly with the mixture, but don't make it too thick or it will leak. Evenly scatter on the sliced garlic, black pepper, fennel, dill, and rosemary.

Roll the pork up, wrapping it over itself, starting with the loin side, until you have a nice, round roast, with skin all around. If your loin is separate, place it in the middle of the belly and roll it together, wrapping the belly around the loin.

Get someone to hold the two sides of the skin so that the "seam" of skin is as tight as possible, and facing upward.

Cut a length (about 18 inches) of kitchen twine, slide it under the skin and, very tightly, tie it in a knot. Work your way from one side to the other, while your helper holds the seam together. There should be about 8 strings on a roast this size. Just make sure it's tight—small bulges here and there are totally fine.

Salt the outside skin thoroughly—rubbing it with about 2 to 3 tablespoons of kosher salt—and place it on a roasting rack in your fridge, seam side down, overnight.

Preheat the oven to 325°F.

Roast the porchetta, seam side down on a rack over a sheet pan, for 2½ hours, or until it reaches an internal temperature of about 160°F (all ovens are different, so timing will vary, but good thermometers don't lie). Then raise the heat to 400°F, to crisp the skin. Again, timing will differ here depending on your oven and whether you have convection, so watch it cook, and don't burn it!

Remove the roast from the oven, let it rest for an hour, tented with foil. Slice, and serve.

A Proper Plate of Italian Cured Meats

Since we journeyed to Norcia, it seemed that a discussion on how we put together a fine platter of salumi is in order.

There is a common misconception—ushered in by introduction of the industrial meat slicer—that hams and salami should be paper thin and rolled into fleshy little blossoms, fashioned like roses, on a cutting board. And while that might look pretty, those translucent slices of salumi often lack the bite and flavor you can get by simply cutting meat with a sharp knife. (Also, if you're preslicing, hams and dry-cured salami get waxy and dry when presliced thinly.) If you buy a few pieces of meat and cut by hand, while it might look less artful, the flavor and texture of your meats will often be better. There are exceptions, like coppa, which can become tough if cut too thick.

There is a logic when assembling an arrangement of cold cuts—you want a variety of flavors, textures, and levels of intensity. You should include at least one heavily spiced sausage—a spicy salami, or maybe a boar sausage, laced with licorice-like fennel. There ought to be another salami that's dried and cured with salt and pepper, without chili. We always include headcheese on our cold-cut plate, because Paolo and I both love the offsetting textures of gelatin from the brawn and the meaty goodness from the cheeks and other bits of the head. Don't forget to add something luxuriously fatty, either lardo, guanciale, pancetta, or coppa, made from the salted and sliced neck and shoulder of the pig. Round this out with some very good, raw leg ham—we serve prosciutto di Norcia at Appia, but prosciutto di Parma or Toscana ham are also very fine. Mortadella is a crowd-pleaser, so throw some of that on, too. (Whole mortadella are huge, so a few slices from the supermarket are perfect. We prefer those with green bits of pistachio that pepper the filling.) My favorite thing on the cold-cut plate at our restaurant doesn't come from a master of salumi but is, in fact, leftovers: cold porchetta (see page 28) works wonderfully as a salumi, as it's sweet with fennel and salty and has a nice rim of fat that surrounds tender meat and a crisp skin that transforms into a chewy, caramelized casing after resting in the fridge.

PICKLES AND MARINATED VEGETABLES, TO SERVE WITH YOUR SALUMI

Make sure you always serve your meats with bread and a few pickles and marinated vegetables, to offset the richness and saltiness. Cold cuts are preserved with salt and often nitrates, and some contain nearly as much fat as meat. Because of the nature of salumi, it is best to serve it with something sour, refreshing, or bitter, in order to stimulate your palate. Olives are appropriate. But these marinated vegetables are easy to prepare at home. They also have the benefit of being preserved in pickling liquid or under oil, so they will last for a week or more in your fridge.

PEPERONI ARROSTITI SOTT'OLIO
ROASTED RED PEPPERS IN OLIVE OIL

makes about 1½ quarts

2 POUNDS FIRM BELL PEPPERS (MOSTLY RED WITH A FEW YELLOW MIXED IN FOR COLOR)

2 OR 3 LARGE GARLIC CLOVES, VERY FINELY CHOPPED, OR GRATED WITH A MICROPLANE

¼ CUP FINELY CHOPPED FRESH ITALIAN PARSLEY

2 SALTED ANCHOVY FILLETS, CHOPPED

SALT AND PEPPER TO TASTE

2 CUPS EXTRA-VIRGIN OLIVE OIL, OR AS NEEDED (A MILD ONE, NOT AN EXPENSIVE FINISHING OIL)

1 TABLESPOON WHITE WINE VINEGAR

"I have vivid memories—flashbacks—of the smell of peppers burning on the stove in Latina," Paolo says. "My aunt lived there, near the sea, and my mother and my aunt would cook. During the summer, we would move there, and everyone in my family would stay for a few months, and this was something the family would make together."

There is really no match for the long, fleshy red and yellow bell peppers one can buy in Italy. They are sugar-sweet but also slightly bitter, and enormous.

That said, smaller bell peppers will taste just as good, and we use them in our restaurant. Homemade roasted peppers are infinitely better than the ones you'll find in the supermarket. With this recipe, you taste the smoke from the fire, the green herbaceousness of the oil, a hint of umami from the anchovies, and spice from fresh garlic. They neatly offset the saltiness of cold cuts, with freshness and sweet acidity. Make your own. They're a wonderful condiment.

Burn your peppers deeply. This is best done on a grill over hot coals but you can also do it on a gas stovetop, or in your broiler at the highest heat possible, turning occasionally. If you do it on a stove, place the peppers directly over the flames, on the rings where a pot might be. When all their sides are burned, burn the tops, then the bottoms, and place them in a metal mixing bowl and quickly cover tightly with plastic wrap to steam and loosen the skins.

When the peppers are cool enough to handle, but still very warm, remove the core first, then open flat pieces of peppers on a cutting board, skin side up, and peel the skin off gently with the tips of your fingers. (If the skin doesn't slip off easily, the peppers are probably undercooked.) The stubborn bits of burnt skin should release if you lightly scrape them with the dull side of a knife.

Slice the peppers into ½-inch-wide strips.

Add the chopped garlic, parsley, and anchovies to a mixing bowl, and mash them with the back of a spoon into a rough paste. Add the peppers and toss. Season with a good amount of salt and just a little pepper, and taste. Pour in the olive oil and vinegar. They will keep, covered with plastic wrap, for at least 2 weeks in the fridge if the oil covers the peppers. Make sure to remove them an hour before serving, so that they can reach room temperature, and the oil can soften from solid to liquid.

GIARDINIERA

makes about 3 quarts of pickles

2 CUPS BROCCOLI ROMANESCO
(OR BROCCOLI) FLORETS
(see note)

2 CUPS CAULIFLOWER FLORETS

1 RED BELL PEPPER, CUT INTO
1-INCH SQUARES

1 YELLOW BELL PEPPER, CUT
INTO 1-INCH SQUARES

¼ FENNEL BULB, CUT INTO
½-INCH-WIDE STRIPS

¼ CUP DICED WHITE OR RED
ONIONS

½ CUP RADISHES

⅓ CUP FRENCH GREEN BEANS

FRESH DILL SPRIGS, THICK
STEMS REMOVED

3 CUPS WHITE WINE VINEGAR

½ CUP SUGAR

½ CUP DIAMOND CRYSTAL
KOSHER SALT (⅓ CUP IF USING
MORTON KOSHER)

Note

Romanesco looks like the alien, angular spawn of broccoli and cauliflower, and is very commonly eaten around Rome. If you can't find broccoli romanesco, you can use broccoli, but it doesn't hold up quite as well to pickling.

This is a classic Italian pickle preparation: not-quite-sweet and not-entirely-sour. These flash-pickled vegetables are colorful and refreshing; feel free to add a pinch of chili flakes to your pickling liquid if you'd like a spicy bite with your giardiniera.

Evenly divide the vegetables and dill into quart pickling jars or another container with an airtight lid.

To make the pickling liquid, combine the vinegar, 2 cups water, sugar, and salt in a medium saucepan over high heat and bring to a boil, then remove from heat. Pour the hot pickling liquid over your vegetables.

For the best texture, chill the vegetables and pickling liquid in a larger bowl of ice water, in order to quickly get the liquid cold. When it's cool, seal the jars or container, and place in the fridge.

The giardiniera will be best after a week—but it will be good after one or two days. It can last, refrigerated, for several weeks.

MELANZANE SOTT'OLIO
GRILLED, MARINATED EGGPLANT

makes about 1½ quarts

2 POUNDS LONG PURPLE
EGGPLANTS, OR FAT, ROUND
ONES

COARSE SALT

2 OR 3 LARGE GARLIC CLOVES,
CHOPPED

¼ CUP PARSLEY, LIGHTLY
PACKED AND CHOPPED

GENEROUS PINCH OF DRIED
OREGANO

1½ TEASPOONS CHILI FLAKES

EXTRA-VIRGIN OLIVE OIL, TO
COVER

Paolo's lived outside Italy for almost twenty years, and like anyone—even though he's a professional chef—he still misses his mother's cooking. "On my way home from Italy, I would always bring back my mother's roasted eggplant. It just tasted different when it was made with her hands. This is her recipe," he says. Years ago, when I first met Paolo, he pulled a plastic container of these out of a suitcase, with a loaf of bread.

This is something we always keep on hand at our restaurant. The same was true at Paolo's childhood home. It uses extra-virgin olive oil, and, if seasoned correctly, it's perfect (don't be shy with the salt and chili). What you want here is a slippery, delicious slice of eggplant that is spicy from both the raw garlic and the chili, sweet from the vegetable itself, smoky from the stove, and a bit bitter from its skin. The eggplant will be gobbled up with cold cuts but is just as welcome on a sandwich, or with burrata and tomatoes, or in salads, or as bruschetta with anchovies, or simply on its own. Versatility at your fingertips.

Slice the eggplants lengthwise into planks about ¼ inch thick.

Get a large cast-iron pan very hot, over medium-high heat. Do not add oil to the pan, but rather salt the pan, so the grains are equally scattered across the bottom of the pan, like a dusting of sand, then lay in as many slices of eggplant as will fit comfortably. Scorch them, and turn them as they start to char. You want a lot of dark color on each side, but do not let them actually burn fully black. Cook all the eggplant slices this way, making sure to add salt to the pan between each round.

When all the eggplant is cooked, start to layer it in a small (8 × 8-inch) casserole: Place a single layer in the bottom of the casserole. Season evenly with salt (taste first, to see if it's needed), then sprinkle with some of the garlic, parsley, oregano, and chili, and cover with a generous pour of olive oil.

Repeat this process until all your eggplant slices are gone. You'll have something like a lasagna of marinated eggplant. Make sure there's a thin layer of olive oil on top to preserve them. Under oil, these will last 2 weeks in the refrigerator.

PASTA ALLA NORCINA CON PRIMO SALE

PASTA, LIKE IN NORCIA, WITH SHEEP CHEESE

serves 4 as a main course,
or 6 as a starter

SALT AND PEPPER

6 OUNCES FRESH PORCINI
MUSHROOMS, OR OTHER
FLAVORFUL WILD MUSHROOMS
IN SEASON

2 TABLESPOONS EXTRA-VIRGIN
OLIVE OIL, PLUS MORE IF
NEEDED

1/2 POUND NORCIA (OR SWEET
ITALIAN) SAUSAGE, CUT INTO
1-INCH-THICK SLICES

3 1/2 OUNCES SMOKED HAM

3 OUNCES PEAS (PREFERABLY
FRESH)

14 OUNCES TUBETTI, MEZZE
MANICHE, OR PENNE PASTA (OR
ANY SMALL TUBULAR DRIED
PASTA)

2 TABLESPOONS BUTTER

FRESH THYME LEAVES, TO
TASTE

1/4 CUP GRATED PRIMO SALE
CHEESE OR ANOTHER MILD
SHEEP CHEESE

Inside the walls of a medieval town like Norcia, there are no supermarkets. This is bad when you want water or milk, or cheap beers and cereal, but good when you want a delicious dinner. It forces you to cook simply, with whatever artisanal ingredients are available. But if you're going out to dinner, there is a pasta dish on nearly every restaurant's menu there, called pasta alla Norcina, which means literally, "pasta in the style of Norcia." It's full of cream and sausage, befitting the town's history of butchery. But it took a while for us to get Paolo to cook it.

He really didn't want to do it. Paolo's cooking has a certain Roman sensibility that I've come to understand. One aspect of it is that he hates cream in pasta; I've never seen him use it. "They didn't use cream before," he explained. "It's a recent thing." (He also muttered something about it being a trashy pub pasta. "It's an alfredo with sausage, dude." I tend to like those sorts of things, so this didn't sway me. I also tried ordering it in Il Clown, the pub next to where we were staying, and they didn't have it. "This is a very sophisticated pub," Paolo explained. It wasn't.)

But because this chapter is devoted to Norcia, and the lands surrounding it, I twisted his arm, and he finally made a pasta that's inspired by the alla Norcina. It uses primo sale—a sheep cheese that undergoes a quick salting and aging process, like a young pecorino—instead of cream. The rest remains, mostly, the same as the original (though Paolo added peas for brightness). And it's delicious.

Bring a pot of water to boil for the pasta, and salt it well.

Cut the mushrooms into 1/2-inch dice. Add the olive oil to a large, heavy-bottomed sauté pan, and set over medium-high heat.

Brown the mushrooms in the pan. Let the mushrooms cling to the pan for a minute or two before agitating them; you need to get the water out and then continue browning them until deeply caramelized. Timing will differ depending on the type of mushroom, so keep an eye on it. Add more olive oil if the mushrooms have swallowed all the oil. Season with salt and pepper.

Add the sausage and the ham to the pan and brown these as well.

Blanch the peas for 1 minute in the boiling water. Remove the peas with a slotted spoon and reserve. (If you're using frozen peas rather than fresh, there's no need to blanch, but do defrost them first.)

Add the pasta to the boiling water and cook until al dente as you sauté the mushrooms and pork. (When cooking the pasta, take a coffee cup and dunk it into the starchy water when the pasta is nearly done. You won't burn your hands, and now you have a starchy medium to thicken your sauce. Usually, you'll need about ¼ cup to emulsify a quick pasta like this, but you'll need to use your intuition.) Drain the pasta.

When the mushrooms, ham, and sausage are browned, add the peas and sauté for 1 minute. Then add the pasta, the butter, and enough reserved pasta water to create a light, emulsified sauce; shake the pan so that the fats and the water become one.

Season with thyme and salt and pepper to taste. Finally, stir in the cheese so that it blends into the sauce.

FAGIOLI CON LE COTICHE

BEANS COOKED WITH HAM SKIN

*serves 4 as a main course,
or 8 as a starter or side dish*

1/2 POUND CURED HAM SKIN

EXTRA-VIRGIN OLIVE OIL, AS
NEEDED

1 GARLIC CLOVE

1/3 CUP VERY FINELY DICED
CARROT

1/3 CUP VERY FINELY DICED
CELERY

1/3 CUP VERY FINELY DICED
ONION

PINCH OF CHILI FLAKES

THICK STRIP OF LEMON ZEST
(FROM ABOUT 1/4 LEMON)

1 FRESH ROSEMARY SPRIG

2 BAY LEAVES

6 1/2 CUPS VEGETABLE STOCK
OR WATER, PLUS MORE IF
NECESSARY

1 (14-OUNCE) CAN SAN
MARZANO TOMATOES, CRUSHED
BY HAND

1 POUND DRIED BORLOTTI
BEANS, RINSED, PICKED FREE
OF STONES, AND SOAKED IN
COLD WATER OVERNIGHT

GREMOLATA *(recipe follows)*,
FOR SERVING

Raw hams, cured with salt, are available in a multitude of styles across Italy. Their skin isn't really edible if just sliced along with the meat. It's leathery, salty, and tough. So it's cut away.

"In my father's shop—he was a *norcino*—we would sell a lot of prosciutto, so we had a lot of leftover skin. And we would eat it often," Paolo tells me. When you braise ham skin with beans, everything coalesces into a silky, earthy, fatty sort of thing. The skin becomes soft, and its fat melts and then seasons the beans. After a slow simmer, it becomes delicious. And when done with love, rather special.

What you're looking for here is a few ribbons of cotiche (the name for the skin), and a lot of beans, and, if you're feeling fancy, a finish of nice gremolata or just a scrape of lemon zest from a Microplane and a circular benediction of good olive oil. One more thing: After I've cultivated a relationship with a butcher, they've always given me the skin for free. Don't be afraid to ask yours for some.

Bring a small saucepan of water to a boil, add the ham skin, turn the heat down to a simmer, and cook about 1 hour, until softened. Add water to the pot if needed to keep the ham skin submerged. Strain the skin and, when cool enough to handle, slice it into 1/4-inch-thick ribbons. Discard the cloudy ham water.

Place a large, heavy-bottomed pot on the stove. Add some olive oil to coat the pot, and the clove of garlic. Heat over medium heat until the garlic browns, then remove and discard it. Add the carrot, celery, and onion and cook, stirring, for about 10 minutes, until well softened. If they start to brown, lower the heat.

Add the chili flakes, lemon zest, and the cooked ham skin. Cook for another 3 minutes over medium heat. Then add the rosemary, bay leaves, vegetable stock, tomatoes, and beans.

(recipe continues)

Bring the mixture to a boil and then turn the heat down to slowly simmer until the beans are creamy and tender, but not breaking apart. This takes vastly different amounts of time depending on the age and hydration of your beans, but count on about 2 hours. Make sure they don't cling to the pot, and add more stock or water if the beans become too dry. The dish should be thick—about the same texture as American-style canned baked beans. Remove the bay leaves.

Finish this dish in bowls with a splash of olive oil and a swirl of gremolata.

GREMOLATA

makes about ⅓ cup

4 GARLIC CLOVES

5 SPRIGS FRESH ROSEMARY, LEAVES REMOVED FROM STEM

ZEST OF ½ LEMON

SALT

¼ CUP EXTRA-VIRGIN OLIVE OIL

Finely chop the garlic, rosemary, and the lemon zest. Then pound these with a mortar and pestle with a healthy pinch of salt until you have something like a pesto. Stir in the olive oil. (You can also do this in a food processor, though it doesn't save that much time.)

STUFATO DI PAOLO
PAOLO'S STEW

serves 4 as a main course

3 TABLESPOONS EXTRA-VIRGIN OLIVE OIL

1/3 CUP FINELY DICED CELERY

1/3 CUP FINELY DICED ONION

1/3 CUP FINELY DICED CARROT

1/4 POUND GUANCIALE, SKIN OFF, CUT INTO 1-INCH-BY-1/2-INCH STRIPS

2 GARLIC CLOVES, CRUSHED

1 WHOLE DRIED PEPERONCINO, BROKEN INTO A FEW PIECES BY HAND

2 FRESH OR DRIED BAY LEAVES

2/3 CUP WHITE WINE

1/2 POUND SPLIT CICERCHIE OR BORLOTTI BEANS, SOAKED IN COLD WATER OVERNIGHT

1/2 POUND DRIED LENTILS, PICKED OVER

1/2 POUND FARRO

1 POUND (4 LINKS) ITALIAN SAUSAGE OF YOUR CHOICE, IN THE CASING

1/2 POUND SWISS CHARD (CLEANED), STEMS DICED AND LEAVES CUT INTO RIBBONS

SALT AND FRESHLY GROUND BLACK PEPPER

GRATED PARMESAN, FOR FINISHING

GRATED PECORINO, FOR FINISHING

GRATED LEMON ZEST, FOR FINISHING

2 TABLESPOONS GREMOLATA (see *opposite page*)

You're probably noticing the proliferation of beans, lentils, and preserved pork in these recipes. That's because they are staples of this region, and also because when we visited this area, it was just emerging from the gray grip of winter. The brilliant vegetables you might find in Rome weren't available. And so we cooked with the climate, improvising with what we had, and admiring how diverse the dishes built on those main ingredients can be.

This is a soupy sort of stew made with the pulses that grow in the mountains. On our last night in Umbria we had a bunch of leftover guanciale, some colorful Swiss chard that was just coming into season, and bags of beans and lentils. With no tomato, this dish revels in the creamy nuttiness of the beans and the chewiness of farro, backed up with the salty funk of guanciale.

In a large, heavy-bottomed pot, heat the olive oil over medium heat until it begins to shimmer. Sauté the celery, onion, and carrot, stirring so they don't get too much color, until soft, for about 10 minutes.

Add the guanciale and cook until most of its fat has rendered, and it starts to become crisp and a little bit browned. Add the garlic, peperoncino, and bay leaves. Cook for another 2 minutes.

Deglaze with the white wine, stirring the pot to scrape up all the brown bits.

Add the beans and lentils, and enough water to cover the beans by an inch. Bring to a simmer, adjust the heat to maintain a gentle simmer, and cook for 1 hour, covered. Check the doneness of the beans. If they're still very hard, keep going.

When the beans are crisp-tender, add the farro and another 2 cups water. Continue cooking for 30 minutes. Then add the sausages and the stems of the chard and continue simmering for 30 minutes, stirring occasionally. Taste and season the stew with salt.

Check to see if everything seems cooked, the flavors have melded, and the texture of the beans and grains feels right to you. Keep cooking if anything is too firm. If the stew seems too dry—or if it sticks to the pot—add more water.

When the stew tastes right to you, add the chard leaves and cook for just another minute or two and adjust seasoning with salt and pepper if needed. Remove the bay leaves. Let the stew rest off the heat for 10 minutes.

Serve the stew in bowls, with plenty of Parmesan, pecorino, grated lemon zest, and gremolata.

LENTICCHIE DI CASTELLUCCIO CON SALSICCIA

LENTILS FROM CASTELLUCCIO WITH SAUSAGE

serves 4 as a main course

1/2 POUND CASTELLUCCIO LENTILS OR OTHER DRIED LENTILS

EXTRA-VIRGIN OLIVE OIL, AS NEEDED

1/3 CUP DICED ONION

1/3 CUP DICED CARROT

1/3 CUP DICED CELERY

SALT

4 LINKS FENNEL SAUSAGE (12 TO 16 OUNCES TOTAL)

1/4 CUP WHITE WINE

1 (14-OUNCE) CAN SAN MARZANO TOMATOES

1 DRIED ITALIAN CHILI

4 CUPS VEGETABLE STOCK OR WATER

GREMOLATA, FOR SERVING (see page 46)

We saw Castelluccio just three months before it fell. When we were there, the hilltop village was resplendent, lit in rays of sunlight that poked through heavy gray clouds which shuffled eastward. Castelluccio sits on a prominent hill, a knob of civilization in a severe, empty valley. It is with so much sadness that I write this: After the earthquake of October 26, 2016, much of the 13th-century village was destroyed. But the minuscule lentils, for which the area is famous, are still planted outside the ruins of the town.

In nearby Norcia, every butcher sells bags of these legumes, as they're a perfect companion to their pork sausages. The delicate lentils also pair well with a fat cotechino sausage, made from the meat, back fat, and skin of pigs, which Romans traditionally eat around the New Year. It's fine to use other varieties of lentils for this dish, but they will probably be larger and tougher, and take a bit longer to cook. But please, use dried lentils—canned ones, with their tired, mushy texture, are not an acceptable substitute.

Empty the lentils into a strainer and sort. There may be some rocks in there and you don't want to trade a tooth for a stew. Place the lentils in a medium pot with 2 cups cold water and bring to a boil. Remove from heat, let rest 5 minutes, and then drain.

Warm a good glug of olive oil, enough to cover the bottom of a medium-sized heavy pot, over medium heat. Add the onion, carrot, and celery and cook over low heat for about 10 minutes, until soft. Season with a pinch of salt, stirring frequently to avoid color. Then add the sausages, and raise the heat to medium to brown them a bit. When the sausages are browned all over, deglaze with the white wine, and let it cook until the liquid reduces by half.

Crush the tomatoes by hand, then add them, along with your chili, which you should break in half before tossing in. Finally, add your lentils and vegetable stock or water. (Don't use chicken stock because you really want to taste the earth in your lentils.) Cover, and simmer until the lentils are tender and the flavors have come together, 45 to 60 minutes. The doneness depends on many things—the age and hydration of your lentils, the size, and even the altitude. So you'll need to cook with your instincts. You might want to start checking them after 20 minutes.

When the lentils are tender and the dish is the consistency of a thick soup, it's ready. Serve in shallow bowls, and finish with a teaspoon of gremolata.

FAGIANO IN UMIDO, IN DUE SERVIZI
STEWED PHEASANT, TWO WAYS

serves 2 as a main course,
with leftovers to sauce pasta for 4

1 (3-POUND) PHEASANT

¼ CUP OLIVE OIL

SALT AND FRESHLY GROUND
BLACK PEPPER

1 MEDIUM CARROT, 1-INCH DICE

2 CELERY STALKS, 1-INCH DICE

1 MEDIUM ONION, 1-INCH DICE

2 GARLIC CLOVES, CRUSHED
WITH THE BACK OF A KNIFE

2 BAY LEAVES

2 SMALL SPRIGS OF FRESH
ROSEMARY

10 WHOLE BLACK PEPPERCORNS

2 JUNIPER BERRIES, CRUSHED
WITH THE BACK OF A KNIFE

1 CUP WHITE WINE

1 CUP CHICKEN STOCK

For the second service

BUTTER

1 POUND PAPPARDELLE OR
OTHER FRESH PASTA

FRESHLY GRATED PARMESAN

FRESH THYME LEAVES

BAY LEAVES

SPRIGS OF FRESH ROSEMARY

JUNIPER BERRIES (OPTIONAL)

On the way out of Norcia, we stopped at a butcher who specializes in game. And though the birds weren't in season, we bought a pheasant to cook somewhere along the way. Game, especially pheasant, hare, venison, and boar, is common in the mountains in central Italy, and makes for a special treat. (These meats are also available in some specialty stores and butchers in the United States.)

Because pheasant is a free-ranging bird, the meat is quite tough if you don't cook it low and slow (this is especially true for wild, as opposed to farm-raised, pheasant). Here, we stew the pheasant *in umido,* over the fire in a big pot with wine. When the pheasant is cooked, it tastes like a firmer, meatier chicken. It's lighter than pigeon, darker than quail. At first, this was a main course, but Paolo and I realized that it could function as a delicious pasta sauce the following day.

CUT THE PHEASANT: Remove the legs and thighs, then divide the legs and thighs into two pieces at the joint. Cut through the cavity and back rib bones with a heavy knife, to cut out the back, and split that in two. Split the rest of the bird in half, lengthwise, and then cut each breast into two pieces. Pat all the pieces dry with paper towels.

Pour the olive oil in a large, heavy-bottomed pot and heat it over medium heat.

Season the pheasant with salt and pepper, and brown it evenly in the olive oil. This will take some time, but you want a nice, all-over browning. Cook in batches and do not crowd the pan.

Remove the pheasant from the pot and add the carrot, celery, onion, and garlic. Cook them, stirring, until softened, about 10 minutes. Add the bay leaves, rosemary, peppercorns, and juniper berries and continue to cook for another 2 minutes.

Deglaze with the white wine and cook until it reduces by half. Add the chicken stock and the pheasant. Bring it to a simmer, then lower the heat to low, cover, and cook for about an hour, until very tender. Remove the bay leaves.

FOR THE SECOND SERVICE: Reserve a generous cup of the meat from the legs and wings before you serve the pheasant as a main course, and reserve most of the braising liquid. Keep the carcass and put it in the fridge with the sauce. The next day, let the stew come up to room temperature, and remove all the delicious bits of meat that cling to the bones, from the back, under the wings, the neck, and the legs. The sauce for our pasta is the braising liquid, rich with collagen and fat, with all the little bits of meat, rounded out with a few pats of butter stirred in. Eggy, wide pappardelle is perhaps the best medium to hold this simple sauce; the flavor of game clings to the noodles. With a pound of fresh pasta, this should be enough to serve four. Finish with some good Parmesan, and fresh thyme, bay, and rosemary, and perhaps a juniper berry or two, which all complement the distinct flavor of the pheasant.

A Detour to Amerigo

In the fall, several months after our visit to Norcia, Paolo and I returned to Italy to continue our trip up north out of Rome. We headed this time to Tuscany, to visit Paolo Parisi, a farmer and friend of ours, who we would invite to cook at our restaurant in Bangkok. This book hadn't taken shape just yet, but the origins of it—of long trips into the countryside to meet farmers and friends—had.

And at the last moment, we decided to detour north, toward Bologna.

After eating lunch at the Four Seasons in Florence, Paolo told Chef Vito Mollica that we were on our way to Modena. Paolo had worked with the Four Seasons for many years, and he and Vito were old friends. We were making a pilgrimage of sorts, off of our planned route, to eat at the celebrated Osteria Francescana. The chef nodded and winked, knowingly. "That's great." But then he narrowed his eyes, and said, "You must go to Amerigo. It's a trattoria in Savigno. A special one. Near Bologna. It's perfect for you guys."

Two days later, we hopped in our tiny Fiat and raced past the archways of old Bologna—which might be Italy's most beautiful city—then through its industrial outskirts. Soon we wound into the hills in darkness, passing shadows of grapevines that produce sweet, bubbly Lambrusco. It was just a degree or two above freezing, and as we circled back down the hills into Savigno, a stag jumped across the road. It was tall and muscular, and it stared right at us. We met the giant stag again at the road's next traverse, and the one after that. We lost sight of him as we entered the town—whose sign proudly proclaims it to be "Savigno—Città del Tartufo." The City of Truffles.

Now, Savigno isn't a city. It's a village, in the hills of Emilia-Romagna, where farmers with dirt-caked fingernails drink at a bar called Free Beach. When we parked at 7 p.m., the streets were eerily empty. The lights were off at Amerigo, and we weren't quite sure if they'd turn on. And so we drank Campari at Free Beach, where fizzy white and red wine are on tap, and where they serve potato chips, nachos, and hot dogs for apertivo hour. And waited.

Savigno's pride—besides its wines and truffles—is Amerigo dal 1934. It's one of the best restaurants I've ever eaten in. Part of it might have been the chill in the air, the wood smoke that whispered out of chimneys, the changing of the seasons, the silence—but the restaurant knows that, and it captures the essence of it all. You cannot separate Amerigo from Savigno; one thing is not possible without the other.

Our meal began on the second floor, as radiators clanked and the waitress poured us glasses of local sauvignon blanc. Then came a string of dishes—earthy and deep, rich with what was outside—that had Paolo and me grunting with pleasure. There was a first course of polenta enriched with Parmesan, topped with thin slices of headcheese whose fat and gelatin melted into the silky grains beneath. Then there was a stew of creamy white beans with plump, pan-seared porcini mushrooms draped on top. This was real food. Honest and exciting in its sincerity.

After the first course, we decided to stay in Savigno for the night, instead of driving back to Bologna. We ordered more wine, and our waitress booked us a room in a local inn (Amerigo has rooms too, and they are elegant in a decidedly deco style, but they were full).

What came next was a pile of feathery black truffles, completely obscuring the fresh pasta beneath, which had been simply tossed in butter and black pepper. And then another pasta course, handmade tortelli filled with

aged Parmesan cream and sautéed with smoky ham. It was like macaroni and cheese from a sacred realm. Paolo ate a lasagna with layers of green sauce, venison, and wild mushrooms. "It's the best lasagna I've ever tasted," he said, between shakes of his bald, red head.

When I took a bite of his lasagna, my thoughts returned to the stag walking through the forest, searching for somewhere to sleep.

By the time the mains came—a veal cheek in red wine, and a massive cut of black pig, simply grilled and served with chunks of sweet fat from the rim of the chop—we had already eaten too much. Dizzy with food and wine, we worked our way through the meat, then stumbled across the street. If you ever go to Amerigo, I suggest you do the same. Eat and drink deeply. Intoxicatingly. Then sleep.

I woke at dawn, in a room so cold I was unable to sleep. A crucifix hung above the bed, covered in purple glitter, sparkling like Lambrusco. The Jesus was dark-skinned, which, in the early morning chill, was striking to my tired eyes.

The vines outside were starting to turn yellow. The mist was lifting.

We dressed and left, but the memory of that meal never left us.

We're so thankful for Amerigo. The food and the specific character and soul of that restaurant really opened our eyes to the possibilities of refined trattoria cooking.

While the food we serve at Appia is inspired by the cuisine of Rome, it's the spirit of Amerigo, of sincerity and a polished simplicity, that we hope to capture.

TORTELLI ALLA AMERIGO

serves 4 to 6,
but with quite a bit of fondue leftover

1 CUP HEAVY CREAM

5 OUNCES GRATED
PARMIGIANO-REGGIANO, PLUS
MORE FOR FINISHING

1 POUND PAOLO'S EGG PASTA
DOUGH *(page 83)*

SEMOLINA FLOUR, AS NEEDED

SALT

½ CUP UNSALTED BUTTER

½ POUND GOOD COOKED
SMOKED HAM, ½-INCH DICE

1 BRANCH OF FRESH SAGE

Note

Most of the Parmesan fondue
will be used for filling the
tortelli, but the rest should
be used for another dish as
a sauce. Keep it. It's so delicious. If you have extra tortelli, these are also wonderful
deep fried, as a crispy snack.

This is our recreation of Amerigo's pasta with Parmesan, cream, and ham. It's a head-whirling sort of dish; the ingredients don't shout, but rather whisper in your ear, with a discreet deliciousness.

In a small saucepan over medium heat, reduce the heavy cream by half, whisking as it boils on the stovetop. Be careful: Cream boils over easily, and if it does, you'll spend 20 minutes cleaning your stovetop like we did when we made this the first time. If it's starting to boil over, whisk more quickly, or take it off the heat for a bit.

When the cream is reduced, quickly whisk in the 5 ounces grated Parmesan, until you have a slurry of cheesy deliciousness that's thick but liquid. Put it in the fridge to set; transfer it to a wide, shallow container if you're in a hurry. This will take an hour in the fridge, less in the freezer.

Using a pasta machine, roll out sheets of egg pasta dough in progressively decreasing settings, until you have something thin and delicate, but not too hard to handle. Cut the sheets into 2-inch squares. Lay the squares out on a table dusted with semolina flour, and lightly dust the pasta squares with semolina as well.

When the cheese fondue is cold and set, scoop about ¾ teaspoon of it onto each square of pasta. Get a cup of water, and put it beside you. With your fingertips, lightly wet the edges of 1 square of pasta, then fold the pasta over the filling, creating a triangle. Press out the air, wet your finger and trace the edge of one side, and press the edges together to seal. Hold the triangle in your hands, with the filling facing toward you. Poke the "belly" of the triangle with your finger, creating a little dent in the filling, and then fold the two bottom corners of the triangle toward each other. Wet each corner lightly and press them together. You'll need 10 to 12 pieces per person.

Bring a large pot of salted water to a boil. In a large saucepan over medium heat, melt the butter and gently brown the ham, about 5 minutes. Turn off the heat.

Boil the tortelli for 3 minutes, testing its doneness. Reserve a cup of the pasta cooking water, and then drain.

Raise the heat under the ham and butter until the butter browns. Add the sage and the tortelli. Add about 3 tablespoons of the reserved pasta water and shake the pan; the sauce will bind together and become cloudy and rich. Divide into bowls, remove the sage, and top with more Parmesan.

BUTCHER SHOP RAGÙ

serves 4 as a main course, or 6 as a starter
(with enough sauce for 10 to 12)

Note

This recipe is even better with the addition of roasted cherry tomatoes. Preheat the oven to 350°F. Simply cut about 6 ounces (one small container) of cherry tomatoes, and toss them with olive oil, salt, and a pinch of fresh thyme and oregano. Spread on a baking sheet and dry in the oven for 30 to 45 minutes, until they lose about half their water but do not burn, occasionally shaking the pan. Add the roasted tomatoes to the pasta just before serving.

After Amerigo, we stopped in Bologna for a night, before heading south to Tuscany. Bologna was gloomy and wet, as is often the case in this city whose covered arches stretch for miles. And we ate Ragù all' Bolognese, for obvious reasons.

"When I was a kid," Paolo explains, "my father would bring home end-cuts, offal, and different meats that he didn't sell in his butcher shop that day—and we would use it for pasta and lasagna." This recipe is Paolo's recreation of how his mother would treat this hodgepodge—by turning it into a Bolognese-style ragù with a bit of tomato and red wine, enriched with chicken liver, cooked for several hours until the meats melded into one another. The technique is more important than the meats, which can change; ground chicken, veal, pork, duck, and even game would work (though chicken liver should always be included). As such, let this recipe become the framework for a sauce that will one day become your own.

We serve this with roasted cherry tomatoes, Parmesan, and fresh fettuccine, and you can certainly use that at home. In this recipe, I've substituted trofie, which is one of my favorite pastas. It's simple but time-consuming to make—basically you roll small balls of dough betwixt your fingers, then drag them out on a wood surface. But there's another reason for the trofie: Just after we'd broken ground on the restaurant, Paolo and I invited a few friends, and the then-designer of the restaurant, to one of several dinners at my apartment. Paolo's wife, June, and my wife, Candice, rolled out the trofie for an hour, to feed the six people that were coming. There was a warm, excited feeling in the air—we were starting something. That night, Paolo showed me how to make this sauce, and I started to understand his basic philosophy of cooking and how flavor is developed.

The dinner party was resoundingly strange—a bizarre clash of personalities. The restaurant designer, whom I'll call Q, refused to drink any wine that one of the other partners brought, and even went as far as pouring a glass of (very expensive) Etna Rosso into my sink, in favor of his own cheap Primitivo. His eyes darted nervously around the room, and he told us peculiar stories. By the end of the evening, after more than a few bottles of wine, it was clear we needed to find someone else to design our restaurant, and that we might never see Q again. And, perhaps because of this weird

(recipe continues)

1 POUND CHICKEN LIVERS

1/2 CUP EXTRA-VIRGIN OLIVE OIL

2 POUNDS GROUND BEEF

2 POUNDS GROUND PORK SHOULDER

SALT AND PEPPER

1 CUP FINELY DICED CELERY

1 CUP FINELY DICED CARROTS

1 CUP FINELY DICED ONION

PINCH OF SMOKED PAPRIKA

3 WIDE STRIPS OF LEMON ZEST, PLUS MORE, GRATED, TO FINISH

1 1/2 CUPS RED WINE

1 (14-OUNCE) CAN PEELED TOMATOES, PREFERABLY SAN MARZANO, CRUSHED BY HAND

6 CUPS VEGETABLE STOCK

2 BAY LEAVES

FRESH THYME LEAVES, TO TASTE

FRESH ROSEMARY LEAVES, TO TASTE

1 POUND FRESH TROFIE (see Appia's [Almost] Eggless Pasta Dough, page 84) OR FETTUCCINE

GRATED PARMESAN, TO TASTE, FOR FINISHING

vibe, the trofie never made it onto our menu. So I decided to bring it back, because bad memories sometimes recall good ones, too.

This recipe makes enough sauce for about twelve people. But it freezes well, and as it takes a long time to make, you'll be happy that you've got another dinner's worth in the freezer.

Trim the chicken livers of any fat or connective tissue, and finely chop them to a fine paste.

Heat the olive oil in a wide, heavy-bottomed pot or Dutch oven over medium heat until it shimmers.

Add all the ground beef and pork to the pot and stir, seasoning with salt and pepper. What you want is for all the water in the meat to evaporate, and then for the meat to begin cooking in its own fat. This takes time—30 to 40 minutes. You only need to stir every 3 or 4 minutes. The objective is for some of the meat to stick to the pot and brown, forming a crust on the bottom of the pot.

When you have a good crust on the pot, and some crispy bits of meat mixed in there, you're ready to lower the heat, and add the celery, carrot, and onion and reduce the heat to medium-low. Add the smoked paprika and the lemon zest strips. Keep stirring, making sure that the sweating vegetables dissolve the crust on the bottom of the pot.

Raise the heat to high and deglaze with the wine until all liquid has evaporated—scraping the bottom of the pot with a wooden spoon.

Add the tomatoes and cook, stirring, for 10 minutes. Add the vegetable stock and bay leaves, then stir in the chicken liver.

Simmer for at least 3 hours, partially covered, over a very low heat. If the sauce looks too dry before it's done cooking, replenish with some water.

When the sauce has developed deep flavor and the surface of the sauce jiggles at the pressure from the back of a ladle or spoon—"almost like a gelatin," as Paolo explained to me—then it is done. Remove the bay leaves and add the fresh thyme and rosemary.

Bring a large pot of well-salted water to boil.

Add the trofie, and cook until the texture is elastic and there is no raw flour in the middle, usually 4 to 6 minutes. (Less if using fettuccine.) Reserve about 1 cup of the pasta water. Drain the pasta.

Add the pasta to a deep sauté pan or nonstick wok, and sauté over medium-high heat with as much sauce as you'd like, adding splashes of the reserved pasta water, until the sauce combines with the starchy water to create an emulsified, shiny pasta. Add cheese and grated lemon zest, and serve.

Paolo Parisi the Eggman

Eight or nine years ago, before Paolo and I had a restaurant together, he had a pop-up at a friend's bar in Bangkok. At that time, Paolo was living in Beijing and preparing to return to Thailand to open a restaurant.

Paolo wasn't sure where, or with whom, he'd open. But he'd thrown out his back, and called me to ask for help. We'd cooked Thai food together, but not much Italian. And the food we made was delicious but confusing for me, as a cook trained in Asian things. Paolo mostly guided from his chair, occasionally standing up to taste, or stir, or instruct. He threw a fistful of rosemary into a stew of chickpeas and vegetable stock and loosened it with more olive oil than I thought possible ("Chickpeas and water, oil, some rosemary?" I thought . . . "What the fuck?"). We rolled and sewed a porchetta, and roasted it. We served bread flown in from Forno Roscioli in Rome, and, memorably, we made a carbonara—that Roman classic—with eggs from Tuscany. The egg farmer's name was Paolo Parisi. On the label, a bald man with a thick, graying beard smiled. He looked a lot like the Paolo

that sat beside me. But older. And smaller.

Three years later, after we'd opened Appia, I suggested that we go see Paolo Parisi, whose eggs we had used in that first carbonara. So, after our meal at Amerigo, and a night in Bologna, we sped south on the A1 to Pisa, shadowing the old Via Aurelia that headed up the coast of Tuscany. We were meant to spend one night; we didn't leave for four, maybe five days.

Parisi is a fascinating sort. He carved out a niche with his eggs and his hams, which are rare and delicious things. He's a famous farmer, which is an odd thing to be in the first place. But he's also an inventor of kitchen equipment, and a promotor of fancy products. As he chain-smoked cigarettes he explained to me how this all happened. "I was selling surgical equipment in Genoa, where I was born. And I made a lot of money. And then I lost it. All of my money, and my life, so that I could live here. I slept through the first eight winters without a heater," he sighed. Don't feel sorry—Parisi lives in a paradise, a half hour from the tower of Pisa, in an elegant, strange house full of art and kitchen equipment and surrounded by sheepdogs that laze in the sun. An artist, a farmer, a surgical equipment salesman, an inventor . . . only he knows.

He took us into his kitchen, where a skinned goat hung on a hook, slowly dripping blood on slate. The kitchen is decorated with hundreds of saucepans from a company that sponsors him. He was the Italian ambassador for Weber Grills. He wears colorful scarves and smart corduroy pants at home, or Carhartt coveralls when he wanders his woods. The woods are decorated with the heads of animals nailed to trees—a jarring taxidermy.

That first night, we ate a cut of steak from his friend's farm, roasted in an oven of his own invention, which has drawers that open like doors, swinging out to the left or right, on different elevations above the flame. Parisi sliced it thin and sprinkled it with sea salt, and we ate it with our fingers from the cutting board. We also sampled the hams that hung from the ceiling of his kitchen; they are more like Spanish Iberico than prosciutto. And tender, sweet guanciale—perhaps the best we'd ever tasted. A risotto bubbled on the stove, and at 11:19 p.m. he ran out into the darkness without a word and returned with a handful of wild marjoram, which he folded into the rice before we ate it. The starch after the meat. A sin, in this part of the world. He doesn't care.

The following day, we went for a walk on his farm where we picked wild fennel and asparagus, thyme, and pimpinella. Parisi moves with an injured gait, a slowness that doesn't extend to his staccato speech. He knelt down and picked up fossils of oysters in the dirt. "They're relics of an inland sea that covered this part of Tuscany. A sea! Imagine swimming in all of this?" His eyes lit up. Most of his farm is wild, and uninhabited by anything more than wild boars rutting under his fence lines and a few sheep and goats. "It's not very good land," he said grumpily, "so I decided to raise chickens."

Parisi's chickens are unique, like him. He has created a feed formula that incorporates goat's whey and grain, so that the eggs grow fat and full of protein. They are almost cheesy. They are also stamped with a number. His visage appears on the cartons that are shipped in air pillows to expensive restaurants across the earth. He puts thyme seeds in the paper packaging, so that customers might bury them, and something might grow. My wife planted some outside our window in Bangkok. Nothing happened.

Despite his fame, Parisi's farm is a half-realized dream. It's full of rusting inventions like smokers and grills and iron sculptures. And there's a huge pot which he travels with across Italy, cooking pasta without water—using only sauce. There is a food truck that bears his name, in a bold, deliberate signature. That afternoon we traveled to Lucca—more than an hour away—to drop off the goat that was hanging in his kitchen.

After another long drive through Tuscany, up through Bolgheri, we returned to his house, to cook carbonara. It was, unsurprisingly, also strange: It's essentially uncooked.

But as he described it, I understood this dish to be a marker of Parisi's philosophy. Of purity. Of a weird and touching worship of simplicity and bowing to the natural world. "I cooked this dish for the first time in 2010. I wanted to keep the integrity of each ingredient—the eggs, the pork and its fat, the cheese—and the heat changes these things too much," he said. He grated cheese and then cracked eggs in the well of feathery pecorino and Parmesan. He ground pepper over it, and added parsley. Then ribbons of raw guanciale. He warmed the mixture over a double boiler to about body temperature, stirring it so that the eggs and cheese emulsified into an unset custard. It was rich, barnyardy, intense but also, almost, subtle. The final step was the addition of hot pasta. The pasta gently warmed the sauce.

"A Roman would look upon my pasta with disgust, like I was an animal," he said, as we stumbled up the hill behind his kitchen to eat. "But I wanted a carbonara that I could eat beside the pool . . ." he explained. We got to the pool. It was empty. It was surrounded by what looked like agave. "I think you can make tequila with these," I said. Paolo Parisi looked at the plants with interest. The wheels turned in his head.

PARISI'S RAW CARBONARA

serves 4 as a main course,
or 6 as a starter

SALT AND FRESHLY GROUND
BLACK PEPPER

1 1/3 POUNDS FRESH
PAPPARDELLE, OR 1 POUND
DRIED SHORT PASTA, LIKE
PENNE

1 1/2 TABLESPOONS
EXTRA-VIRGIN OLIVE OIL

1/4 OF A MEDIUM WHITE ONION,
JULIENNED

4 EGG YOLKS AND 2 EGG
WHITES—THE BEST EGGS
YOU CAN FIND—AT ROOM
TEMPERATURE (*see note*)

2 TABLESPOONS HEAVY CREAM

1/2 CUP FRESHLY GRATED
PECORINO ROMANO

1/2 CUP FRESHLY GRATED
PARMESAN

1/4 CUP CHOPPED FRESH
PARSLEY

4 OUNCES SMOKED GUANCIALE
(OR SMOKED PANCETTA), SKIN
REMOVED, CUT INTO THIN
MATCHSTICKS

Note

If your eggs are cold from the fridge, place them in a bowl with some warm tap water for a few minutes, to let them come to room temperature before using.

A book on Roman food has to include a carbonara, but this carbonara is unlike any you'd find in Rome, or anywhere else, for that matter. It's our interpretation of Paolo Parisi's recipe. The egg farmer inspires us with his products . . . and his eccentricity. He joined us in Bangkok the following year to serve this dish, but his final salvo of the dinner was even more unusual—a simple bun, with a piece of tender beef between it. A complicated man, serving unbelievably simple food.

Bring a tall pot, filled about halfway with well-salted water, to a boil over high heat.

Add the pasta to the boiling water. While the pasta is cooking, place a metal mixing bowl over the pot of boiling water to create a double boiler. When the bowl is hot, add the olive oil and the onion and slowly warm the onion in the oil. (Make sure the pasta water doesn't boil over, creating a mess of your contraption.)

Meanwhile, in a mixing bowl, beat the eggs, as little as possible so that they're just broken, and then add the cream, three-quarters of the cheese, and the parsley.

When the pasta is al dente, reserve a cup of the pasta water and drain the pasta.

Add the pasta to the double boiler and toss, coating the pasta. Add the guanciale, and toss again. Then add the egg mixture, remove from the heat, and continue to stir, adding a little reserved pasta water if necessary, to create a custard-like sauce. Finish with lots of black pepper and some more of the cheese, if necessary.

Eat beside a pool.

INSALATA DI PANZANELLA
A SALAD OF TOMATOES AND BREAD

serves 2 to 4, as one appetizer out of several

3/4 POUND CHERRY TOMATOES, AS RIPE AS POSSIBLE

1/4 OF A MEDIUM RED ONION

1 TABLESPOON RED WINE VINEGAR

3 THICK SLICES SOURDOUGH BREAD

EXTRA-VIRGIN OLIVE OIL, AS NEEDED

SALT AND PEPPER

1/2 TEASPOON COLATURA DI ALICI (ITALIAN FISH SAUCE) OR GOOD SOUTHEAST ASIAN FISH SAUCE

1 TEASPOON BALSAMIC VINEGAR

1 TEASPOON WHITE WINE VINEGAR

5 CELERY LEAVES

5 FRESH BASIL LEAVES

1/4 CUP ROBIOLA CHEESE

3 PICKLED (WHITE) ANCHOVY FILLETS

"I feel the arrival of summertime when panzanella is on the table," Paolo says. "It's a way to use an overabundance of tomatoes, and old bread. In summer I'd work at my father's bakery, and we'd make *fresella*, a toasted, crusty bread, not unlike a bagel. I would toast the bread and make the salad, when the bakers would leave their shift at around 10 a.m. But panzanella is more of a central Italian staple, especially in Tuscany."

A classic panzanella recipe is an idea, rather than an exact and instructional sort of thing. Chunks of country bread (you'll need something crusty to stand up to the marinade) are soaked in the juice you'll remove from the hearts of tomatoes. Those tomatoes, and perhaps some red onion, and a little celery and parsley, and maybe a few greens, are then tossed with olive oil and red wine vinegar, and salt and pepper. With this framework, you can go wherever you'd like with your old bread and ripe tomatoes. Add some cucumber, arugula, mint or other herbs, caper berries, even good canned tuna . . . it's up to you.

The recipe below is our version of the panzanella. It focuses more on the tomatoes than the bread, and it does take a bit more time, as it requires you to peel small tomatoes, lightly pickle the onion, and toast the bread. But the results are worth it, as we also include creamy Robiola cheese to stand up to the acidity of the dressing, and a few white anchovies and basil and celery leaves to create depth of flavor and brightness.

Bring a medium pot of water to boil over high heat. Wash the cherry tomatoes and cut a small cross on the bottom of each. Blanch the tomatoes in the boiling water for 10 seconds, then scoop them out and drop them into a bowl of ice water. (Your objective is not to cook the tomatoes, but rather to loosen their skins, and make them easy to peel. If they cook too long, they will lose their freshness and sweetness.) Peel the tomatoes and place them in a large bowl.

Slice the red onion in a thin julienne and soak it in ice-cold water for a minute or two to remove some of the bite, and then strain. Sprinkle red wine vinegar over the onions and marinate for at least 5 minutes.

(recipe continues)

Cut the bread into 1-inch cubes, and heat a nonstick pan over medium-low heat. In a mixing bowl, toss the croutons with enough olive oil to coat them, and season with salt and pepper. Toast in the pan until golden brown on all sides. Cool the bread cubes off-heat.

Season the cherry tomatoes with the fish sauce, balsamic vinegar, white wine vinegar, salt, pepper, and 2 tablespoons extra-virgin olive oil.

Tear the celery and basil leaves and add them to the marinating tomatoes.

Toss the tomatoes with the bread and onions, and allow the bread to soak up the marinade for 5 minutes in order to soften. Plate your salad and finish with pinches of Robiola cheese, along with the pickled anchovy fillets on top.

APPIA'S CHICKEN LIVER PÂTÉ

*makes about 4 cups, plenty for a dinner party
with some leftovers*

6 TABLESPOONS EXTRA-VIRGIN
OLIVE OIL

1 POUND WHITE ONIONS,
JULIENNED

1 POUND CHICKEN LIVERS
(see note)

2 FRESH SAGE LEAVES

2 BAY LEAVES (FRESH IS BEST)

KOSHER SALT AND FRESHLY
GROUND BLACK PEPPER

3/4 CUP DRY WHITE WINE

1/4 POUND UNSALTED BUTTER,
COLD, IN 1-INCH CHUNKS

FLAKY SEA SALT, FOR FINISHING
(MALDON IS BEST)

Note

When purchasing the chicken livers, make sure they are shiny and bright crimson, not a dull red. If very fresh, they should also be slippery and soft and smell of almost nothing at all.

"I never thought I would be famous for something as simple as chicken liver pâté," Paolo says to me, about a dish that has become a big part of our restaurant's identity. "It's a Tuscan specialty, it's not a Roman thing. Sometimes, it even annoys me. But when my son was born, I went to visit my mother, and I took her, and my son, Giulio, and my wife, June, to the hilltop town of Montepulciano. When we got there it was snowing, and we were starving, and the first thing we ate was Tuscan-style chicken liver crostini. It was grainy, and a little oily, but it was very satisfying."

Two years later, Paolo and I left Parisi's farm and headed back to Rome, on the A1, shooting south. Hungry and almost out of gas, we pulled into La Bettola del Buttero, a roadside restaurant and hotel. It sits just by the tollbooth where Tuscany and Umbria meet, in a small town called Fabro. As soon as we walked through the door, we knew we'd stumbled upon something unique. A huge fire roared in the hearth and chefs dragged the coals from the center of the blaze outward, under grills, where T-bones charred and sausages sizzled. We began to eat.

While the fire was impressive, and the steak was cooked well, once again the chicken liver was grainy. "I'm going to do this, but much better, at the restaurant," Paolo swore.

And so, since the opening of Appia, we've been making this recipe for chicken liver pâté. It's creamy and more refined than the one we ate by the roadside. I love when I come to the restaurant in the afternoon and it's being prepared. The pan of onions and browning chicken livers and herbs and wine fills the entire room with a delicate, fragrant steam. It smells, to me, like Christmas.

The pâté is smooth and spreadable and, because of the melted onions and the care of the cooking, and the oil and butter, it's addictive. You can fold some into a meat ragù if you'd like to give the sauce a bit of backbone. Serve it with toasted or (better yet) grilled bread, lightly scrubbed on one side with a peeled clove of raw garlic, and some crispy Maldon salt for seasoning, and maybe a small plate of our Giardiniera pickles (page 36).

(recipe continues)

Heat 2 tablespoons of the olive oil in a large nonstick skillet over medium heat. Add the onions, then lower the temperature to medium-low, and cook for 20 to 30 minutes. You're aiming to melt the onions here, and it's a slow process, but it allows you to prepare the livers and all your other ingredients. Stir occasionally, making sure they don't cling to the pan and burn, because if they do burn, you'll need to start over. Check on them every few minutes.

Meanwhile, clean the chicken livers by removing any stringy connective tissue, yellow fat, and any bloody bits with a small paring knife. Rinse the livers and pat them very dry with paper towels.

When the onions are evenly browned and have reduced by about half in volume, add your sage and bay leaves, and cook for 2 more minutes. Then push the onions to the side and raise the heat to high. When the pan is very hot, add the chicken livers to the pan in one layer.

Fry the livers and onions and season with plenty of kosher salt, and a few turns of the peppermill.

When the livers are caramelized, and nice and brown on the outside, add the white wine and reduce wine by half.

The livers are cooked once there is no blood inside them; cut into one to check. Taste one. Are they the correct amount of salty? Could you serve them, like this, as a dish? If so, they're ready. Remove the bay leaves and discard.

Add half of the liver and onion mix to a large food processor and start pureeing. Add a few chunks of cold butter and some of the remaining olive oil, and keep going. When it's almost smooth, add the remaining liver and onion mixture, the remaining butter chunks, one by one, and the remaining olive oil and puree until you have a smooth paste. Taste again for salt and texture. It should be smooth, like a gelato.

When this cools, it will taste less salty, and you will need to finish it with some flaky sea salt.

Transfer the mixture to an airtight container and refrigerate immediately.

Before serving, remove the liver pâté from the fridge for 20 or 30 minutes to warm up a bit; it's best at just below room temperature, not ice-cold.

PAOLO'S HOMETOWN, FALCOGNANA

After our trip north to Emilia-Romagna and Tuscany, we returned not to Rome, but to Paolo's hometown of Falcognana. It's a small town about twenty minutes' drive outside of the city, and I've eaten some of the simplest but most memorable meals of my life there. At Paolo's mother's table, to be exact. I've visited Pia in Italy many times, and she has also come to Bangkok to cook at Appia. What follows are some of her recipes—the ones that have most influenced Paolo and our restaurant. But before that, Paolo wanted to tell you about his mother himself.

TO—AND FOR—MY MOTHER, PIA

How can I speak to you at this point? How can I explain to you all the emotions I have in my chest?

It took so long to write this book, that now you won't see it with the same eyes. It's too difficult for you to cook anymore, and the last few years have taken away so many of your memories. So I'll tell our story for you, Mamma.

I can't explain the satisfaction of opening a restaurant that serves your recipes, and all the inspiration you gave me, and our team, when we first opened Appia. I remember you rolling out your dough with Kevin. Laughing with our pastry chef, Jason. Cleaning the puntarelle and the artichokes while our cooks watched, studying your experienced hands. Teaching us

how to make your tiramisu. Scolding me when it was wrong. It created an atmosphere of family, of sharing, of love. But I'll start at the beginning of your story.

My mother, Pia, was born in 1936, in Alatri, and when she was one, just before the war, her family moved to the outskirts of the fascist city of Littoria. The town was built in 1932 after the Canale Mussolini (the Mussolini Canal) drained the malarial Pontine Marshes, reclaiming land that hadn't been used since the fall of the Roman empire. People, mostly poor, moved from all over Italy to the area. Many were given a house and some land to farm.

After the war they changed the name from Littoria to Latina because of the specter

of war and the history of fascism that hung over the town. But in the 1950s, Latina was a young place, like a sort of Italian Wild West, where families from across Italy were brought together, creating a melting pot of dialects, traditions, food, and culture.

My grandfather was a fisherman, and so eels and fish were a staple in the family kitchen, as was game from my great-uncle's hunting preserve. My mother was the third of six children, but she married last. Because of this, she became the cook in her household; all the married brothers and sisters and their children would arrive on weekends, and Pia would cook for the whole family.

One day, in her early thirties, she went to visit her friend in the hospital. There she met Guido, a *norcino*—a butcher—from Rome. They married when she was thirty-five. My brother, Stefano, was born a few years later, and my mother had me when she was forty.

And so a family that loved food was born. My father, already cutting meat for twenty years, had just opened a deli that sold delicious things from the best producers across Italy. We didn't eat industrialized food, and my father had a passion for the highest quality products. He would keep the deep red, irregular chunks of the prosciutto close to the bone instead of perfect slices because of the complexity in taste. When he cut into a giant wheel of Parmigiano to sell to customers, he would collect the crumbs that fell from the middle of the wheel, keeping them on the side, like jewels, to bring home. And whatever he brought, my mother would cook.

Good food was the backbone of their relationship. My mother took her job of raising the family and cooking very seriously, and her approach to cooking was almost spiritual.

She always used to say, "You see my sister? She rushes too much in the kitchen. She doesn't add love to her dishes, and because of this, she puts stress on the ingredients. You can taste it." And so I suggest you, too, add love to yours.

As I became a more mature cook, my mother became my muse. She gave me the opportunity to do something different in life, something that came from my soul, because of the way she raised me.

Her empathy, and love, and her insistence on inviting people home to share her cooking was what made me become a chef.

She taught me how to communicate with people through the medium of food, and to know, intimately, the products I was cooking. She no longer cooks, but her recipes, and her legacy remain.

These are some of the things she taught me. Please, cook them.

—— PAOLO

CHICKEN SOUP WITH QUADRUCCI PASTA, AND A SALAD OF WARM CHICKEN

serves 4

Broth

1 WHOLE CHICKEN, ABOUT 3 POUNDS

1 MEDIUM CARROT, CUT INTO 1-INCH PIECES

1 MEDIUM WHITE ONION, HALVED

2 CELERY STALKS, CUT INTO 1-INCH PIECES

10 WHOLE BLACK PEPPERCORNS

1 BAY LEAF

SALT AND FRESHLY GROUND BLACK PEPPER

1/2 POUND QUADRUCCI PASTA, OR OTHER LITTLE BITS OF FRESH PASTA

3/4 CUP FINELY GRATED GRANA PADANO OR PARMIGIANO-REGGIANO

GOOD EXTRA-VIRGIN OLIVE OIL, FOR FINISHING

Bollito

PICKED CHICKEN MEAT AND VEGETABLES FROM THE BROTH

RED WINE VINEGAR

EXTRA-VIRGIN OLIVE OIL

2 TABLESPOONS CHOPPED FRESH PARSLEY LEAVES

SALT AND PEPPER

After winding our way from Emilia-Romagna to Parisi's farm to the small Roman town of Falcognana, a pot of chicken soup was awaiting our arrival, cooked by Pia, Paolo's mother. It's a rich, clean broth given heft with bits of pasta and served with a simply dressed salad of the simmered meat, called bollito. Pia's simple dishes always outshone most of what we'd eaten on the way home to Rome.

This is a soup that Pia would make with the ends of her fresh fettuccine, which she would cut into a pasta called *quadrucci*, meaning "small squares." They freeze well, and come in handy. If you don't have the time to make them from scratch, you can easily buy fresh fettuccine and cut that into 1/4-inch squares.

The soup is also best when the pasta is slightly overcooked, and left to rest, as the pasta starch thickens the broth. Finish with Grana Padano or Parmesan and a few drops of olive oil. But make sure you add the cheese just before serving, or it will clump and sink to the bottom of your soup.

MAKE THE BROTH: Cut your chicken into 10 pieces: 2 drumsticks, 2 thighs, 2 wings, and halve each breast (see page 121). Place the pieces into a stockpot and cover with water. Add the carrot, onion, celery, peppercorns, and bay leaf, and bring to a boil over high heat.

Lower the heat and simmer for 1½ to 2 hours, skimming off all the foam, and adding more water as it reduces. You want to finish with about the same amount of liquid as you started with.

When your broth is ready, and the chicken meat is very tender, strain out and reserve all the solids and return the liquid to the pot. Season it well to taste with salt and freshly ground pepper and take it off the heat.

Pick the meat from the bones, and add it—along with the celery, onion, and carrot—to a salad bowl. Season well with salt and pepper.

Bring the broth back to a boil, add the pasta, and cook until slightly overcooked, about 5 minutes. Remove from the heat, and set aside to rest for 5 minutes before serving. Taste and adjust seasoning if needed. Serve with grated cheese on top, and a whirl of oil.

After you finish, or perhaps at the same time, serve the salad of chicken and boiled vegetables with a simple dressing of red wine vinegar, olive oil, parsley, and salt and pepper, all to taste.

PIA'S AND PAOLO'S EGG PASTA DOUGHS

makes about 3 pounds pasta,
12 main course portions (or 6, in Paolo's house)

Pia's Egg Pasta Dough

2 POUNDS PLUS 3 OUNCES
ITALIAN "OO" FLOUR

10 EGG YOLKS

1 TABLESPOON SEA SALT

1 TABLESPOON OLIVE OIL

ALL-PURPOSE FLOUR, FOR
DUSTING THE SURFACE
WHILE KNEADING

Paolo's Egg Pasta Dough

14 OUNCES SEMOLINA FLOUR

11 OUNCES ALL-PURPOSE
FLOUR, PLUS MORE FOR
DUSTING

10 EGG YOLKS

1 TABLESPOON SEA SALT

2 TABLESPOONS OLIVE OIL

"When I was a child, you couldn't go to the store to buy pasta—you made pasta—four or five days a week, in different shapes, in different styles," Pia said to me once, as I watched her work in her kitchen.

I asked her what she thought makes a perfect pasta dough. "The outside should have the texture of velvet," she explained, nonchalantly. "It needs resistance . . . elasticity . . . but not too much." She breathed a little heavier, pressing her weight down on the dough, the tendons in her thick wrists showing. Her hands have made a lifetime of pasta.

"Pasta is my greatest love. I can eat so much pasta. As a kid, when I would return home and see my mother making a minestrone instead of a pasta—my mother tried to make me eat vegetables—I would scream and cry. This is the pasta my mother would make; it is her recipe, not mine," Paolo says.

What follows Pia's recipe is Paolo's own recipe for egg pasta dough. Both use the same method; the difference is that Paolo's has more elasticity than his mother's—there is more egg, and a different blend of flours. Developed in a restaurant kitchen, it is a bit more durable, a bit chewier, and more suitable for pasta machines, while Pia's dough is best for hand-rolling with a pin if you want to do that. "To be honest, I prefer the texture of my mother's dough, which is more delicate," Paolo says.

And what follows that is the nearly eggless dough we use at Appia for leaner, chewier pastas, like trofie and cavatelli.

These recipes are for the doughs themselves; to finish them, roll them out with a pin or in decreasing settings in a pasta machine until they reach your desired thickness, and cut the shapes you desire, like wide pappardelle or thinner fettuccine. To be honest, the world of pasta shapes is enormous, far more than we can cover in this book, and it is easiest to direct you to the internet to find videos on how to cut or form different pasta shapes.

Note that these recipes produce about 3 pounds of pasta dough; smaller batches of dough can be tricky to work with. Well-wrapped in plastic, the extra dough can be stored in the fridge for up to 4 days, or frozen.

(recipe continues)

CHOOSE EITHER TYPE OF PASTA DOUGH: Pile the flour in a mound in the middle of your clean work surface. In the middle of your flour, dig out a crater, like a volcano. Add the egg yolks to the center of your crater. Add the salt and olive oil to the eggs.

Take a fork and first beat the eggs inside the crater, and then, from the outside in, fold the eggs into the flour.

As soon as it's solid enough (it'll look like a bunch of dusty balls), drop the fork and start to use your hands, working from the outside in, to make a ball of dough.

Once you have a single ball of dough, you'll need to knead it on a surface dusted with all-purpose flour. Just like bread dough, you'll press heavily in the center of the dough, pushing it away from you, then fold it over, turn a quarter of a turn, and repeat until you have an elastic dough.

After about 10 minutes of kneading (you should be tired, this is work), press your finger into it, 1 inch deep. Does the dough slowly bounce back, and return to shape? If so, then it's done. If not, keep kneading. Let rest at least 1 hour, covered with a clean dish towel or wrapped in plastic wrap, before rolling and cutting or putting into a pasta-making machine.

APPIA'S (ALMOST) EGGLESS PASTA DOUGH

2 POUNDS PLUS 3 OUNCES
ITALIAN "00" FLOUR

2 CUPS WARM WATER

1½ OUNCES PARMESAN, GRATED

4 EGG WHITES

Use the same method as above, but first mix together the water, cheese, and egg whites before adding them to the crater of flour. Proceed as above.

CONIGLIO ALLA CACCIATORA
RABBIT, IN THE HUNTER'S STYLE

serves 4 as a main course

2 POUNDS RABBIT (1/2 OF A
LARGE ONE), CUT IN 8 PIECES,
WITH ORGANS (*see note*)

SALT AND PEPPER

1/4 CUP EXTRA-VIRGIN OLIVE OIL

2 GARLIC CLOVES, LIGHTLY
CRUSHED

2 BIG SPRIGS OF FRESH
ROSEMARY

1 1/4 CUPS WHITE WINE

GREMOLATA (*see page 46*)

"My grandmother on my father's side raised rabbits across the street from my home. Just for our family. This dish is simple, and one that we've cooked for generations, but it takes touch, and attentiveness. Rabbit is a fragile, lean animal. But when cooked well, it's one of my favorites," Paolo says. We put it here because it is something we both remember eating at Pia's table, on one of those nights before returning to Bangkok. A final, fortifying meal, after so many days on the road.

The recipes for cacciatora vary significantly. *Cacciatora* means "in the style of the hunter," but people have hunted all across Italy, in vastly different climates with different products. A hunter in the hills of Campania or Sicily, in Italy's warmer south, might cook this dish with tomato. But in the mountains of central Italy, and Rome itself, it is almost always cooked with wine, vinegar, and (sometimes) olives. This recipe is even simpler—employing only white wine—which enhances, rather than masks, the lightness of the rabbit.

Rabbit isn't a forgiving meat—it's extremely lean—so you must tend to it carefully. Don't undercook it as it will be tough; don't keep it on the heat for too long or it will be dry. Its flavor is clean and meaty, light but satisfying, and a joy to eat when cooked well. Taste, and trust your instincts. And allow it to rest in the juices and relax after cooking for at least ten minutes before serving it.

Pat the rabbit pieces dry with paper towels and thoroughly salt and pepper them.

Heat the oil, garlic, and rosemary in a heavy-bottomed pot or Dutch oven over medium-high heat.

When the garlic and rosemary are at a firm sizzle, add the rabbit pieces, cooking in batches if necessary to not crowd the pot. Brown the rabbit well on both sides. You want lots of color in this case; it should cook for 3 to 5 minutes per side. Remember how I said some pieces cook faster than others? Well, the organs cook even faster than that. So add the liver and heart last to brown, then remove and set aside. When you braise the dish, you will add these back in the last 5 minutes to cook in the rich liquid.

Slowly add the white wine, while shaking the pot in order for the oil and the wine to become one. This is an important step in many braised Italian dishes. What we're after is a cloudy sauce that is yellowish brown and is not separated. Dishes where water or wine and oil are emulsified take on an almost creamy texture. Taste it. The wine will still taste strong. Don't worry, it will cook down, and soften, just like the rabbit.

When you've achieved a nice, unified sort of sauce, turn down the heat to a bare simmer, cover the pot, and simmer for 45 minutes to an hour. If your pot lid isn't super tight, the wine will likely evaporate during the cooking time; add splashes of water occasionally if necessary to keep the pot from going dry, ending the process with enough liquid for a sauce. The meat should be soft, not chewy. If it is, continue to cook for as long as you need until it relaxes. Add the organs for the last few minutes. Season to taste with salt and pepper. Serve as a second course (after pasta) with some crusty bread for soaking up the delicious sauce, and the gremolata for a fresh, herbal condiment.

SCAROLA AGLIO E OLIO

SAUTÉED ESCAROLE WITH GARLIC, PINE NUTS, AND OLIVES

serves 4 as a side dish

1 LARGE OR 2 SMALL HEADS OF ESCAROLE

2 TABLESPOONS OLIVE OIL

PINCH OF CHILI FLAKES

1 SALTED ANCHOVY FILLET, CHOPPED

2 GARLIC CLOVES, CRUSHED

¼ CUP WHITE WINE

2 TABLESPOONS PINE NUTS, TOASTED

1 TABLESPOON RAISINS (OPTIONAL)

10 BLACK GAETA OLIVES, PITS REMOVED

SALT AND PEPPER

Escarole is a very versatile vegetable. You can eat it raw in a salad or sauté it for a classic trattoria-style *contorni* (side dish). It works perfectly as a sweet and bitter foil for the rich, succulent rabbit recipe on page 86.

Split the heads of escarole in half, separate the leaves, and wash them. Shake them well to dry.

Add the olive oil to a large pot over medium heat. Add the chili, anchovy, and garlic. Sauté until the anchovy dissolves. Raise the heat to high, add the escarole, and sauté for 2 minutes, until it starts to wilt. Now add the wine, pine nuts, raisins, and olives, cover, and turn the heat to low.

Let it stew for about 10 minutes, or up to 15, until tender. Check to see if you need to add a splash of water to keep the pot from scorching before the escarole is ready. The cooking time depends on the size of the escarole; if the hearts are thick and large, you'll need to cook it longer. Season well with salt and pepper and serve.

PIA'S TIRAMISU

serves 8

5 EGGS, SEPARATED INTO YOLKS AND WHITES (ABOUT 5 OUNCES OF EACH)

I CUP SUGAR

1 POUND MASCARPONE CHEESE

COCOA POWDER, FOR DUSTING

18 OUNCES PAVESINI COOKIES

2 CUPS (16 OUNCES) ESPRESSO OR VERY STRONGLY BREWED COFFEE, ICE-COLD

This is a recipe that we will never change. It is Paulo's mother's, and when we opened Appia she came to Bangkok, from Rome, to taste his version of it. Pia scolded her son, in the kitchen of his first restaurant, because it wasn't *quite right*. It was too creamy, she declared. Apparently there was too much mascarpone between the layers.

But we fixed that.

Tiramisu is something that people riff endlessly on. There are modernist versions, deconstructed ones, ones that look like pies or cakes. Ours has two very important distinctions:

1. It contains no alcohol.

2. We use pavesini cookies—a lighter, airier, fluffier version of lady fingers with an aromatic, vanilla scent. Pavesini cookies are mostly egg whites and sugar, and they mop up espresso, but less than lady fingers. They expand, like coffee- and vanilla-scented clouds, and when spread with a light layer of marscarpone, egg, and sugar, what you get is an airy dessert.

One last thing: This is the most perfect thing imaginable for breakfast, with a coffee. I know that sounds hedonistic, and it is. But try it. I can't imagine a better way to start my day.

Using a very clean hand mixer or stand mixer, beat the egg whites until they form stiff peaks. Remove and reserve.

Using that mixer, beat together the egg yolks and sugar until the color changes from a bright yellow to a creamy off-white. Add the mascarpone, beat for another 5 minutes, and set aside.

Gently fold the egg whites into the creamy mascarpone and egg mixture.

Line a 10 × 12-inch lasagna pan with parchment paper.

Start the assembly with a thin layer of mascarpone mixture (about ¼ inch) on the bottom of the pan and then sprinkle some cocoa powder on top. (The easiest way to do this is using a small sieve, filling it with cocoa powder, and tapping the side of the sieve with your hand so the cocoa is distributed evenly. It's the only way to do it correctly, actually.)

(recipe continues)

Make sure the coffee is cold! You cannot use hot coffee or this whole house will fall down—the heat from the coffee will break down the cookies, melt the marscapone, and basically, waste an hour of your life.

One by one, quickly dip your pavesini cookies in the coffee, just a one-to-two-second swim in the dark, and make a tight layer of them over the mascarpone, like you're making lasagna.

Cover with a slightly thicker layer of mascarpone. Just enough to blanket the cookies. Then sprinkle with cocoa powder.

Repeat this step 3 more times (so there are four cookie layers), finishing with a cocoa powder dusting on top.

Cover the pan with foil and place in the fridge for a minimum of 4 hours, but preferably overnight. Remove from the lasagna pan by setting a plastic-lined sheet tray over the top and, smoothly and without hesitation, flipping it over neatly. (Or just serve it directly from the pan. It won't look as pretty, but it will still taste like a light, fluffy cloud—like an almost weightless cake.)

Dust again with cocoa, and it's ready to serve for dessert. And breakfast, the following day. Trust me on this one.

Two

LAZIO, AND
THE ROADS
SOUTH

LONG AFTER we arrived back in Bangkok, my thoughts often returned to our trip to Norcia and over to the mountains of Umbria. After a few months at the restaurant, Paolo and I planned another long trip, but this time we would stay in Lazio, to eat and cook and explore.

Rome lies within the region of Lazio. For centuries, before the ancient Romans expanded outward, Lazio was their larder. Much later, after the fall of the Roman Empire, the roads eroded, and what was left was again local; the food of Lazio was the beginning and the end of Roman food. The landscape of Lazio itself is very diverse—lowland marshes, rugged coast, and mountains abound in its five provinces—and it boasts dishes marked by both Mediterranean and mountain climates.

But there is something Lazio lacks that other places in Italy have in abundance. It is not glamorous; it does not ooze a cultivated elegance. Though Lazio has beautiful beaches, medieval hilltop towns knocked out of stone, rolling hills and vineyards, and Rome itself, it is not Sicily, or Piedmont. You don't look at Lazio through the same golden prism that you do when driving through, say, Tuscany, with its manicured fields and too-perfect hamlets where not a single paving stone or roof tile is out of place. And that is actually what I love most about Lazio. It's a place for its people; it hasn't succumbed to tourist hordes and property management companies. It is pure. Imperfectly so.

Once a land of the ancient civilizations of the Etruscans, Latins, and Sabines, Lazio now stands as an area deeply rooted in agriculture and, especially, animal husbandry. Running from the blond, undulating hills south of Tuscany to Abruzzo's craggy peaks, then south down into the Pontine Marshes toward the region of Campania, the landscape changes abruptly. It is magnificent occasionally. It is also plain at times. But it is a great place to eat real food, unblemished by the corrosive forces of tourism.

The shepherd and his flock might be the most prominent figures in the eating culture of Lazio. As Frederika Randall writes in her book *The Lazio Countryside and Its Cheeses*, "Cheesemaking is as old as pastoral life itself, and animals have been grazing these plains and hills since long before the Romans rose to power. Homer, in *The Odyssey*, describes the making of Pecorino (ewe's milk cheese), telling how the one-eyed giant Polyphemus, returning to his cave, milks his sheep, adds rennet to the milk, and when the curd is set, pours it into rush baskets, just as it is done here today." That pecorino, along with guanciale and pasta, forms Rome's triumvirate of tastes.

In this chapter, we'll show you classic recipes from the Lazio countryside. We'll gather peas and fava beans and artichokes from a lazy farmer's field, to make the dish of vignarola. We'll also meet the people who press the olives to make the oil that we finish our salads with in Bangkok. And we'll explore the rugged orchards of Gaeta, where we uncover the best oils we've ever tasted, in the hands of a renegade farmer at Valle d'Itri.

We'll introduce you to a remarkable shepherd, Loreto Pacitti, in the tiny mountaintop village of Picinisco. His determination and wisdom inspire us, and in visiting people like him, you go straight to the heart of the cuisine; you can feel the pull of the powerful back-to-agriculture movement in modern Italy. Pacitti left a career in Rome to return to the countryside and continue the work of his ancestors, herding eight hundred sheep on the steep mountainsides of the Ciociaria, where transhumance—a great migration of animals—has occurred for more than two thousand years. Shepherds pasture their sheep in the south of Italy to avoid the winter snow, and return to the steep alpine pastures of central Italy in summer. The spine of the Apennines has been their highway for millennia.

Lazio also has a long coastline that stretches north from Tuscany to the shadow of Vesuvius. The Sabine—the rolling hills that greet the Apennines—are dotted with sheep and groves of olives. The lakes of Bracciano and Bolsena offer squirming eels and freshwater fish. Following the old roads out of Rome—the Via Salaria east, the Via Aurelia back to Rome, and the Via Appia southward—we explore overlooked pockets of one of Italy's most underrated regions, in search of deliciousness. Rome has cast a shadow across the continent for two thousand years, keeping the surrounding countryside mostly out of our sight, so we set out to see it.

A Trip to the Hotel Roma

For me, spaghetti amatriciana is the ultimate comfort food—tomato sauce infused with the fat of guanciale and the funk of pecorino. For Paolo, the dish is suffused with memories of his childhood. It's considered one of the classic Roman dishes, but it actually comes from the mountains on the border of Lazio and Abruzzo, two hours by car from Rome. As the name suggests, it originated in the town of Amatrice.

"I spent weeks there as a kid," Paolo explained one night as we ate the dish in Bangkok, "at a place called the Hotel Roma. There were two brothers, and they made the best amatriciana in the world. And they loved me, because I ate so much of it." I laughed as he continued, "From the window of the dining room, you could see my uncle's pastures on the top of the mountain. He was one of the most famous pecorari—a wealthy shepherd." As we were discussing this, Paolo sighed. "We should go back."

Three years later, we did.

The Hotel Roma housed a tattered, cavernous dining room, facing sloping green fields that curve up into steep, ancient peaks. In late May, the snowmelt filled the angry streams, and tumbling rain clouds passed as quickly as bright sunlight. The sky in this part of Italy tends to roil, as winds rise up against a mountain range that cleaves the country in half.

During the 18th and 19th centuries, much of Italy was agrarian, and very poor. But the shepherds who owned the grazing rights to these fields grew rich. The wealthy shepherds and the butchers in nearby Norcia bought up land in modern Rome—as investments, but more importantly, to sell their products.

Amatriciana combines these two tribes—the shepherds and the butchers—in one dish. Sheep cheese and pig fat is its essence, with pasta as their foil. And at the Hotel Roma they served it in massive, shimmering piles.

On Saturdays and Sundays, hundreds of hungry diners headed here to feast: families;

sightseers from Rome; hikers following ancient shepherd paths; and gangs of bikers, who unbuttoned their leather pants as they left. The meal cost twenty euros. The wine was all-you-could-drink and better than it should've been—a simple Montepulciano d'Abruzzo sat on each table in repurposed 1-liter Pepsi bottles, their labels removed. The kitchen was a blur of mothers and daughters tossing pasta and frying lamb chops and offal on the flattops. The pasta flew out of the kitchen and onto wheeled carts, where it was piled on plates in great, greasy tangles.

I write this in the past tense, because the Hotel Roma is, sadly, now gone. It was a victim of a great earthquake just weeks after our visit and these photos are among the last ones of that grand, gluttonous spectacle.

That afternoon we ate local hams and sheep sausage and mozzarella, beans and white celery, and coratella, a stew of lamb innards and artichokes. What followed was more amatriciana than I'm comfortable with. The server decided how much you'd get, and if you didn't finish your dish, it wasn't taken kindly. Then another pasta arrived atop a squealing cart—this time a shiny pile of spaghetti alla gricia—essentially, carbonara without the eggs. I shivered. A new plate was slapped over my tomato-stained one. And then we ate. And gulped wine, and when we gave up, drank some water to quiet the sodium. And still, it wasn't over.

The final salvo was a massive platter of meat—sweetbreads, veal, lamb chops, and sausage, all cooked simply on the grill, and drizzled with oil. We ate valiantly, and then stretched out on park benches in the town square, as the sun shone through the rolling clouds.

So Paolo returned to the Hotel Roma. He came, he fought, and I think he got conquered. One last time.

SPAGHETTI ALL'AMATRICIANA
SPAGHETTI IN THE STYLE OF AMATRICE

serves 4 as a main course,
or 6 as a starter

10 OUNCES GUANCIALE

1/2 CUP WHITE WINE

1 (28-OUNCE) CAN SAN MARZANO TOMATOES, DRAINED OF JUICE AND CRUSHED BY HAND

1/2 TEASPOON CHILI FLAKES

SALT AND FRESHLY GROUND BLACK PEPPER

1 POUND DRIED SPAGHETTI

PLENTY OF FRESHLY GRATED PECORINO

Note

A quick primer in saltiness (which I'll attribute to David Chang, though I think he attributed it to someone else). You can't tell if something is salty by tasting it once. Something that is correctly salted should taste a touch too salty the first time you taste it. Wait a few seconds. Taste it again. Does it taste too salty this time, or correct? If it still tastes too salty, there you go. Add more tomato and a little wine. If on the second taste it doesn't taste salty enough, add some salt. But don't let the first impression of your taste buds be your ultimate judgment. I usually taste something three times before I season it.

Remove the thick, outer skin from your guanciale and scrape off some of the pepper on the guanciale's outer surface by running the dull edge of a knife against it. Cut it into thick lardons—about half the length and nearly the same thickness as your index finger.

Brown the pork in a heavy-bottomed pot or deep frying pan over medium-high heat until brown and crispy on the edges. Your pork will be swimming in a considerable puddle of fat.

Lower the heat to medium-low and slowly add the white wine while shaking the pan aggressively back and forth on the stove. This will allow the pork fat and the wine to emulsify into a sauce. It should appear almost creamy and yellow if you did it right.

Add the tomatoes, a pinch of chili flakes, and bring it to a simmer, and cook over low heat, covered, for 45 minutes to an hour. You may need to add salt, depending on your guanciale's saltiness. We rarely do. It really depends on the length and depth of the cure on the pork, though, so let your tongue be your guide (see note). The sauce will be ready when the pork is very tender, with the flavors well-blended.

Bring a large pot of well-salted water to a boil over high heat. Add the spaghetti. Scoop out and reserve some pasta water—about 1/2 cup—to add to the sauce if necessary. Drain the pasta when it's al dente.

You will need to re-emulsify the sauce before serving; because of the high fat content, amatriciana will "split" into liquids and fat. Don't be alarmed. Just stir it vigorously and shake the pan and it will come together again.

Add the pasta to your pan of sauce and raise the heat to high. Stir. Add plenty of pecorino, to taste, and cook, stirring well, for 1 minute. If the pan seems dry, stir in splashes of the pasta water. Season with lots of pepper, and top with more pecorino. Finish with more pepper and serve.

The Roman
Countryside

From Amatrice, we headed west, down the mountains, and back into the fertile Mediterranean hills near Rome. In this part of Lazio, the Campagna Romana, the climate is warm, and the sea is within reach. There is still the strong pull of the shepherd, but fish is also abundant here. The markets are full of artichokes, puntarelle, sweet peppers, tomatoes, and zucchini. There are dozens of cheeses unique to the area, and wild herbs and vegetables are easy to forage. Simply put, it's a wonderfully diverse cradle of food. The recipes that follow are from the countryside surrounding Rome, and southward.

INSALATA DI PUNTARELLE
PUNTARELLE SALAD

serves 4 as a light starter, or as a component of an antipasti course

10 OUNCES PUNTARELLE STEMS
AND CORES (*see note*)

1 GARLIC CLOVE, MINCED

4 SALTED ANCHOVY FILLETS,
2 CHOPPED AND 2 WHOLE

2 TEASPOONS COLATURA DI
ALICI (ITALIAN FISH SAUCE) OR
GOOD SOUTHEAST ASIAN FISH
SAUCE

2 TABLESPOONS PLUS
1 TEASPOON EXTRA-VIRGIN
OLIVE OIL

3 TABLESPOONS RED WINE
VINEGAR

SALT AND PEPPER TO TASTE

Note

To prepare the puntarelle,
first carefully remove the
large green leaves with a
paring knife. They are too
bitter to eat raw; you can
reserve them to blanch and
sauté with garlic and chili,
or pickle them with other
vegetables. You will need 10
ounces of the cleaned stems
and cores for this dish.

Puntarelle, a slightly bitter chicory, is an essential ingredient in Rome and greater Lazio. This is a perfect starter to a rich pasta, such as Amatriciana (page 107).

We're not using the leaves in this salad, but rather the thick stems and the core. You can often find cleaned puntarelle in the market, on ice.

There is a simple kitchen tool for the preparation of puntarelle that consists of thin, guitar-like strings pulled tightly across an opening of wood. You push the vegetable through and it comes out in strips. If you can find one of these, buy it. They're cheap and useful for raw salads of this sort. (In Italian, this tool is called a *taglia puntarelle*—literally, a puntarelle cutter—which gives you a sense of how much Romans love puntarelle.)

If you can't find puntarelle where you live, I recommend substituting raw green asparagus. The thick-stemmed variety is best. Peel the tough skin, and cut the asparagus into matchsticks.

Cut out the fibrous bits from the thick core of the puntarelle. The small buds and stems of the core need to be cut in half and subsequently into long strips that are about ¾ inch thick.

Now, cut these pieces into thin strips. Cut each section in half, and lay the vegetable flat-side down on your cutting board, lengthwise, while gently rocking your knife and slicing them into ribbons (or, pass them through your *taglia puntarelle*). Once cut, place the puntarelle into an ice bath for 30 minutes. This reduces the bitterness of the vegetable, keeps it cold and crisp, and makes it curl up nicely. Puntarelle should always be kept chilled after it is cut (if you have extra, place it in an airtight container under a damp paper towel in the fridge). Otherwise, it will turn brown.

In a salad bowl, combine the garlic, chopped anchovies, fish sauce, olive oil, and red wine vinegar. Use the back side of a fork to crush the anchovies. Then vigorously whisk the ingredients back and forth with the fork to make your dressing. It doesn't need to be perfectly emulsified.

Drain the puntarelle from the ice bath, quickly dry it with paper towels or in a salad spinner, add it to the salad bowl, and toss it with the dressing. Season with salt and pepper, to taste. Don't be shy with seasoning.

Let your salad rest, ideally for 20 to 30 minutes before serving, to absorb the acid, oil, and the umami of the anchovies. Serve with the remaining anchovy fillets draped on top.

BRUSCHETTA, ANY WAY YOU LIKE IT

Bruschetta is not unique to Lazio. It's eaten across Italy, in countless styles. In fact, when we're on the road, exploring different parts of Italy, it's the perfect way to eat. As we journeyed across Lazio and southward, so many of our meals were made with a simple cheese knife, whatever local vegetables and salumi we had on hand, a loaf of bread, and olive oil.

At Appia, when we were bored, Paolo, our chef Kevin Ching, and I used to have bruschetta competitions. We would slice thick pieces of sourdough, toast them, and fire up the meat slicer. One of us might top the bread with ribbons of thinly sliced porchetta and marinated eggplant and melt pecorino over the top with a torch, then finish with a drizzle of honey or some toasted walnuts. Someone else would spread soft Robiola cheese over the toast, then add roasted red peppers (see page 35), and drape good, salted anchovies on top, with leaves of Italian parsley and the best oil in the restaurant. Our zucchini salad (see page 114) is equally at home over sourdough, with lots of shaved Parmigiano-Reggiano and extra-virgin olive oil. Chicken liver pâté (see page 73), with pickled red onions and flaky sea salt also makes a genius bruschetta. But the one that kills every time is soft, spicy 'nduja sausage, spread evenly across the warm bread so that it melts, topped with a spoonful of runny burrata that drips luxuriantly onto the plate, with plenty of good green olive oil, Maldon salt, pepper, and a little chopped parsley.

I'm going to let you decide what to put atop your bread. Because it really does depend on what you have on hand. What you're looking for is a rich ingredient, an acidic component, and a salty one. And think about balance and contrast in texture when you build your bruschetta. It can't be too dry, though it shouldn't be too wet. A little crunch, from nuts or seeds, and fresh herbs or chili will elevate your bruschetta to the next level. Cold cuts like mortadella are perfect, perhaps with toasted pistachio nuts, pickles, and maybe some black pepper. Or spicy salami with stracchino cheese (like a looser cream cheese), or simply ham and pickles.

AS FOR THE BREAD ITSELF, DO IT THIS WAY: Slice sourdough bread about ¾ inch thick and brush one side with olive oil. Crisp it over coals, in a hot pan, or in a broiler.

Take a raw garlic clove and scrub the crunchy, toasted side of the bread with the garlic. It will slowly disappear, as the bread acts like sandpaper to a soft piece of wood. Don't over-garlic; you want the garlic there in the background, a subtle reminder rather than an overbearing introduction to your bruschetta.

Then top your bread slices with whatever you like. With solid bread, bruschetta will hold up for 20 minutes or more. This allows you to get into the kitchen and cook, and your guests to marvel at the ingenuity of your bruschetta-building skills.

INSALATA DI ZUCCHINE CRUDE

RAW ZUCCHINI SALAD WITH PARMESAN AND MINT

serves 4 as part of an antipasto course

2 SMALLISH ZUCCHINI (10 OUNCES ALL TOGETHER)

1 MEDIUM SHALLOT, VERY FINELY DICED

3 TABLESPOONS PLUS 1 TEASPOON EXTRA-VIRGIN OLIVE OIL

1 1/2 TEASPOONS RED WINE VINEGAR

5 LARGE LEAVES OF FRESH MINT, PLUS SMALLER ONES TO FINISH THE DISH

SALT AND PEPPER

2 OUNCES PARMIGIANO-REGGIANO

Zucchini is one of the most popular vegetables around Rome—it is eaten raw and sautéed, and its flowers are stuffed with cheese and anchovies and then battered and fried. In this dish, we run raw zucchini lengthwise down a mandoline for perfect, thin strips. Those tender green ribbons are dressed with red wine vinegar and olive oil. Then the salad is finished with fresh mint and good Parmesan. It is an exercise in simple restraint and a refreshing foil to many of the heavier dishes in the region.

If you take the time to roll the dressed strips, the salad becomes beautifully three-dimensional, and it's rather easy to do.

Wash the zucchini and slice them, ideally with a mandoline, from bottom to top, about ⅛ inch thick. If you slice them too thin they will be limp and watery; too thick and they can't be curled into rings without breaking (still, this is okay—you can simply arrange them on a plate and serve without rolling).

In a medium bowl, mix together the shallot, olive oil, vinegar, mint, and salt and pepper to taste. Toss in the zucchini and agitate it with your fingertips, to massage the dressing into the vegetable.

Take a slice of zucchini and roll it up. Place the roll, with the seam down, on a serving plate. Repeat with all the slices; we usually stack them in a flat-topped pyramid, but you don't have to. Finish the dish with Parmesan shaved into ribbons with a vegetable peeler or coarsely grated, and a few more tiny sprigs of mint.

INSALATA DI BACCALÀ

A SALAD OF SALTED CODFISH AND TOMATOES

serves 4 as a small appetizer with other salads

10 OUNCES BACCALÀ
(SALTED COD)

½ CUP LARGE-DICED CARROT

½ CUP LARGE-DICED CELERY

½ CUP LARGE-DICED WHITE
ONION

6 OUNCES CHERRY TOMATOES

SALT

1 GARLIC CLOVE, FINELY
CHOPPED

EXTRA-VIRGIN OLIVE OIL

½ MEDIUM RED ONION

1 TABLESPOON SALTED CAPERS

2 OUNCES WHOLE BLACK
OLIVES, PITS REMOVED (WE
LIKE THE SMALL, PUNGENT
GAETA OLIVE FOR THIS DISH)

2 TABLESPOONS ROUGHLY
CHOPPED FRESH PARSLEY

½ LEMON, SEEDED

In the trattorias of Lazio, many places cook a certain dish on a certain day. And on Wednesday and Friday—the days of *magro*, or fasting—that dish usually consists of fish. "Different businesses have different schedules," Paolo explains. "Fishermen don't fish on Sundays. Butcher shops are closed on Thursday afternoons. Things aren't always available all the time; for this reason, and also for religious traditions, restaurants and families work around what they can get, when they can get it. On Tuesday and Thursday, for instance, my father would fill a marble vat with baccalà, to prepare it for sale the following day. And unfortunately, I had to handle it every time, so I didn't eat it for many years."

Baccalà is sold throughout the Mediterranean in different shapes and sizes—from thin tail pieces to thick, flaky chunks from the loins of big codfish. The price often reflects the quality of the cut. But the way that you treat it—soaking it several times, in changes of cold water, over a few days—is just as important as the price and thickness of the meat.

This is a recipe that you must keep an eye on—and you'll start it a day or two before you serve it. If handled correctly, the codfish is sweet and flavorful, yet salty and firm. It's obvious, once you taste it, why salted cod has been taken to sea ever since ships first sailed. It lasts so long, and yet it tastes so good.

Two days before you begin to cook this dish, start soaking your codfish in a container of cold water in the fridge. Replace the water every 4 hours or so. You can let it rest overnight, but don't forget to change the water as soon as you wake up in the morning.

After 2 days of baths, much of the salinity in the codfish should be gone.

Bring 2 quarts of water to a boil over high heat in a small pot with the diced carrot, celery, and white onion. Add the codfish and turn off the heat, and let it steep for 30 minutes.

Remove the codfish from the water, and let it dry on a rack or on a kitchen towel for about 30 minutes, until cooled. Taste a bit. If it's frighteningly salty, repeat the boiling process and blanch it again, though it may break up. If that begins to happen, stop and work with what you've got. If the fish is bland, you can re-season it with salt.

(recipe continues)

Flake the fish according to the natural grain of its flesh—this will make sense to you as the meat begins to break apart in your hands. Keep the grain rather than tearing or chopping the meat. Every piece of fish is like a fingerprint—try to maintain its unique shape and break it into bite-size pieces.

Scatter the pieces of flaked fish on a large, flat plate; this is a composed salad, so it's not tossed but rather assembled in pieces and then dressed.

Halve the cherry tomatoes (or quarter, if they're big) and season them with salt, the finely chopped garlic, and olive oil in a small bowl. Shave the red onion very thin, then soak it in cold water for 5 minutes and drain. Rinse the capers in water, drain, and dry them with paper towels, then crack them open with your fingers.

Arrange the tomatoes on the plate with the fish. Add slivers of the onion between the flakes of fish. Add the capers and olives and scatter the parsley on your salad. Then drizzle with quite a bit of olive oil, then squeeze the lemon on top. Serve.

FAVE E PECORINO ROMANO

FAVA BEANS AND PECORINO CHEESE

serves 4 as a snack

WHITE WINE, FOR DRINKING

2 POUNDS FRESH YOUNG FAVA BEAN PODS

7 OUNCES PECORINO CHEESE, BROKEN INTO SMALL CHUNKS

"Primo Maggio—May 1st—is Labor Day in Italy," Paolo says. "It's also the day of fava beans and pecorino. Many people from Rome leave the city and do the *scampagnata,* a picnic in the Lazio countryside, to celebrate spring, and nature, with friends and family, and eat things of the season, and drink wine. Especially with fava beans and pecorino. After lunch, you sit, slowly opening the pods, eating the beans with cheese. It's not prepared, it just happens."

Good aged pecorino stagionato is hard to find outside of Italy, unless you've got a fine purveyor of Italian foods near you. But the white, salty pecorino Romano is also perfect for this snack. There is also a great wine, grown in central Italy, that shares the same name—Pecorino. This is an ideal match, in my opinion.

Gather some friends. Pour the wine. Slowly break open pods of fava beans, and eat the beans raw with chunks of pecorino. Summer is coming.

POLLO CON I PEPERONI

CHICKEN SMOTHERED WITH PEPPERS

serves 4 as a main course, with bread

2 LARGE PEPERONI (ITALIAN BELL PEPPERS)—1 YELLOW AND 1 RED. THESE SHOULD BE VERY LONG AND LARGE; IF YOU'RE USING THE MORE COMMON BASEBALL-SIZED ONES, USE 4

1 (3-TO-4-POUND) CHICKEN, CUT INTO 10 PIECES (*see note*)

SALT AND FRESHLY GROUND PEPPER

¼ CUP EXTRA-VIRGIN OLIVE OIL

2 GARLIC CLOVES

1 MEDIUM WHITE ONION, JULIENNED

1 FRESH BAY LEAF OR 2 DRY

PINCH OF CHILI FLAKES

½ CUP WHITE WINE

1¼ CUPS CANNED WHOLE SAN MARZANO TOMATOES, DRAINED AND HAND-CRUSHED

CHOPPED FRESH PARSLEY, FOR FINISHING

CRUSTY BREAD, FOR SERVING

Note

Separate the wings from the breast by running your knife around the joint and then pulling it free. Take off the legs by bending them back away from the breast and cutting them at the joint, and then separate the thigh from the drumstick by opening the joint between the two and severing it. Whack each breast into two pieces. Use a cleaver or heavy chef's knife for this pleasurable job.

The peppers in the markets of Lazio are luxuriously large and sweet—with just a hint of bitterness.

Words cannot explain how much I love pollo con i peperoni. "Don't tell me!" Paolo said, as we read these recipe notes together. It's a dish of chicken smothered and braised in bell peppers and their juices; it's nourishing and sweet and savory. I often cook it for my family or for people I care about because it's simple and it also allows you to drink and enjoy the company of your guests. Just remember to buy or bake a lot of good bread, take some nice butter out to soften, and maybe make a salad to serve alongside.

Cut the peppers by removing the stem end and discarding it. Remove the bottoms and keep those. Cut the remaining pepper into 4 sides, and then cut those sides into 4 pieces each. Remove the seeds and the white pith.

Pat the chicken parts very dry, and season them with salt and pepper.

Pour the oil into a heavy-bottomed pot that has a lid. A Dutch oven is the best option. Heat it over medium-high heat until shimmering-hot.

Add the garlic to the oil, and as it begins to brown, add the chicken pieces in batches. Don't do this all at once; your pan will be crowded and the oil temperature will plunge and it will take longer for the chicken to brown. If you're in a hurry, use two pans. Sear the chicken until richly browned, 3 to 5 minutes per side. Remove the chicken from the pot.

Add the peppers, onion, bay leaf, and chili flakes and sauté, stirring, about 12 minutes, until they begin to soften. Season with a few pinches of salt. When the peppers and onion are softened, deglaze with the white wine, and shake the pot over the stove to emulsify the wine and the oil.

Add the tomatoes and chicken, and make sure all of the chicken is covered by the peppers and their juices. Bring the pot to a simmer, turn down the heat to a gentle simmer, cover, and cook for 30 to 45 minutes, until the chicken is cooked through, and the sauce is reduced. Add water if the mixture becomes too dry. You want a stew that is not very liquid; your peppers and chicken should stand alone on the plate with a small amount of rich sauce. Remove the bay leaves.

Season with salt and pepper, and a sprinkling of parsley. Serve with sourdough with a sturdy crust, and a couple of bottles of cold, crisp white wine—a falanghina or a good, local Frascati Superiore would be perfect.

The Olives of Itri

On a hot May morning, Paolo, Jason, and I headed south out of Rome in search of great olive oils. We were driving directly parallel to the ancient Via Appia Antica, and occasionally on the Via Appia Nuova (the "new Appia"), which is framed beautifully by huge pines, their elegance counterbalancing the recklessness of those who drive along it.

Lazio is most famous for gaeta—a small olive that is picked green around December for pressing into oil, or left on the trees to mature until early spring to make black olives for brining. The olive is named for a magnificent seaside town with an old fort perched on stern cliffs about two hours south of Rome. As you drive down into Gaeta you pass through hundreds of acres of gnarled old olive trees that cling to steep, grassy hills.

But before we got that far south, we stopped near the ancient Gardens of Ninfa, at a factory and farm called Agnoni. After winding around small lanes we skidded to a stop, at a gate that looked grand for this humble corner of Lazio. We were buzzed in, and met by a huge German shepherd and her owner, Viviana—the woman who runs Agnoni with her two sisters. The family business began two generations ago; their grandmother used to go door-to-door in the village, selling her jams and conserved vegetables—artichokes, peppers, red onions. They were, apparently, far better than anyone else's. And so her son, who is now about seventy years old, got the recipes. The matriarch's legacy lives on—in green, bitter oils, huge jars of jams, and—especially—those preserved artichokes. Her portrait sits just beside the production room where women trim and pickle vegetables. Everything is cleaned and packed by hand, and shipped across Italy. Their products are wonderful; if you ever come across Agnoni artichokes or preserves, buy a jar.

But we were there for the oil. You see, we'd been bringing Agnoni oils to tables in our restaurant for years. They make many oils; the best one is made from a cultivar called Itrana. Viviana led us deep into a grove of olive trees,

some of which are five centuries old. (One of the trees on their property is protected by government decree. They are not allowed to prune it or harvest olives from this tree. It is sacred, this magic tree, huddled in tall grass.)

After seeing the trees from which some of our favorite oils come, we left Agnoni and continued south, following the Appia the entire way. On the right, the Pontine Marshes stretched to the sea. Until the marshes were drained by Mussolini after almost fifteen hundred years, this area of Lazio had been malarial and uninhabitable. After the fall of the Roman empire, no one could control the mosquitoes. On the left, the crooked range of the Ciociaria rises up.

And suddenly, the land is arid, desertlike, distinctly different. The Via Appia Antica winds through shallow canyons, and fruit trees make way for cacti and olive trees. Forts peek out from hilltops. Campania, and Mount Vesuvius, are close. This is olive country, one of many in Italy. But perhaps the best one.

We had heard from friends that there was a sublime olive oil from this area, made by a woman named Serena. We headed to her shop. Inside, a man with rubber boots was producing the purest olive oil I'd ever had. As he poured us small cups to taste from a plastic barrel, he said, "We lost everything this year—150,000 euros worth of olives, at least—to a frost. All we have is a little oil to sell." But that oil was exquisite. It smelled of freshly cut grass; it tasted of mint, thyme, and lavender. "You can extract more oil at a higher temperature," he explained, "and get even more oil, if you add water to the process. I add no water, and press it very cold. I want only the purest oil."

Fifty-pound sacks of salt sat on the floor. Red pickling jugs hugged the corners of the shop, empty. And then Serena emerged, tall and handsome, from the back. "Our olives are more for eating than for oils," she explained, without introducing herself. "These are Itrana olives, and it took us fifteen years to get the D.O.P. [a certification of origin]." She rolled her eyes. "Ah . . . Italy."

We tasted some olives from the small crop they had been able to save. They were nothing like olives I've tasted elsewhere. There was salinity of course, but interwoven with a bright sweetness, and notes of clove and nutmeg, even juniper. "I'll take you to my olives," Serena said, meaning her trees. "Though since I lost my crop, I haven't returned."

We climbed into her Mitsubishi truck, and she left the town, heading up into the hills. "I am a producer of olive oil," she explained, fatalistically. "My father was a merchant, and I went to London to study import and export, but I returned here to produce oil. He was very angry with me. I'll never tell him, but he was right. Farming. It's a dream. And then . . . it's a struggle."

She drove the creaky truck around steep mountain curves, above the town of Itri, to the top of an orchard. You could see the sea, and Gaeta, in the distance. On this hilltop, the wind was suffused with the scent of wild herbs. Serena pulled the emergency brake to a stop, the truck skidded a bit, and we got out. Olives littered the ground. "This is the spot where—how do I say?—I've asked the kids to make a cremation for me."

It was still, and hot, and shriveled olives dried on flat stones. "We can no longer predict the season here, and it interrupts the long rhythm of farming. Last March, it dropped to minus ten degrees [Celsius]. And I lost everything." She continued, "Here is not Tuscany. I go to my brother's house in Tuscany, and everything is perfect. The houses, perfect. The animals, perfect. Here, we're hanging off the side of a rock, depending on the climate."

From there we curled around to another orchard, near Serena's home, where she has 2,500 olive trees. A wild boar had decimated her fence, and she yelled "Mamma Mia" before rounding another snake of a corner. "People will spend fifty euros to fill their car with petrol but they won't spend fifteen euros for a bottle of olive oil, which will feed them for weeks. I left the co-op because they forced me out. I wanted quality; they wanted quantity. There was nowhere to go.

"These, these are my olives and my oils. *Solo mio*. Not oil from Morocco or Tunisia, not oils put into a laboratory and acidified and manipulated. To sell my oil in the European Community I can only write 'Olives from Italy.' But it is much, much more personal, and particular, than that. And for that, I had to change my label, and the identity of my own oils. And for that, I might lose everything."

We had a *merenda*—an afternoon snack— at Serena's home, and later, drove to visit her friend who raises black pigs—the miale nero casertano breed—and we drank wine. They were both, seemingly, alone. Fighting against the land, and also married to it. "Do you want to buy my farm?" her friend asked us. She and our host lay in the sun, tanning, beside a small pool. The pigs—huge black hogs—snorted in the background.

After an hour or so, we drove back to Itri. We ate sausages with fennel seed and coriander and Serena explained to us how her town was destroyed during World War II when the Americans landed and made their way north from Sicily. Her home had been a *frantoio*—a place to press olives—before a bomb fell on it. It's been repaired, but the old house and the repaired parts don't quite seem to match.

Our final hour with Serena was spent at the top of the cathedral that sits on the very top of a hill over Itri. It was quite a climb, and we panted as she scrambled up the stairs.

On the way out of town, we passed massive factories, like Mancini, which produce hundreds of thousands of liters of oil, shipped across the world. "See what I'm fighting against?" she asked.

We did. As the car wound around the olive trees, the factories cut an ugly slash through the landscape. And then we reached the sea, heading north toward Anzio. We saw people sitting beside the ocean, eating fish and dipping bread, some in oils that were honest, and some that were not.

ZUPPA DI ARZILLA CON BROCCOLI

A SOUP OF SKATE AND BROCCOLI ROMANESCO

serves 4 as an appetizer

EXTRA-VIRGIN OLIVE OIL

1 1/2 POUNDS SKATE WINGS, SKINNED AND FILLETED, BONES RESERVED FROM THE FISHMONGER

1/3 CUP LARGE-DICED ONION PLUS 1/2 CUP FINELY DICED

1/3 CUP LARGE-DICED CARROT PLUS 1/2 CUP FINELY DICED

1/3 CUP LARGE-DICED CELERY PLUS 1/2 CUP FINELY DICED

3/4 CUP DRY WHITE WINE

1 GARLIC CLOVE

1 POUND BROCCOLI ROMANESCO

4 SALTED ANCHOVY FILLETS, CHOPPED

1/2 CUP CANNED SAN MARZANO TOMATOES, CRUSHED

SALT AND PEPPER

A HANDFUL OF SMALL FRESH PASTA, LIKE QUADRUCCI (OPTIONAL)

CHOPPED FRESH PARSLEY, TO FINISH

"The main fishing ports of Rome are Civitavecchia and Anzio. Just before World War II, Anzio thrived, and was the most important port south of Rome. In wintertime, the fishermen would come with a great catch, and my family would go there to buy *arzilla*—Roman slang for skate—because it's cheap, but delicious. And it's amazing for this soup, which my mother taught me to cook," Paolo says.

Mild, gelatinous, and not at all oily, skate is a delicate fish ideally suited for soup. Chicken soup is the ultimate comfort food; but this is a worthy substitute, because it has many of the same qualities. Find a skate that is slick and clean and fresh, and ask your fishmonger to clean it for you, reserving the bones. Simmer it and pull the meat from the tiny, cartilaginous skeleton and what results is a soup that is so round and rich that you might forget that it came from the sea.

MAKE THE STOCK: Start by filming a heavy-bottomed pot with olive oil and heating it over medium heat. Roast the reserved bones of the fish in this, turning occasionally, letting them release their moisture, and eventually begin to brown, about 10 minutes.

Add the large-diced onion, carrot, and celery and sauté, stirring occasionally, for 10 minutes or until they start to soften. Deglaze with 1/2 cup of the wine, let it come to a simmer, and reduce by half. Add 2 quarts and 1 cup cold water, raise the heat to high to bring it to a boil, then turn the heat down to a simmer and cook for 30 minutes, skimming the scum off the surface. Strain the stock, return the liquid to the pot, and keep warm.

MAKE THE SOUP: In another heavy-bottomed pot over medium heat, heat a generous glug of olive oil. Add the finely diced onion, carrot, and celery. Crush the garlic with the back of your knife and add it to the pot. Cook, stirring occasionally, until the vegetables are soft, about 10 minutes.

Meanwhile, prepare the romanesco by cutting the small spindles from the core with a sharp paring knife. Peel the core and then cut into 1/2-inch dice.

(recipe continues)

When the vegetables in the pot have softened, add the chopped anchovy fillets and cook until they dissolve in the oil. Then add the remaining ¼ cup white wine and reduce for 3 minutes, or until it's almost entirely evaporated. Add the tomatoes and stir.

Add the romanesco to the pot and add half of the fish stock you prepared. Season the skate wings with salt and pepper, then add them to the soup.

Put a lid on the pot, bring to a boil, then lower the heat to a slow simmer and let it cook gently for 15 minutes. The skeleton structure of the fish is made of collagen, which will thicken the sauce naturally. After the flavors have developed and the romanesco is soft, add the rest of the fish stock.

Remove the skate wings; if there are bones in the wings, use your fingers and a fork to scrape the meat from the small, soft bones. When you're finished, return all the meat to the pot. If you're using pasta, add it to the soup and cook it for 3 to 5 minutes while you are handling the skate.

When the pasta is fully cooked, season the soup well with salt and pepper. If you'd like, remove about one-quarter of the soup and blend it in a blender, and then add this back to the pot to give it more body. Finish with some chopped parsley and extra-virgin olive oil, and serve.

AGRETTI IN AGRO

AGRETTI WITH LEMON

serves 4 as a small side

½ POUND AGRETTI

LEMON WEDGES

EXTRA-VIRGIN OLIVE OIL

SALT

Grown by the sea, along the coast of Lazio and further south, agretti can be irrigated with salt water. Historically, it was used to make soda ash, to produce stained glass in Italy. Now this succulent—which speaks of the ocean—is simply for eating.

Similar to sea beans (otherwise known as samphire), agretti can grow in gardens as well as in salt marshes. It has both the green, vegetal expression of the earth and the mineral saline taste of the Mediterranean.

Bring a medium saucepan full of water to a boil over high heat. Blanch the agretti for 15 seconds, then run cold water over it or dunk it in an ice bath. Serve it with lemon wedges and a splash of olive oil and, maybe, a pinch of salt.

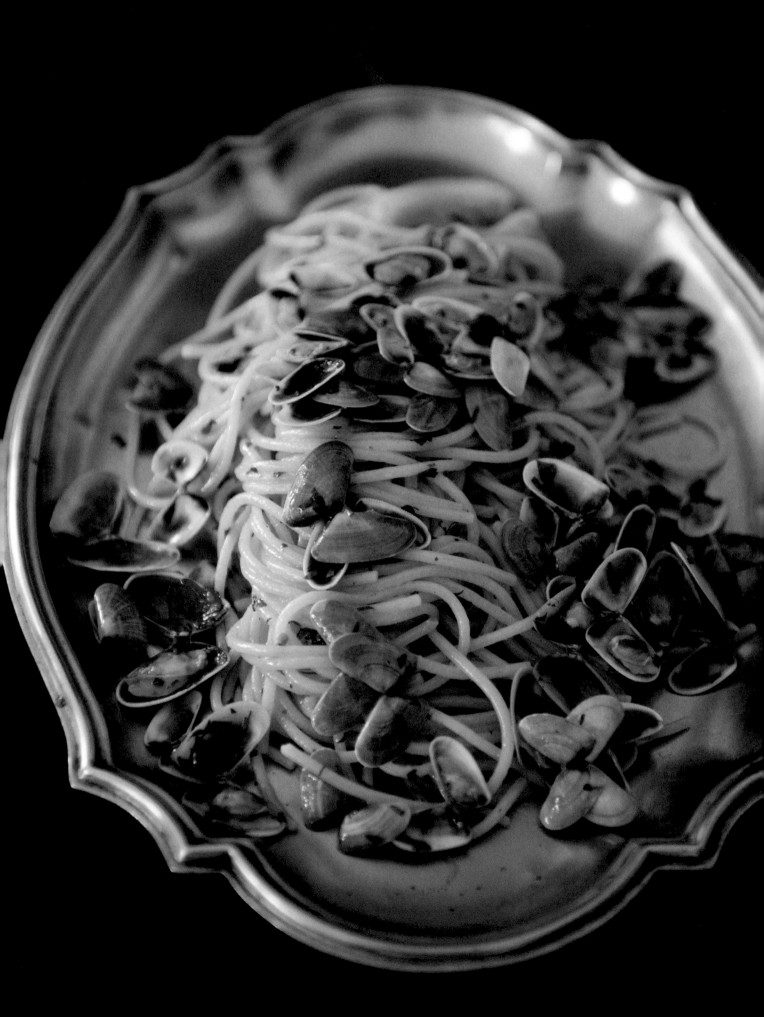

SPAGHETTI CON LE TELLINE
SPAGHETTI WITH SMALL WILD CLAMS

serves 4 as a main course, or 6 as a starter

1 POUND TELLINA OR OTHER TINY CLAMS

SALT

1 POUND DRIED SPAGHETTI

¼ CUP EXTRA-VIRGIN OLIVE OIL

2 GARLIC CLOVES, CRUSHED WITH THE SIDE OF A KNIFE

CHILI FLAKES, TO TASTE

½ CUP WHITE WINE

FISTFUL OF FRESH PARSLEY LEAVES, PLUS A LITTLE MORE

HERBED BREAD CRUMBS, IF YOU HAVE SOME ON HAND *(see page 198)*

Note

For Paolo's mother's version of this dish, use 2 pounds of Manila clams. After the clams have opened, add ½ cup of crushed San Marzano tomatoes—just the tomatoes, no juice—and a few scrapings of lemon zest. Let these warm together over low heat for 5 minutes, and then add the cooked pasta.

"Roberto, an old friend of mine and an avid fisherman, came to us one day," Paolo tells me. "He had a bag full of tiny clams called tellina. He had been gathering them in Anzio for two days, raking the sand to search for them. Tellina are so difficult to find, and when they're wild, and from a friend, they are such a rare and special present. He asked me to cook them, and so I did, and here is the recipe." These tiny clams, often harvested by hand in the Mediterranean waters of Lazio, are prized for their flavor. They are also occasionally available in markets along the coast, in Anzio or Ostia. The recipe works for little cockles or other small clams, but feel free to increase the amount of clams if yours are a bit shell-heavy.

Soak the tiny clams in salt water (in seawater, if possible) in the refrigerator for 2 days, so they spit out whatever sand is inside them. They live in the sand, and you need to get it out. Change the water several times. When your clams have exorcised the seabed, drain them.

Boil a large pot of water, and salt it well. Pop the spaghetti in the pot, stir for the first 30 seconds, and cook until al dente. Drain the spaghetti.

While the pasta cooks, get a large sauté pan ripping hot over high heat. Add the olive oil, garlic, and a little chili and cook until just fragrant. Add the clams and the wine and bring to a boil, covered. When the clams open, after just a couple of minutes, add the spaghetti and cook for a minute or two, stirring and flipping the noodles over themselves. Add a fistful of parsley. Taste to see if the pasta needs some salt. It probably won't.

Serve on a platter topped with some herbed bread crumbs, if you have them, and a flurry of more parsley.

On Shepherds, Cheeses, and Returning to the Countryside

The food of Lazio, and of Rome itself, has been shaped for centuries by the *pecorari*, the people who care for, milk, and occasionally slaughter sheep. It is difficult to overestimate the importance of lamb to the Roman dinner table. Baby lambs are roasted with rosemary. The offal is prepared in countless ways. Sheep's milk becomes many kinds of cheese. Pecorino, from *pecora*, the Italian word for sheep, is grated atop most pastas; sheep ricotta is spread on bread and made into cakes and pastry. You'll see animals grazing just outside the ancient city walls, often on the side of the busy highway.

Exploring the sheep cheeses of Lazio is, as with so many other Italian traditions, like peering into a dimly lit, ancient cave. It's easiest to understand by spending time with the shepherds. Their history is one of listening to the land and the agrarian rhythms that echo through it. The cheese springs from this knowledge.

Paolo owns a small stake in a pecorino cheese facility, Caseificio de Juliis, which is behind his childhood home in the village of Falcognana, just twenty minutes from downtown Rome (if Paolo is behind the wheel). The owners, Fabio and Paolo de Juliis, are Paolo's childhood friends. A year ago, they decided to sell a portion of their business, and thus began our foray into cheese making and shepherding.

We visited the factory one November morning. It's small, with room for no more than four people to work. Since 1966, the boiler has clanked to life in the predawn light, heating a 200-liter vat of sheep's milk. Giuliana, the matriarch of the operation, occasionally wandered in to chat or to hand us small cups of sweet coffee from a Moka pot. On this morning, they first made pecorino for aging; it was packed in salt, and later would be packed in *vinaccia*, the remains of red grapes after pressing, or wrapped in chestnut leaves. For three months or longer, the cheese would mature on wooden racks, just a hundred feet from where it was born..

We ate cheese for breakfast. The Caciofiore, a cheese whose curd is set with wild artichoke rennet, was creamy and soft, with a subtle taste of nutty decay, and the faint tingle of active fermentation. The pecorino, shot through with small holes, was still young, grassy, and a little gamy; the salt had not yet penetrated all the way through. When I returned to the small building that houses the cheese making, the workers were sitting, eating steaming baskets of ricotta with spoons. Warm whey dripped onto the concrete floor from larger baskets of ricotta sitting on stainless-steel shelves.

In Oretta Zanini De Vita's seminal book on Lazio's cuisine, *Popes, Peasants, and Shepherds*, she explains: "The best lambs on the Roman market were the ones from the Ciociaria, and this is why lamb and sheep's milk cheeses are common in popular cooking."

A few days after that first meal, we went to the Ciociaria for the first of our meetings with Loretto Pacitti, a farmer who made a pecorino that Paolo's mother had served us. Like shepherds in centuries past, Pacitti travels to Rome several times a month to sell his cheese at the Mercato di Campagna Amica del Circo Massimo, a farmer's market open only on weekends. We arrived at his house and had to wait about an hour for him. He apologized; it was his birthday, and he had had to visit family first. Pacitti, a dapper forty-five-year-old, took us on an hour-long walk through the mountains above his village of Picinisco. The Monti della Meta and other mountains form a border between Lazio and the regions to the east and south, Abruzzo, Molise, and finally, Campania.

Earlier in his life, he had left the Ciociaria for what was then obligatory military service, and then went on to earn a university degree in business development. Soon after, he decided to return to Picinisco. "It was only after my university that I realized what a treasure I had in my old home—the honesty of the people, and the food," he explained. "I wanted to preserve that way of life by living it myself. This farm represents twenty years of research—my family at first made only ricotta and pecorino di Picinisco." Pacitti has ambitiously expanded the family business, adding more cheeses, but also opening a small *agriturismo* and restaurant, which members of his family help him run.

The research he described is that of mastering the making of an ancient cheese, Conciato di San Vittore, for which he is now best known. He learned how to make it from an old cheesemaker, Teodoro Vadalà, who brought the cheese back to the marketplace along with Vincent Mancino, proprietor of Rome's Pro Loco DOL. (The initials stand for *di origine laziale*—"from Lazio.") Conciato di San Vittore comes in a rich, creamy white version and a sharper one laced through with blue mold. It was on the verge of extinction before Vadalà reintroduced it and Mancino marketed it in his Lazio-centric restaurant and shop.

The cheese was originally created by shepherds to hold up during the difficult period of transhumance, the ancient migration of shepherds and their flocks from Lazio and the mountains of Abruzzo and Umbria south to the bottom-of-the-boot pastures of Apulia, Calabria, and Basilicata, and then back again. The men followed the grass, pasturing the sheep high in the north in the summer. The walk south, for the winter, took months, and for sustenance they carried cheese, foraged, and sometimes ate one of their animals.

Pacitti's cheese is packed in wild mountain herbs, the most important of which is *santoreggia*, a form of winter savory, "which has antibiotic properties," he explained. It protects the outside of the cheese from bacteria and other microorganisms, while others inside thrive and develop flavor. As we walked through the forest, Pacitti plucked *santoreggia* from a path that leads his sheep to pastures at over three thousand feet, where the best summer grasses grow, thick with herbs and flowers that affect the milk. "We also use juniper, fennel, and wild rosemary to preserve the cheese," he explained, "as they keep insects away in our caves."

I asked what makes the cheeses of the Ciociaria different from those of coastal or northern Lazio. "The milk here is always raw, and I remove the rennet from the

stomachs of animals to set the curd. We have always been a poor place, producing *prodotti artigianale* [artisanal products] because we lack machinery and investment. The cheeses are aged naturally, in non-temperature-controlled conditions, so the product is wild. And the pastures, which all the local shepherds share, have a great biodiversity. The mountains are high, and as the animals graze at different altitudes during different seasons, the milk changes greatly. The industrial Romano is a fixed thing." He meant the *denominazione di origine protetta* (DOP) cheese pecorino Romano, which most people would consider the good, "authentic" stuff. "It is not touched by nature as ours is."

That afternoon, we ate another of Pacitti's cheeses, a soft, creamy Caciofiore. The milk, rather than being curdled by animal rennet, had been curdled by rennet from wild artichoke flowers. That form of rennet was mentioned by the Roman agronomist Columella in *De Re Rustica* in the first century A.D.

Paolo and I returned in the freezing weather of early December 2016 to see Pacitti again at Casa Lawrence, his agriturismo, named for D. H. Lawrence. The writer stayed here briefly in the 1920s; parts of his book *The Lost Girl* take place in Picinisco.

Inside the house, a tiny restaurant operates on weekends, and a few rooms are available for guests to spend the night. A family sat by the fire, tearing chunks of local sourdough and eating it with thick slices of Pacitti's cheese. Farmers neatly tucked their fingers around slices of bread and cheese, popping them in their mouths as they talked. We mistakenly assumed the guests were part of Pacitti's family—the hospitality here is so great that it's difficult to distinguish between paying guests and those who live and work here.

The meal began with a cake of polenta with blue Conciato on top, the sweetness of the cornmeal delicately offsetting the powerful blue. A simple, warm mound of ricotta and olive oil was fresh and pure, as was a frittata with potato and leeks. A few slices of Pacitti's

cheese called Marzolina, which I'd never tasted before, were soft, almost stringy but at the same time crumbly, like ricotta. As the people at the table beside us drank wine and discussed Italian politics, Paolo and I ate a dish of *fegatino*, made from the lamb's pluck—its heart, lungs, kidney, and liver—stewed with onion, white wine, and a little tomato, in the tradition of southern Lazio. The tomato softened the pungency of the liver and the earthy funk of the offal; the fegatino was deliciously fortifying in the cold.

Then came a pasta with bitter local broccoli rabe and sausage and another pasta, cacio e pepe. Two older women from the kitchen, one of whom cooked with a portable oxygen tank slung over her shoulder, emerged to smile and ask how everything was. The food was honest and good, and they could tell we appreciated it for what it was. Just as our stomachs were bursting, Pacitti spread the embers on the hearth to make a bed of coals, and set in place a simple iron grill. On it he put milk-fed lamb seasoned only with salt, which he took from a deep terra-cotta pot on the mantel.

"When you focus on the tourist, rather than the land, you lose the sense of community and the connection between land and animals. You mine your soul," Pacitti said. As we talked, the cooks, aunts, and uncles gathered around the fire. A winemaker arrived with some of his wines for the visitors to taste. When we finally left, it was very dark and very cold. The sheep had been herded for the winter into stables, where they eat hay with a bit of local farro and corn, to fatten them and keep them warm. We heard the distant clang of their bells.

A few days later, Paolo and I drove north to Bracciano, still in Lazio but in an area called the Tuscia, which lies mostly in Tuscany and was settled by the Etruscans long before the Romans consolidated their power. The sheep for our own milk and cheese were soon to be delivered from a local farm, called L'Isola del Formaggio. We went there to meet the owner, Sergio Pitzalis, to see our sheep,

and to taste his cheese from land and methods of production different from Pacitti's. "He makes a delicious Gorgonzola di Pecora," Pacitti had told us.

Compared with the severe Ciociaria, the land here was gentler. The hills rolled and were flat, open on top, with fields and olive trees—the Sabine and the Tuscia produce some of Italy's best oils. Below the hilltops, the creases and the steep, small valleys were filled with oaks and chestnuts. Beside the parking lot of the cheese factory, *mirto*, or myrtle, was planted. The workers produce a strong, delicious, tart-sweet liqueur from its berries.

L'Isola is less ambitious than Casa Lawrence, without a restaurant or rooms. It has just a small cheese shop, with the pink, plastic-beaded curtains that fill the entrances to many cheese shops in rural Italy. The glass door itself was littered with Slow Food stickers and other marks of approval for its cheese.

Inside, in the back half of the room given over to cheese making, a spry cheesemaker was perched above a steaming steel pot of sheep's milk, stirring the curds with a wooden staff. He reached in with a slotted scoop to fill white plastic baskets with curd. These curds sweat whey that goes into vats (to feed the pigs) or down the floor drain. The steady trickle of whey made a gentle splashing noise that is the soundtrack of cheese making.

"Don't take my photo!" shouted the man. But after ten minutes he was posing and hamming it up for the camera. His name was Tonino. A shepherd and cheesemaker from Sardinia, he had grown up on an eighty-acre farm. "After my military service, in 1971," he told us, "I was taking the train back to Rome on my way home. I passed through this part of Lazio, and saw the landscape, and thought it would be very good for raising sheep and making pecorino." He still thinks that pecorino Sardo, the DOP cheese from Sardinia, might be better. "In Sardinia we have the best grass, and the water is very pure, but instead of focusing on agriculture, they developed the petrochemical industry there. We all know that won't last, that it's not sustainable. People in Lazio appreciate agriculture more. It's easier to sell cheese here and make some money."

As Tonino stirred the vat of curds, breaking them into small pieces that he would strain, he repeated something I'd heard many times over the last few years in Italy—that young, educated people were returning to a life of agriculture. "People in Sardinia and here in Lazio, young people, are realizing you can make good money from sheep," he said. "And the work is satisfying. I always wanted to learn English, and to travel, but I'm happy that I chose this profession. It must be a good way to live, if educated young people are doing it."

SHEEP'S RICOTTA WITH HONEY AND CARAMELIZED FIGS

serves 4 to 8

1 POUND FRESH SHEEP'S OR
COW'S RICOTTA

1 POUND FIGS

1/4 CUP LIGHT BROWN SUGAR

GOOD FLORAL HONEY

FRESH THYME LEAVES,
TO FINISH

FRESH MINT LEAVES,
JULIENNED, TO FINISH

We make ricotta from our sheeps' milk, and we have a fig tree, and we have bees that produce honey. So here's what we make with these gifts.

One couldn't ask for a simpler dessert when figs are in season. If you happen to have a fig tree, or know someone who does, you understand that a harvest of figs is a frenetic thing. All of a sudden, they're everywhere. Splattered across the ground, sticking to your shoes, feeding birds and boars and bees. The fig tree doesn't hold back when it's time.

When choosing figs, make sure they're purple and give gently to the touch. Green figs are, as you might expect, not very sweet. But the fruit is delicate and its window between ripe and rotten is very short.

Sometimes we serve this dish as a salad, with the addition of hand-cut Tuscan ham, and arugula tossed with olive oil and salt and pepper.

Take the ricotta out of the fridge and let it shake off its chill. Cut your figs into halves. Spread the brown sugar over a plate.

Place a nonstick pan over medium-high heat, and quickly drop a few figs in the sugar, cut side down. Working in batches, place the figs sugar side down in the pan and allow them to caramelize for 30 seconds, then remove.

Arrange the figs artfully, around nice spoons of ricotta on a plate. Drizzle with honey, and finish with thyme leaves and julienned mint leaves.

PAOLO'S PASTA OF ASPARAGUS, GUANCIALE, ARTICHOKES, PEAS, AND SHEEP'S RICOTTA

serves 4 as a main course,
or 6 as a starter

SEA SALT AND PEPPER

1 CUP FRESH SHEEP RICOTTA
(OR COW'S RICOTTA,
IN A PINCH), AT ROOM
TEMPERATURE

ZEST OF 1/2 LEMON

2 TABLESPOONS EXTRA-VIRGIN
OLIVE OIL

4 OUNCES MEDIUM-DICED
GUANCIALE

2 MEDIUM ARTICHOKES,
CLEANED (see page 276),
JULIENNED

2/3 CUP ASPARAGUS TIPS AND
SHOOTS, CUT ON AN ANGLE
INTO 3/4-INCH PIECES

1/4 CUP PEAS

1/3 CUP WHITE WINE

1 POUND TONNARELLI OR
FETTUCCINE (OR OTHER FRESH
EGG PASTA)

GRATED PECORINO

FRESH CHOPPED MINT

There's usually something or other around that you can make a delicious pasta with, and one night, that's what happened—Paolo and I had arrived on a flight to Rome, and we raided his mother's fridge for dinner. He remembers, "Everything in this dish came from around my house. The cheese was from De Juliis, our tiny cheese factory. My brother, Stefano, had foraged the asparagus. The artichokes and peas were from our neighbor's farm. The pork, okay, I'm not entirely sure where that came from, but I do know my mother had made the pasta the day before."

And so Paolo cooked the guanciale, melting the fat in a pan. The artichoke sizzled in the pig fat, followed by the asparagus, and then it all came together with the ricotta and a few sprigs of mint.

Bring a pot of water to boil for pasta, and salt it well.

Meanwhile, put the ricotta in a mixing bowl. Add the lemon zest, some sea salt, pepper, and the olive oil, and whip together.

In a large sauté pan or wok, cook the guanciale over medium heat, until the fat is rendered and the pork is crispy. Add the artichokes and brown them a bit, then add the asparagus, and later the peas, to fry in the pig fat and crispy pork until cooked, about 4 minutes. Deglaze with the white wine and turn the heat off.

Drop the pasta in the water and cook until there is no raw flour in the middle. Turn the heat back up to medium-high heat under the guanciale pan. Save a cup or so of the pasta water and drain the pasta.

Add the pasta to the guanciale pan, and stir. Add a splash of pasta cooking water and then toss the pasta by flipping it off the lip of the sauté pan or wok, back over itself.

When the pasta has absorbed the sauce, dump it into the bowl with the ricotta, so that the ricotta and pasta create a sauce. Flip it in the bowl or stir aggressively, several times. Adjust the seasoning with salt and pepper, pecorino, and chopped mint to taste.

CORATELLA

A STEW OF THE PLUCK OF THE BABY LAMB

serves 4

1½ POUNDS CORATELLA—
LIVER, HEART, LUNGS, KIDNEYS,
AND SWEETBREADS OF A BABY
LAMB (*see note*)

1 POUND ONIONS, JULIENNED

¼ CUP EXTRA-VIRGIN
OLIVE OIL

SALT AND PEPPER

2 BAY LEAVES

CHILI FLAKES, IF YOU'D LIKE

1 CUP WHITE WINE

1 ROSEMARY SPRIG

Note

This may be obvious, but you're going to have to find a butcher who can supply you with the pluck—and it needs to be very fresh. In the United States, lungs are not permitted for sale by the USDA, so you may need to go to the source—a shepherd. Or omit the lungs, if you can buy all the other organs.

This is Paolo's favorite dish, and we were lucky enough to eat it at Pacitti's home. I like to think of it as a shepherd's dinner. Each spring, nearly all the male lambs are slaughtered—otherwise they fight with each other, and cause more problems in the flock than they solve. So they're eaten, and the mothers and daughters remain to graze, and produce milk.

The "pluck"' (the lungs, liver, heart, kidneys, and sweetbreads) of the milk-fed baby lambs are removed, all attached to the windpipe. This looks like a bunch of grapes on the stem. The organs are then removed, separated, and sliced (the windpipe, in parts brittle and rubbery, is one of the few bits that is discarded). The rest is stewed with lots of sweet onions, rosemary, and white wine. Sometimes artichokes are added. An earthy gravy results; it is deep, sweet, and gamy, with contrasting textures and tastes from the different organs. It's not a conventionally beautiful dish, but you may fall in love with it all the same. *Coratella* is served as an antipasto, as a main course, or as a *secondo*—after a pasta.

Remove the organs from the windpipe, and then remove the excess fat that jackets the outside of them. Now you should have 2 lungs, 2 kidneys, 2 sweetbreads (a long one, and a round one), a liver, and a heart.

Start with the lungs, which are spongy with tough bronchial tubes inside that are the texture of hard plastic. Remove these—the big ones at least. Then slice the lungs into slices, about 1½ inches long by ¼ inch thick.

Move on to the kidneys: Cut them in half, and remove the vein inside. Cut each half in 2 pieces.

Cut the sweetbreads like the lungs.

Take off the cap of fat from the heart and remove the aorta (the large artery). Cut the heart in half, remove any blood, and again slice it like the lungs. Remove any veins or fat around the liver, slice it in half, and again, cut into strips like the lungs.

If you get all these ingredients very, very fresh, you don't need to do anything but cut them. If the freshness is in question, you might soak the organs in water with a little splash of red or white wine vinegar for 30 minutes.

Place the onions in a sturdy pot with the olive oil and a healthy pinch of salt and sweat them over medium-low heat, allowing them to slowly break down. Stir often. It should take about 20 minutes to get them very soft and taking on a golden color. Add the bay leaves and chili flakes, if using.

Add all the organs to the onions and sauté for about 5 minutes, to take the rawness off. Season well with salt and pepper. Deglaze with the white wine, add the rosemary, bring to a simmer, and cook, covered, for 20 to 30 minutes, to cook through. Remove the bay leaves. You should have a thick slurry of a stew, that is nearly, but not quite, dry. Season with salt and pepper one more time if needed, and serve.

CAVATELLI WITH LAMB RAGÙ

serves 4 as a main course,
or 6 as a starter

SALT AND BLACK PEPPER

3 CUPS LAMB RAGÙ *(recipe follows)*, PLUS MORE AS NEEDED

1/2 CUP LAMB STOCK *(recipe follows)*, PLUS MORE AS NEEDED

FENNEL POWDER, TO TASTE

1 POUND FRESH CAVATELLI PASTA (USE APPIA'S [ALMOST] EGGLESS PASTA DOUGH *recipe on page 84*, OR BUY A GOOD ONE)

3 1/2 TABLESPOONS UNSALTED BUTTER, COLD, CUT INTO SMALL CHUNKS

CHOPPED FRESH PARSLEY

GRATED PARMESAN CHEESE

1/3 CUP ROMANESCO "FONDUE" *(recipe follows)*

FRESH TARRAGON LEAVES, FOR FINISHING

FRESH MINT LEAVES, FOR FINISHING

FINELY GRATED PECORINO, FOR FINISHING

This dish is, we admit, a little more involved than most in this book. It's delicious—chewy cavatelli pasta with a rich lamb ragù and a fondue of broccoli romanesco. "This is a restaurant dish," Paolo says. "It has a lot of components, but if you strip it down, without the stock, and just blanch the romanesco, it's easy. And it's here because its two main ingredients connect Lazio's lamb-eating tradition and broccoli romanesco with cavatelli, which is one of my favorite pastas."

Although you can do many things with cavatelli, we think it's at its best with a salty, slow-cooked, caramelized meat ragù. In this recipe, we've used lamb, with just a little tomato and red wine, and a few spices. The most essential thing you want is to taste the lamb itself—not a sweet and sour tomatoey thing—and how it complements the texture and taste of the pasta.

Bring a large pot of well-salted water to a boil for the pasta.

Meanwhile, in a large sauté pan or shallow wok, combine the lamb ragù and lamb stock and heat over medium heat. Season with fennel powder, salt, and pepper.

Add the cavatelli to the pasta pot and boil for 7 minutes or until it is just cooked. Drain the pasta and add it to the pan with the sauce. Sauté on high heat for a minute or two, just to meld the flavors. If it looks too dry, add some more lamb stock.

Turn off the heat and add the butter, parsley, and a generous amount of Parmesan. Toss together quickly in the hot pan to form a smooth sauce.

Serve the cavatelli topped with a few teaspoons of the romanesco fondue. (We put it in squeeze bottles at the restaurant, but a few half-teaspoon dollops will work, too.) Top with some fresh tarragon leaves, mint, and grated pecorino.

(recipe continues)

LAMB RAGÙ

makes about 1½ quarts

2¼ POUNDS BONELESS
LAMB SHOULDER (TO GRIND
YOURSELF) OR GROUND LAMB

1 TEASPOON FENNEL SEED,
TOASTED AND GROUND

½ TEASPOON SWEET PAPRIKA

SALT AND PEPPER

¼ CUP EXTRA-VIRGIN
OLIVE OIL

1⅓ CUPS MEDIUM-DICED
ONION

1⅓ CUPS MEDIUM-DICED
CELERY

2 BAY LEAVES, DRIED OR FRESH

½ CUP RED WINE

1⅓ CUPS CRUSHED CANNED
SAN MARZANO TOMATOES
(CRUSH AFTER DRAINING THE
JUICE), HARD BITS REMOVED

¾ CUP LAMB STOCK (*recipe
follows*) OR WATER

Note

Whenever you grind meat, it needs to be very cold, right above frozen. Ideally, chill all the parts of your meat grinder in the freezer, too. The process of grinding meat—the meat gets forced by a large screw through a tube that then pushes it through a steel plate—creates a lot of heat. If your meat is not extremely cold, the fat will melt and the end result will be a grainy, off-texture ragù. You can, and often should, season the meat mixture *before* you grind it, especially when making sausages.

IF USING THE LAMB SHOULDER: Remove the large layer of fat. Cut the lamb into 1-inch pieces in order to feed it through your grinder. Marinate the lamb meat with fennel seed, paprika, salt, and pepper for at least 1 hour. Then chill in the freezer until very cold (but not frozen), about 20 minutes (see note). Using a meat grinder, grind the lamb using a large plate (meaning the one with big holes, rather than small ones).

IF USING GROUND LAMB, simply season it with the fennel seed, paprika, salt, and pepper, and let it rest for 1 hour.

In a large, heavy pot, heat the olive oil over medium-high heat. When the oil starts to lightly smoke, add about a quarter of the ground lamb and spread it to cover the pot. Let it sear. You want the lamb to cling to the bottom of the pot, and almost burn, before scraping it off with your spatula, removing it to a bowl, and then adding another batch.

This process will take 15 to 20 minutes. When all the meat is dry and browned and removed from the pot, add the onion, celery, and bay leaves. The vegetables will release their own liquids, and while that happens you'll need to scrape the bottom of the pan again, scraping off what's left of the brown bits. Add the seared meat back to the pot.

Deglaze with the red wine, until it reduces by half, less than a minute. Add the crushed tomatoes and the lamb stock. Bring to a boil, lower the heat to a gentle simmer, and cook slowly for 3 hours, covered, until it's reduced, and almost gelatin-like. In case it becomes too dry, add some lamb stock or water. Remove the bay leaves. Season with salt and pepper to taste.

LAMB STOCK

makes 1 very rich quart

8 TO 10 POUNDS LAMB BONES

1/4 CUP EXTRA-VIRGIN
OLIVE OIL

2/3 CUP LARGE-DICED ONION

2/3 CUP LARGE-DICED CELERY

2/3 CUP LARGE-DICED CARROT

1/2 CUP RED WINE

1/2 CUP CRUSHED CANNED
SAN MARZANO TOMATOES

PINCH OF DRIED THYME

3 FRESH SAGE LEAVES

1 SPRIG OF FRESH ROSEMARY

Preheat the oven to 400°F. Roast the lamb bones on a sheet pan in the oven until brown, 30 to 40 minutes.

In a large pot, heat the olive oil over medium heat, and add the onion, celery, and carrot. Sauté for 10 minutes, stirring occasionally, until cooked and the onion is translucent, but not brown.

Add the lamb bones, red wine, and tomatoes to the pot and bring the wine to a boil over high heat until it is thick and reduced by half. Add the thyme and sage and rosemary and 6 quarts water. Bring to a simmer, reduce the heat to maintain a gentle simmer, and cook, partially covered, for at least 5 hours, until you have about 1 quart of stock. Strain. If necessary, reduce the stock to get to 1 quart.

ROMANESCO "FONDUE"

makes about 1 cup

1/3 CUP FINELY DICED ONION

2 TABLESPOONS EXTRA-VIRGIN
OLIVE OIL

1/2 POUND BROCCOLI
ROMANESCO (OR BROCCOLI)
FLORETS

SALT

1 BAY LEAF, PREFERABLY FRESH

1 BIG PIECE LEMON RIND (FROM
1/4 LEMON)

In a small saucepan, sauté the onion with the oil over medium heat for 5 minutes, stirring, until the onion has softened. Add the romanesco or broccoli. Season with salt. Add enough water to cover the vegetables. Add the bay leaf and lemon rind. Bring it to a simmer, then lower the heat to maintain a gentle simmer and cook, tightly covered, for 30 minutes, or until the vegetables are very soft, and the liquid is nearly completely evaporated. Remove the bay leaf and lemon rind. Blend the romanesco and the liquid until smooth with a blender or food processor, and cool down in your fridge or freezer.

The Vignarola Incident

Each year, the growing seasons of fava beans, artichokes, and peas cross over, in a green eclipse. And during this time, Romans make *vignarola*—a dish that sings of springtime, and connects them to the countryside of Lazio.

Rome is special in so many ways; its proximity to the countryside is one. The city doesn't sprawl like other capitals in Europe. There is little industrial decay—there is less sadness as you leave its wondrous, frustrating center than, say, Paris. In fact, as soon as you drive out of the old city walls, you're spit into a yellow-tinted, static suburbia for just a few kilometers, and then it's pastoral. Grape and kiwi vines mix with amber houses. Sheep graze between highways. This connects the city, its people, and the countryside, in a manner that most places don't.

One spring evening we left downtown Rome and headed to Paolo's house, which is a twenty-minute zip from the edge of town to Falcognana. Falcognana looks like any Roman suburb until you reach the top of the hill (there are four, maybe five streets). In

the distance, shade pines dot old pathways; a crumbling estate lies barren in the distance.

Paolo and I went to the tiny factory where a childhood friend of his makes cheese. We were waiting until eight p.m.—the perfect time to pick peas and fava beans in the countryside, according to Stefano, Paolo's brother.

After a few drinks, the cheesemaker, also named Paolo, emerged from his house with a board of soft cheese. His customary athletic gear tightly hugged his ample belly (he is a cyclist, I'm told, though he looks like a man who makes, and eats, a lot of cheese). I asked him why we picked the beans at this time—if somehow the cool night air imparted sweetness, or the lack of sunlight put less stress on the plants. "Yes," he laughed. "And, the farmer who rents that plot of land over there is lazy. He doesn't pick his fava beans. He goes home at seven o'clock. So we're going to steal them at eight."

We gathered artichokes, peas, and favas, and wild chicory and wild asparagus from the weed patches surrounding the plantings. The

four of us stopped, occasionally, to split open the pea pods with dirty thumbnails and pop them in our mouths. They were bursting with sweetness—more fruit than vegetable. "You could make ice cream with these!" our Paolo said, with excitement.

The favas, which Romans often eat raw, were the opposite of those sweet peas—bitter, with hints of clove and nutmeg and lots of tannin. We pried inside the cottony pods for more, until it was dark, and then we headed home for more wine and to cook the dinner which we'd just plucked from the earth. We lit a fire to grill a baby lamb, which is so common here in spring. The lamb was cut roughly. Not the seam cuts that isolate individual muscles, which Italians have mastered with pigs or cows, but rather a simple separation of parts.

The peas, favas, and artichokes which Paolo's mother, Pia, had cleaned made their way into a pot, to simmer. I manned the grill, and cooked the lamb medium-rare. Paolo took a bite and shook his head. "Jarrett, lamb is cooked medium-well here, and rested." I felt a slight bit of shame. But it makes sense to me now; lamb, especially young, is best when the blood becomes one with the meat. The fat crisps. The meat relaxes. It's better that way.

We ate the vignarola with bits of lamb neck, ribs, chops, and legs cut in cross-section. We drank white wine, and kicked a flat soccer ball around the yard.

"To cook with ingredients like these is truly gratifying," Paolo said, in a rare, wistful sort of way.

VIGNAROLA

SAUTÉED ARTICHOKES, PEAS, AND FAVA BEANS

serves 4 to 6 as a side

2 OUNCES GUANCIALE, SKIN REMOVED, CUT INTO MATCHSTICKS

2/3 CUP JULIENNED ONION

2¹/3 CUPS THINLY SLICED ARTICHOKE HEARTS, FROM ABOUT 2 LARGE CLEANED ARTICHOKES (*see page 276*)

SALT AND PEPPER

1¹/2 TABLESPOONS EXTRA-VIRGIN OLIVE OIL

1/4 CUP WHITE WINE

2 CUPS SHELLED FAVA BEANS

1¹/3 CUPS SHELLED FRESH PEAS (OR FROZEN, IF NOT IN SEASON)

CHOPPED FRESH MINT, FOR THE STEW, AND SOME MORE TO GARNISH

First, crisp the guanciale in a large sauté pan over medium heat. When the fat from the pork is fully rendered and the bits are crisp, add the onion and sweat for 5 minutes, stirring, until translucent.

Add the artichokes, and salt them. Add the olive oil to the pan after they suck up all the pork fat. Sauté over medium heat for about 7 minutes. First, their color will fade and they will begin to soften. Then, they will brown a bit. Don't agitate the pan too much—you want the artichokes to briefly cling to the bottom, and begin to brown. Then stir a little, shaking them loose. Wait another 45 seconds or so. Repeat this process until most of the artichokes have a nice, brown color.

Deglaze with the white wine, and add the fava beans. (If you're using frozen peas you can also add them now. But if you're using fresh peas don't cook them just yet. You want them to be fresh, green, and not altered much by the cooking process.)

Cook the favas for 3 minutes. If you're using fresh peas, add them now along with the mint. Lower the heat as much as possible, and cover tightly with a lid so it steams for 3 minutes to soften the vegetables. Season with salt and pepper and finish with two or three pinches of fresh, chopped mint.

Three

DOWN THE
VIA APPIA

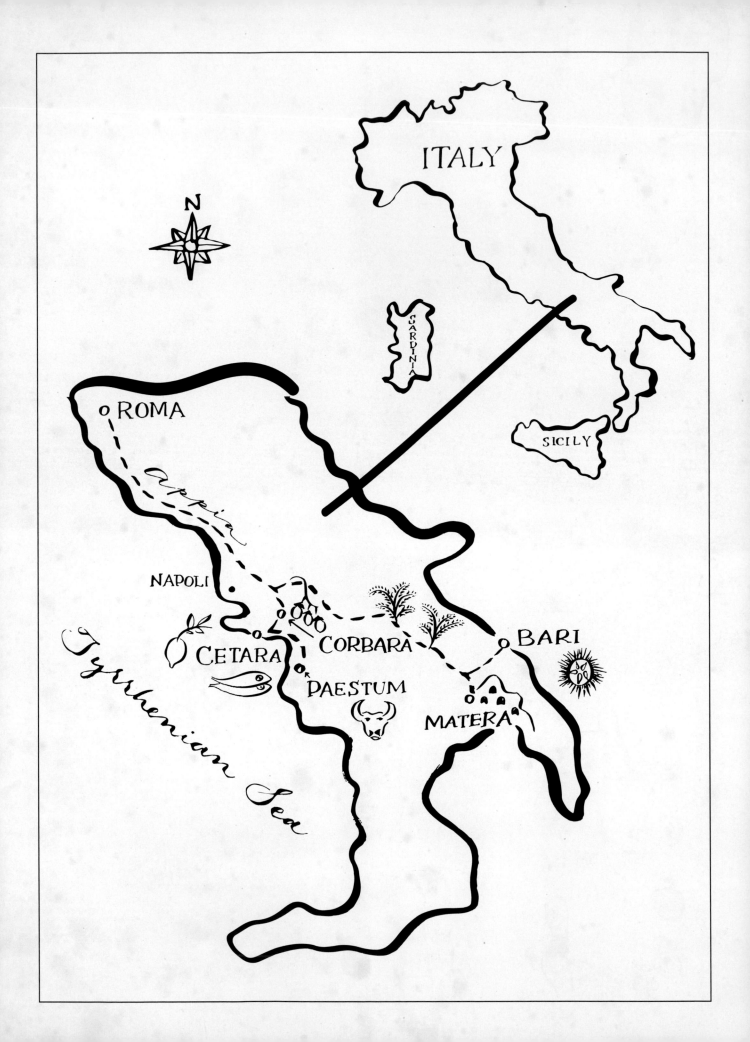

TOMATOES AND mozzarella are inseparable from our understanding of Italian cuisine—especially in the United States, whose earliest Italian immigrants came from the southern part of Italy, where these things are vital.

In Rome, anchovies are nearly as important; long ago, garum, a pungent sauce made from the same small fish, was one of the Republic's principal seasonings. And in Rome, when you eat a crisp, nutty *frittura* of calamari and prawns, or dress a salad, you might squeeze a lumpy wedge of lemon over it. That lemon's sour juice is tempered by a rich sweetness, without the bitterness we associate with industrial citrus from the supermarket.

These things and more spring from the seas and the volcanic earth of Campania, in the countryside surrounding the city of Naples. The shores of this part of the Mediterranean are steeply walled and starkly beautiful. The things that grow in the dark volcanic soils here are special, indeed. Here also lies the second section of the Via Appia, as the Romans once slowly made their way across this part of Italy that was deeply influenced by the ancient Greeks. It runs through groves of olives and undulating fields of wheat.

This land, and those who worked it, shaped Roman cuisine profoundly.

In this chapter, we'll meet producers including Luigi Dicrecenzo, a fourth-generation lemon farmer who scampers around the steep slopes above Cetara with his dog, Hercole, continuing the town's ancient tradition of harvesting Italy's best lemons. Later, he cooks his lemon pasta for us, as we drink prosecco out of the lemons' knobbled, hollowed-out skins.

Just over the mountains that separate the Amalfi Coast from the sea lies Mount Vesuvius, with its long-gone top and broad shoulders that ease down to the outskirts of Naples. Nearby, quite possibly the world's best tomatoes are grown. From there, the Via Appia turns east and south, across Italy's breadbasket of Apulia, where one sees shimmering oceans of semolina, and where some of the olive trees that dot the countryside date back millennia. Apulia is also the home of burrata, and incredible spreads of seafood antipasti. The Via Appia splits here and ends in two places—our final stop is the ancient city of Matera, where we cook in a thousand-year-old cave carved into the limestone mountainside, before heading back to Rome.

A Look Inside Nettuno, and the Famous Colatura di Alici of Cetara

After weeks of racing around Lazio, we'd arrived in Campania. We followed the Via Appia south, down the coast. We skirted the delicious madness of Naples, and headed straight to the town of Cetara. Because anchovies are essential in the recipes of Rome, and in Cetara, anchovies are nothing short of sacred there.

The town of Cetara ends, elegantly, beside a sheltered bend of sea. The cobblestone street and zigzagging staircases that wind up its cliffs all end there too. Cetara has been a fishing port for centuries, and the sea has always breathed life into the town. The town has a deep gulf in front of it, and because of the tiny migrating fish that gather there, it has become famous. Cetarese fry the fish, pickle them, and pack them in salt. They also brew a very special fish sauce.

Colatura di alici is a pure expression of umami, the Japanese word that encompasses a particular depth of flavor from glutamate. If you sprinkle a knob of buffalo mozzarella or a slice of raw tomato with this sauce, the taste becomes deeper, and more developed. And—like Asian fish sauce—it's creeping into the pantries of restaurants worldwide.

As a writer and cook who has worked with fish sauce in Thailand, I was a bit skeptical at first. For one thing, colatura di alici is expensive. I've been to a few nam pla (fish sauce) factories in Thailand, both industrial and artisanal, and I thought I'd seen what there is to see in the making of fish sauce. But nothing would prepare me for what we saw in the small wood barrels of Nettuno, a famed producer of anchovy products, named after the god Neptune. Yellow, purple, and orange crystals of salt—colored by blooms of fermentation and age—rose up in crusty piles. The production is so small and so personal that I quickly forgot about what it costs. In Thailand and Vietnam, you can find beautifully made fish sauces using only fish and salt, but larger industrial makers usually process their sauces in massive concrete, wooden, or plastic vats. Often, chemicals are added to speed up the

fermentation process, and MSG and caramel coloring are no stranger to supermarket fish sauces. But what makes the fish sauce of Cetara so different from the ones I use in Southeast Asia is viscosity—colatura is a much thicker, richer liquid. It is also less salty than its Asian cousins. Garum, the predecessor of colatura di alici, was made mostly of fish intestines and other guts, salted and left to ferment. (In Thailand, Laos, and Cambodia, there are variations of that, too.)

"We have a deep and cold sea near here, which creates a flavorful fish," explained Nettuno's proprietor, Giulio Giordano. "We use small anchovies—maybe fifty to sixty fish per kilo—for the sauce. The larger anchovies are packed in salt, for eating." We saw three women from the village, all well into their sixties, swiftly removing the heads and gutting the tiny fish with a mechanical flick of the wrist. "First, we clean them—the head is twisted off and the guts free easily, as you can see. They are then salted for the first time. Then, after a rinse, the fish are fanned out in layers, inside the barrel, with plenty of sea salt." Layer after layer is splayed out in a spiral inside the barrel, and as the spiral tightens to a single fish, the process begins again.

Finally, a worn wooden lid with a small hole is placed on top, and a rock, weighing about fifteen pounds, is placed on top of that. The rock presses down on the fish and salt, and the liquor of the fish rises up, through the hole. After a year, or even two, a large pool of oily anchovy essence sits atop the lid. When Giulio decides that the flavor and texture of the colatura is correct, a screw inside the barrel is removed, revealing a hole through which the amber liquid makes a final pass through the salted, compressed fish, ready to add depth and character in a kitchen.

The *terzini*—the name of these barrels—hold about 25 kilograms (55 pounds) of anchovies. After years, this yields about 2.2 liters (a little more than half a gallon) of colatura di alici. Giordano's business has passed through three generations, but he says that this process has remained relatively unchanged here since the 16th century. He points across the street. "The nuns in that convent used to get free anchovies when the fishermen would have a good catch. That's how the preservation began. By chance, they salted anchovies for one or two years—like many food discoveries, they probably forgot and then found them, again—and realized that they were left with a very fragrant, flavorful sauce. A beautiful flavor enhancer. And it made its way into pasta . . . and that pasta, it made Cetara famous."

He tests the fish sauce by dipping the tip of his index finger into the liquid and testing its texture on the surface of his thumb; when it's viscous and almost oily, and when it sticks to his fingertips, it's ready. "During the 1990s we fought against new regulations from the EU to use plastic terzini, and to industrialize the processes," he says, with a smile. "They forced us to change." Fermentation is about colonies of bacteria, and about preserving them, and this process had been perfected over centuries—the bacteria were embedded in the terzini and in the air of this place. Sure enough, in the plastic terzini, the bloom of the proper bacteria didn't occur and the taste of the colatura changed. And so the local producers fought the European Union regulations with the help of Slow Food Italy, and won. "Now, again, we can make it in the ancient way. Even the rocks that weigh down our lids come from an estuary outside. Everything you see before you has been touched by the sea."

SPAGHETTI CON COLATURA DI ALICI
SPAGHETTI WITH ITALIAN FISH SAUCE

serves 4

SALT

½ CUP COLATURA DI ALICI, PLUS MORE IF NEEDED

3 TABLESPOONS GOOD EXTRA-VIRGIN OLIVE OIL

2 GARLIC CLOVES, PEELED, CRUSHED WITH THE SIDE OF A KNIFE

A LARGE HANDFUL OF CHOPPED FRESH ITALIAN PARSLEY, PLUS MORE TO FINISH

1 POUND ARTISANAL DRIED SPAGHETTI (THICKER IS BETTER)

In a convent just outside the Nettuno factory is a restaurant called Al Convento. Paolo and I were invited there, along with Bangkok chef Tim Butler, to eat and cook and enjoy the bottomless hospitality of its owner, Chef Pasquale Torrente, who brands himself as Italy's "King of Anchovies." In fact, he's released a book: *L'Uomo Che Sussurra Alle Alici* (The Man Who Speaks with Anchovies).

Later, Pasquale invited us to his home for a long lunch with his mother. And he brought us into his kitchen to see how he cooks this dish—a simple showcase for colatura and a pure expression of umami and wheat. While high-quality southeast Asian fish sauces may be used as a substitute for colatura in most recipes, for this one we strongly recommend using true colatura.

Bring a pot of well-salted water to a boil over high heat.

In a stainless-steel salad bowl, combine the colatura, olive oil, garlic, and parsley, and whisk together aggressively to emulsify.

Add the spaghetti to the boiling water and cook until al dente. Drain and add it to the bowl with the sauce.

Mix the spaghetti with a fork quickly, until it's evenly coated. Taste for saltiness, and add a little more colatura if need be. Remove the garlic cloves. Serve on warm plates with a sprinkling of chopped parsley on top.

ALICI IN TRE MODI
ANCHOVIES, THREE WAYS

"When I was very young—before Knorr stock cubes and other kitchen shortcuts arrived—anchovies were in everything," Paolo says. "It was sold in fillets and as a paste, as a flavor enhancer, and everyone used it. And so many of my mother's recipes began with a fillet of anchovy. My father had a huge can of salted anchovies in his shop—and people would come each night to buy them, plucked out of the salt with a spoon made from the bone of a pig. It was the base of so many things that we would eat in my home. The role of the anchovy was flavor, not fishiness."

The anchovy, repugnant to some, grows on you. If you spend much time in Italy or Spain, it becomes an addiction. In many places in Rome and southward, meals begin with anchovies, and for good reason. Their saltiness shakes your palate awake, and makes you reach for white wine and hunks of bread.

For our purposes, we're talking about anchovies cured in salt, preserved in oil in tins or jars. (Anchovies pickled in vinegar are also wonderful, but they have a totally different texture and flavor.) Buy the best ones possible—Cetara is home to some of Italy's finest. If you cannot find those, high-quality Spanish brands, like Ortiz, are a fine substitute.

Here are three super-simple, totally delicious ways to serve them. You'll notice they are not entirely unlike one another, but the subtle differences make for distinct flavors.

1. Taken out of the can or jar, placed on a plate, drizzled with the best olive oil you have in your pantry, and placed atop grilled bread.

2. On toasted bread, but this time atop a thick slab of cultured butter. The "Anchovy King" of Cetara, Pasquale Torrente, serves them this way. It's so good.

3. On grilled sourdough, rubbed with garlic, topped with burrata, and draped with one, or maybe two, anchovies, and a drizzle of good olive oil. If you're lucky enough to find fresh buffalo mozzarella, this would be even better than burrata.

ALICI FRITTE

FRIED FRESH ANCHOVIES

serves 4 as a starter

VEGETABLE OIL, FOR FRYING

1 CUP ALL-PURPOSE FLOUR

1 CUP SEMOLINA FLOUR

SALT AND PEPPER

1 POUND FRESH ANCHOVIES,
CLEAR-EYED AND SHINY,
CLEANED (BY THE FISHMONGER,
or see note)

LEMON WEDGES (PREFERABLY
FROM AMALFI LEMONS)

Note

If your fishmonger hasn't already cleaned the anchovies, here's how to do it. First, get a bowl and place it under running water. Use your thumbnail, or a small demitasse spoon—the kind that comes with your espresso. Working from tail to head, scrape off the scales. Then grab the head by the gills, gently push on the belly with your thumb, twist a bit, and pull the head off. The guts should release and come out as well. Rinse the fish under the water, focusing on cleaning out the cavity. Be gentle, and don't tear the torso. Like most cooking chores, you'll pick this up quickly. Once clean, place the fish in another bowl or on a sheet tray. If you're working in a very warm kitchen, as we were when we wrote this, you might want to put a larger bowl or tray of ice beneath the one filled with fish.

If you have silvery fresh anchovies at your disposal, there are few things so simple and rewarding as frying them. Many people expect a fresh anchovy to exhibit the same stubborn saltiness a cured one might display; but they are as different as a cucumber is to a dill pickle. Fresh anchovies are light and lean, crisp and almost sweetly crabby in flavor; the flesh yields easily from the bones as one gobbles them up.

Fried anchovies always remind me of Rome, and of summer. Rome's (recently renamed) airport, Leonardo da Vinci, is just minutes from the fishing port of Fiumicino. Our frequent trips to Rome are often punctuated by a final fritti of anchovies, wrapped in brown paper.

In our method, fresh anchovies, which shine like polished silver, take a quick dive in a 50/50 mix of semolina and all-purpose flour, seasoned with a good amount of salt and pepper, and then dance, quickly, in a pool of hot oil.

What emerges is something so good that with a gentle squeeze of lemon, you might be convinced that this is the most delicious seafood you could ever eat.

In a heavy-bottomed pot over medium-high heat, or in a deep-fryer, heat 2 to 3 inches of oil to 350°F, making sure there are at least 3 inches of clearance to the top of the pot. Use a thermometer to test the temperature.

Meanwhile, mix your flours together in a bowl, and season well with salt and a little pepper. Taste the flour mix for appropriate saltiness—this is your only seasoning save for a few drops of lemon juice. Imagine the saltiness of French fries, or potato chips. This is what you're after.

Dredge the fish in the flour, in batches of about a quarter of the fish at a time. Coat them completely, and drop one in the oil to test. If it bubbles aggressively, the oil is ready. Fry small batches for about 2 minutes, until light brown. Make sure to do this in small batches or else the oil temperature will plunge and the fish won't brown and will absorb too much oil.

Drain the fish on paper towels. Serve immediately, on absorbent paper, with lemon wedges.

ZITI CON GENOVESE DI TONNO
ZITI WITH A RAGÙ OF TUNA AND ONIONS

serves 4 as a main course, or 6 as a starter

1 POUND FRESH YELLOWFIN OR ALBACORE TUNA

3 TABLESPOONS EXTRA-VIRGIN OLIVE OIL, PLUS MORE AS NEEDED

SALT AND PEPPER

ZEST OF 1/2 LEMON, FINELY GRATED

PINCH OF DRIED OREGANO

2 POUNDS WHITE ONIONS, JULIENNED

3 TABLESPOONS WHITE WINE

1 POUND DRIED ZITI PASTA— VERY LONG TUBES THAT YOU CAN BREAK INTO 5-INCH SECTIONS (PENNE WILL ALSO WORK)

5 FENNEL FRONDS, CHOPPED FINELY, NO THICK STEMS

GRATED PECORINO OR PARMESAN, IF DESIRED

We first ate this dish at a restaurant called Acqua Pazza in Cetara, and it was delicious. Genovese, despite its name, is a common dish in Naples and its surrounds. "The Genovese they do in Naples isn't like the one they do in Genoa," Paolo explained. "That one's a pesto." When I ate the Neapolitan Genovese, I was surprised by its sweetness.

Tuna Genovese is a white seafood ragù; there is nothing here to detract from the subtle taste of the tuna but sweet onions, olive oil, and a whisper of fennel in the background. It's traditionally cooked low and slow—the tuna falls apart and becomes one with the sauce. Paolo wanted to shorten the time the fish spends over heat, to retain its texture and taste, so this recipe strays from the traditional, but only in terms of cooking time.

Cut the tuna into 1/2-inch cubes, and toss with the 3 tablespoons olive oil, a few pinches of salt and pepper, most of the lemon zest, and the oregano.

In a deep frying pan or Dutch oven, add oil to generously coat the pan, and cook the onions very slowly over medium heat with a few generous pinches of salt, and a splash of water. Add small splashes of water intermittently if it's browning too quickly at the bottom. Cover the pan as it cooks, but stir often to prevent too much browning. The idea is that the onions will melt, through a long, slow cooking process, and end up a uniform tan color, like natural sugar. This should take 30 to 40 minutes.

Bring a pot of well-salted water to a boil over high heat.

When the onions are ready, add the marinated tuna, and cook it, moving the cubes around gently. Deglaze with your white wine. Cook the tuna for about 5 minutes, or until cooked through but still tender, and set aside.

Cook the pasta until al dente in the boiling water. Reserve about 1/2 cup of the pasta water, and drain the pasta.

When the pasta is done, turn the heat back to medium under the tuna sauce. Add 2 or 3 tablespoons of the pasta water to the tuna, shaking the pan to emulsify the sauce. Add most of the fennel and cook for another minute, tasting for seasoning. Then add your pasta, raise the heat to high, and toss until well combined.

Serve hot, with some more grated lemon zest on top, and the remaining fennel. Add a little grated pecorino or Parmesan, if you'd like.

FUSILLI FRESCHI CON PESTO CETARESE

FRESH FUSILLI WITH A PESTO OF ALMONDS, ANCHOVIES, AND HERBS FROM CETARA

serves 4 as a main course, or 6 as a starter

1/4 CUP SKINLESS ALMONDS, TOASTED, CHOPPED

1 TABLESPOON WALNUTS, TOASTED, CHOPPED

1 TABLESPOON HAZELNUTS, TOASTED, CHOPPED

1 TABLESPOON PINE NUTS, TOASTED, CHOPPED

2 TABLESPOONS GREEN OLIVES, PITS REMOVED, CHOPPED

2 TABLESPOONS BLACK OLIVES, PITS REMOVED, CHOPPED

1 TEASPOON CAPERS, CHOPPED

5 SALTED ANCHOVY FILLETS, CHOPPED

2 GARLIC CLOVES, CHOPPED

PINCH OF DRIED OREGANO

1/4 CUP LOOSELY PACKED FRESH BASIL, CHOPPED

2 PACKED TABLESPOONS FRESH MINT, CHOPPED

3/4 CUP EXTRA-VIRGIN OLIVE OIL

SALT AND PEPPER, TO TASTE

1 POUND FRESH FUSILLI (OR 3/4 POUND DRIED FUSILLI)

YOUNG PECORINO CHEESE, GRATED, FOR FINISHING

Pesto can take so many forms—but some aspects of this dish remain the same. A pesto is an herb-based sauce in which the protein of nuts holds the fragrant herbs together in a rough emulsion with olive oil.

The nuts are interchangeable, though we prefer almonds and walnuts. This dish is loosely based on pestos we ate along the southern part of the Appia, featuring the briny funk of capers and anchovies, and brought back to Rome with the addition of fresh mint (Romans hide a little mint in many things).

If you're making this the old fashioned way—in a mortar and pestle—smash the ingredients from hardest to softest (basically, in the order they appear in the ingredients list). Once you get to the oregano, basil, and mint, slowly add olive oil, and keep bumping the mixture with your stone pestle, agitating the ingredients, and thereby creating a sauce. Season with salt and pepper.

Otherwise, throw the nuts, olives, capers, anchovies, garlic, oregano, basil, and mint in a blender or food processor and let it rip, slowly drizzling the olive oil through the lid as you blend it. Season with salt and pepper.

Bring a pot of well-salted water to a boil over high heat.

Cook the fresh (or dried, if in a pinch) fusilli in the boiling water until it's the texture you prefer. Strain it, and toss with some of the pesto in a sauté pan or shallow wok over medium-low heat. Do this to taste, adding more pesto as you go, though we would use most or all of the pesto in this recipe for this amount of pasta. Finish with some grated pecorino cheese.

COZZE ALLA MARINARA CON 'NDUJA

MUSSELS WITH SPICY SAUSAGE, TOMATOES, WHITE WINE, AND GARLIC

serves 4 as an appetizer

2 POUNDS MEDIUM-SIZED
MUSSELS, VERY MUCH ALIVE
(see note)

2 GARLIC CLOVES

2 TABLESPOONS EXTRA-VIRGIN
OLIVE OIL, PLUS MORE FOR THE
BREAD

2 TABLESPOONS 'NDUJA
SAUSAGE

2 PIECES OF LEMON ZEST,
EACH ABOUT THE SIZE OF YOUR
THUMB

1/2 CUP CRUSHED SAN
MARZANO TOMATOES, OR
1/2 CUP VERY RIPE CHERRY
TOMATOES, HALVED

1/2 CUP WHITE WINE

2 THICK SLICES BREAD,
PREFERABLY SOURDOUGH

2 TABLESPOONS CHOPPED
FRESH PARSLEY

SALT, IF NECESSARY

Note

This is important. If you don't
have access to fresh mussels,
wait until you do. Frozen
green-lipped New Zealand
mussels, for instance, won't
work here, as they are free of
juice, already open, and too
large and leathery in texture.

"Mussels were my Sunday lunch, along with spaghetti and clams. It's the quintessential Roman seafood lunch," Paolo says. "My father used to drive to Torvaianica and buy them in the early spring, when they are fattest. It's also such an easy way to feed a lot of people—just clean them and put them in a huge pot and serve with bread, and follow with some pasta."

On one of our nights on the Amalfi coast, we ate at a restaurant called Pane e Coccos'—the local slang for "bread and mussels." That night, we ate the fattest mussels imaginable. They were bright yellow or white, and occasionally rust-colored; they were briny and addictive. The mussels there were simply sautéed in white wine and garlic, but when we returned to our kitchen Paolo wanted to make something a little more complex. At Appia, Paolo created a mussel dish that incorporates the natural umami of the shellfish, the aroma of garlic, the acidity of white wine, and the spice and fat of 'nduja—a soft, spicy sausage from Calabria.

Debeard the mussels, which means to simply tug off any strings attached to them. If you have any open mussels, tap the shell a few times and wait for it to close. If it doesn't, ditch that mussel.

Slice the garlic as thinly as possible and add most of it to a large sauté pan or Dutch oven with the olive oil. Heat it for 3 or 4 minutes over medium-high heat, until it's aromatic and just golden. Add the 'nduja and let it melt. Add the lemon zest and the tomatoes and cook for 2 minutes. Then, add white wine and turn the heat to high.

Then add the mussels and toss. Cook the mussels over high heat, covered, until the pan gets very hot (when you add cold mussels, the temperature will drop precipitously). The steam will encourage the mussels to pop open. While this is happening, brush the slices of bread with some oil and toast under a broiler.

Cook until the mussels are open; shake the pan vigorously and take a look every minute or so to see how things are going. If the pot is dry but the mussels are still closed, add a few splashes of water to create more steam. When they are all open, finish with the remaining garlic and the parsley. You probably will not need salt, but taste just to make sure.

Lay the toasted bread in a deep bowl, and serve the mussels on top. That bread is a wonderful ending to this dish.

ALICI IMBOTTITE

ANCHOVIES STUFFED WITH SMOKED MOZZARELLA AND TOMATO SAUCE

serves 2 to 4 as an appetizer

1 TABLESPOON OLIVE OIL

1 GARLIC CLOVE, CRUSHED

½ CUP CANNED SAN MARZANO TOMATOES, CRUSHED BY HAND OR PUREED

SALT AND PEPPER

16 LARGE, FRESH ANCHOVIES, CLEANED BY THE FISHMONGER (OR SEE INSTRUCTIONS ON PAGE 170), BUTTERFLIED OPEN

8 LARGE FRESH BASIL LEAVES

8 THIN SLICES (ABOUT 6 OUNCES) SCAMORZA (SMOKED MOZZARELLA)

1 CUP ALL-PURPOSE FLOUR

2 EGGS, BEATEN

1 CUP BREAD CRUMBS

VEGETABLE OIL, FOR FRYING

LEMON WEDGES, FOR SQUEEZING

As we wound our way down the coast, we drove through Campania. Campania is a large, bountiful, and biodiverse region of Italy; it's enjoyed thousands of years of civilization, trade, and agriculture. (The kingdom of Naples was actually a more significant power than Rome for several hundred years.) It has so many delicious foods to eat, and some of the best white wines in Italy (and Aglianico, an inky, versatile red). We stopped in Paestum to stuff ourselves with mozzarella, and admire the Greek temples that still stand there. And then Pasquale, the Anchovy King, brought us to his friend's trattoria, Nonna Sceppa, for a lunch that stretched well into suppertime.

Chief among Campania's treasures are tomatoes—the best in Italy—and anchovies, which are fried, conserved, made into fish sauce, pickled, and, in this instance, stuffed with scamorza. Scamorza is a smoked mozzarella, which is a classic way to preserve the area's soft, very perishable cheese. I've heard many people erroneously claim that Italians "never, ever mix cheese with fish." Yet here we are—in Paestum, eating anchovies that are stuffed with tomato sauce and a slice of cold-smoked mozzarella. Here, the combination of fish and cheese isn't anathema. It's brilliant.

FIRST, MAKE A SIMPLE TOMATO SAUCE: Heat the olive oil in a small saucepan over medium heat until it shimmers. Add the garlic, and remove it when it's fragrant and begins to turn light brown. Add the tomatoes. Reduce the sauce, without burning it, until it has the consistency of ketchup. Stir often. Add a little salt, and taste. Then let it cool in the fridge (you don't want warm sauce to start cooking your fish).

MAKE THE FISH: Place the fish on a cutting board, skin-down, opened up. Season them with salt.

Top a butterflied anchovy with about ½ teaspoon of sauce, just to cover the cavity of the fish. Add a leaf of basil, and finally, a slice of scamorza. Place another anchovy on top of it. You are making an anchovy "sandwich."

When you're finished, place the anchovies in the fridge, on a tray, so that they get cold and the ingredients meld. Twenty minutes should do it.

Set the flour, eggs, and bread crumbs in separate, wide bowls. Season them each with salt and pepper.

Roll an anchovy sandwich in the flour, then in a bath of eggs, and finish by rolling it in bread crumbs. Set it on a platter or a cooling rack; repeat with the rest.

Pour 2 or 3 inches of vegetable oil in a heavy-bottomed pot, making sure there are at least 3 inches of clearance. Heat over medium-high heat until a thermometer reads 375°F. Gently deep-fry the anchovies, a few at a time so you don't crowd the pot, until they're golden brown, 2 or 3 minutes. Use a slotted spoon or a mesh strainer to gently lift the anchovies out. (These things are delicate and you don't want to be fishing around in a ripping hot pot of oil for them with tongs.)

Drain the fried anchovies on a paper towel–lined tray and serve with lemon wedges. If you want to keep them warm, set an oven to warm and place the finished anchovies in there while you fry the rest.

PARMIGIANA DI MELANZANE

EGGPLANT PARMESAN

serves 4 to 6 as a main course

Tomato sauce

2 TABLESPOONS OLIVE OIL

2 GARLIC CLOVES

1 (28-OUNCE) CAN SAN MARZANO TOMATOES, STRAINED OF THE JUICE, CRUSHED BY HAND, STEMS AND HARD BITS DISCARDED

SALT AND PEPPER

Eggplants

2 POUNDS PURPLE EGGPLANTS

SALT, BOTH COARSE AND FINE

6 EGGS

1 CUP ALL-PURPOSE FLOUR, OR MORE AS NEEDED

1 CUP EXTRA-VIRGIN OLIVE OIL, FOR FRYING, OR MORE AS NEEDED

FRESHLY GROUND BLACK PEPPER

1 CUP GRATED PARMIGIANO-REGGIANO (OR GRANA PADANO)

1 POUND FRESH MOZZARELLA, TORN INTO PIECES

10 TO 15 FRESH ITALIAN BASIL LEAVES

"The countryside of southern Italy was poor—extremely poor—for the last several hundred years. And for this reason, people didn't eat a lot of meat. But eggplants have a meatiness that is filling and delicious, and because they absorb a lot of oil, which has always been produced here, and it's made with tomatoes, which grow so well in the soils of southern Italy, I want to put eggplant parmigiana in this chapter," Paolo says to me. "Though it's on almost every trattoria menu in Rome, places like Sicily and Campania grow the eggplants and the tomatoes that make up the dish. And of course, they produce the mozzarella that pulls this vegetarian dish together so deliciously." In fact, Campania is the home of what is arguably the finest mozzarella, made from buffalo milk.

Parmigiana, like lasagna, takes time and effort, but if you organize your mise en place it's easy to do while cooking something slow, like a ragù. It's an unhurried, deliberate process that requires a little bit of planning before one proceeds . . . which is my favorite sort of cooking. It's great as a main course, after a pasta, but just at home as a starter, or as a side dish with steak or fish.

If you have leftovers, it's nice to serve this dish over a bit of warmed tomato sauce, spread in a circle over the plate, like you might when making a pizza, as the eggplant will thirstily soak up a lot of sauce in your fridge.

START THE TOMATO SAUCE FIRST: Heat the olive oil and garlic cloves, starting from room temperature, in a saucepan over medium-low heat. Flip the garlic a few times. After 5 minutes, when the oil starts to shimmer and the cloves are getting some color, discard the garlic, add the crushed tomatoes and salt and pepper to taste, and bring it to a simmer over medium heat. Lower the heat and gently simmer for 30 minutes. You'll want a fairly fresh-tasting and acidic sauce, not one that is very cooked-down.

START ON THE EGGPLANTS: Cut the eggplants in long slices, from top to bottom, about ¼ inch thick. Sweat the eggplant slices by salting them with coarse salt thoroughly on both sides, and placing them on a drying

(recipe continues)

rack (or an oven rack, propped up on two small bowls). Flip the eggplant slices after 15 minutes. Sweat for 30 minutes total.

Beat the eggs, and put them aside. Put enough flour in a shallow bowl or tray to coat all the eggplant slices on both sides.

Dry off the eggplant slices with a clean dish towel, being sure to brush off any visible salt. Put about 2 inches of oil in a deep frying pan or Dutch oven and bring it to 350°F over medium-high heat. Season the flour with fine salt and pepper. Line a sheet tray with paper towels.

Coat the slices of eggplant in the flour, then dredge them in the egg bath, then add them straight into the frying oil. This will be easy if the assembly line is set up right beside your cooktop. To make this process less messy, reserve one hand for dredging, and one for tongs. Don't use both hands interchangeably, or you'll spend more time at the sink washing off gooey flour than cooking and you'll probably burn your eggplants in the meantime. They should cook in about 2 minutes per side, just until golden brown. Remove the eggplant slices when done and drain on the paper towel–lined sheet tray. Do not crowd the pan, and cook in batches until finished. And beware of the temperature of the oil creeping up, and scorching the eggplant.

Build the dish in a deep casserole (about 6 × 9 × 3½ inches): Start with a big spoonful of the tomato sauce, and spread it evenly in a thin layer. Add a big pinch of Parmigiano, like a light dusting of snow.

Then add a layer of eggplant, which should cover the sauce completely (you can cut small strips from a spare piece to fill in the gaps). You want a complete layer.

Add more sauce, just enough to cover the eggplants in a thin layer (be careful—you don't want it too soupy). Top the sauce with about a fifth of the torn mozzarella, another light dusting of parmesan, and then 3 or 4 torn basil leaves and a pinch of salt.

Repeat this process until you reach the top of the casserole, where you'll end with a sprinkling of Parmigiano so you get a nice, blistery, cheesy top.

This dish should rest for at least 45 minutes before you cook it, so the eggplants marinate and soak up some liquid, and the dish becomes one. Meanwhile, preheat the oven to 400°F.

Cover the casserole with foil. Bake it for 20 minutes, until hot, then remove the foil and cook for another 10 minutes or until the top is nicely browned and bubbly. Let it rest for at least 30 minutes before serving. (This is an important step that shouldn't be neglected—if you serve it roaring hot just out of the oven it will be too loose, and it will slip across your plate in greasy pieces, instead of standing there as a delicious, dignified square.)

Under the Lemon Trees on the Amalfi Coast

There is something about lemons in an Italian market. They gleam. In the Mediterranean they're often sold on stems, with green leaves slicked with citrus oil. The lemons of the Amalfi Coast are the best in Italy, and perhaps, in the world. As you might have noticed, lemons, and their skins, feature pretty prominently in this book. And so we went to meet an Amalfi lemon farmer, Luigi Dicrecenzo, a friend of Paolo's brother, Stefano, to learn more about his fruit.

Luigi met us at the top of the hill, beside his industrious Jack Russell, Hercole. Luigi looks the way you might expect a lemon farmer to look, and yet he speaks of the severe landscape, and of lemons, like a poet.

"Here, for hundreds of years, we've seen the fight of the human against nature." He was talking about how violently the mountains drop into the sea here, and the need to engineer a separation between the land and the water. Lemon farms like Luigi's also keep the soil from eroding down the mountains and into the sea. In effect, the lemon farms prevent their tight terraces from sliding into the towns, which also cling to the Amalfi's cliffs. They allow the conversations between balconies to flutter on, as well as for bright, salty pastas to make their way to the table.

Hercole scampered across the stone terraces chasing lizards, which warmed in the sunlight as it slid downhill, from over the mountains behind.

Luigi lovingly cradled the thick trunk of a lemon tree, which he said was a hundred years old. "We are blessed with the lava of Vesuvius," he explained, looking just behind us, "that blocks the colder northern winds yet welcomes the winds from North Africa, across the sea." Luigi has eyes that are penetratingly blue, like the ocean, and the thick, dirtied fingers of someone who works the earth.

I'd been writing about food for almost fifteen years, yet I had no idea that a lemon was something first made by humans. "There are six hundred, maybe seven hundred, cultivars of lemon in the world, and I think they were first cultivated in Florence. But they

188

don't exist in nature. The Mesopotamians bred them as well; perhaps they came from there. My lemons are a graft of *arancia amaro* [bitter oranges] and wild lemons; my lemon trees do not produce fruit until they are grafted with oranges." He instructs us to smell the leaves. The bottom leaves smell of chlorophyll and a slight hint of orange; the top ones are bright . . . lemony.

"We used to send our lemons across the world. To England, America, Argentina. If you treat the fruit correctly, in a constant humidity, a lemon will last for three months. But then the big American fruit companies came," he said, looking deliberately at me and our photographer, Jason, "and produced small, perfectly round, flavorless fruit." Luigi spoke at a machine-gun pace as he described the hard life of a citrus farmer, in the age of Sunkist. "You Americans, you pick with your eyes and not your nose!" he said, sarcastically. Then he held a melon-sized lemon up to my face, an inch from my nose.

Luigi opened a guesthouse, he explained, because his lemons can no longer support his family. "I hope that someday, people will appreciate this art again."

After a long morning climbing the rock terraces of his lemon farm, we walked down the slope. Fireworks popped in the early night sky, outside a small cathedral, in honor of the Madonna of Pescatora, the guardian of fishermen.

That evening, we learned to make Luigi's lemon pasta, and drank sparkling wine from the carved-out skins of his sweet, tart, delicious fruit. The fireworks popped and we drank, looking down at the sea, eating pasta that was bitterly acidic, slightly oily, and entirely of this place.

SPAGHETTI AL LIMONE AMALFITANO

SPAGHETTI WITH AMALFI LEMON SAUCE

serves 6 as a starter

SALT

2 GARLIC CLOVES, SLICED AS THIN AS YOU CAN

5 SALTED ANCHOVY FILLETS

1/4 CUP PLUS 1 TABLESPOON EXTRA-VIRGIN OLIVE OIL

2 TABLESPOONS COLATURA DI ALICI (ITALIAN FISH SAUCE) OR GOOD SOUTHEAST ASIAN FISH SAUCE, PLUS MORE AS NEEDED

JUICE OF ONE AMALFI LEMON (OR A SMALL STANDARD LEMON)

1 POUND DRIED SPAGHETTI (A BRAND WITH A ROUGH TEXTURE THAT WILL CLING TO THE MINIMAL SAUCE IS IDEAL)

2 TABLESPOONS CHOPPED FRESH PARSLEY

CHILI FLAKES TO TASTE

PINCH OF DRIED OREGANO

After we visited his lemon farm, Luigi promised to meet us at our house, a humble little warren on the edge of a cliff (with one of the world's most precarious parking spots—tour buses race behind, and a sharp cliff juts in front). He showed up a few hours later with his fruit, some prosecco, and a bag of good, artisanal dried pasta. Then he began to cook.

His version of this dish was extremely sour—the man loves lemons. We adapted it to round it out with the subtle umami taste of anchovy, plus plenty of the fish sauce that is so crucial to the food here, and a bit of chili and parsley. The Amalfi lemon is a rare thing; standard American ones are lesser but serviceable alternatives, but they're more sour so you might want to reduce the juice a bit to taste. Meyer lemons, I think, would work well, though I haven't tested them in this instance. If you can't find colatura di alici, a good brand of Thai (Megachef) or Vietnamese (Red Boat) fish sauce will also be very good, but the fish sauce will be sharper, and more immediate. This is a cook's recipe; your tongue, rather than my words, is most important.

Bring a pot of well-salted water to a boil.

MAKE THE SAUCE: Chop the garlic and anchovies finely and stir them together in a bowl with the olive oil, fish sauce, and lemon juice (don't use all the juice from the lemon at once; save some and add it later to taste). You can also process this in a food processor.

Cook the pasta in the salted water until al dente, reserving a cup of the pasta water to create the sauce.

Drain the pasta, and dump it into a bowl with the lemon sauce mixture. Add a spoonful or two of the reserved pasta water to help loosen and bind the sauce, and toss the hot pasta until it is coated with sauce and tastes of lemon and salt.

Adjust the seasoning with more fish sauce, lemon, or pasta water. Add the parsley and some chili flakes and oregano. Serve with a nice, crisp white wine, preferably before some fish.

CAPPUCCINO LIMONE

A LEMON CAPPUCCINO, LIKE AT APPIA

serves 6

1 CUP PLUS 1 TABLESPOON
GRANULATED SUGAR

12 EGG YOLKS

6 OUNCES OF LEMON PUREE,
OR BLENDED LEMON PULP,
SCOOPED OUT OF LEMONS,
SEEDS REMOVED (FROZEN IS
OKAY)

15 TABLESPOONS (2 STICKS
MINUS 1 TABLESPOON) COLD
UNSALTED BUTTER, CUT INTO
1-TABLESPOON CHUNKS

1 CUP HEAVY CREAM

2 TABLESPOONS
CONFECTIONERS' SUGAR

ALMOND CAKE *(recipe follows)*,
CUT INTO 12 (1-INCH) CUBES

This is a dish that we call a cappuccino because of its resemblance to the drink, rather than what's inside it. There is no coffee here (though it would be nice with one). It's a beautifully simple dessert, with lemon curd and almond cake, topped with a crown of sweet whipped cream.

Prepare a double boiler by placing a metal bowl on top of a pot of simmering water, without touching the surface of the water. Combine the granulated sugar and the egg yolks in the bowl, and whisk aggressively, until creamy. Then add the lemon, and whisk again, until you have a unified sauce. Keep whisking over the heat until the texture thickens and it reaches about 160°F. Remove from the heat and whisk in the cold butter, 1 tablespoon at a time, until all the butter is incorporated into the curd. Place the mixture in the fridge to chill for 1 to 2 hours.

In a large mixing bowl or in a stand mixer, whip the cream with the confectioners' sugar until it has soft peaks.

Then, in each of 6 mugs or bowls (glass ones are perfect, but whatever works), place 2 cubes of almond cake, followed by ¼ cup lemon curd, and top with generous piles of whipped cream. This dessert is best when you get all the layers on your spoon.

ALMOND CAKE

makes enough for 6 portions of cappuccino limone (opposite),
plus some for snacking

6 TABLESPOONS (3/4 STICK)
UNSALTED BUTTER, AT ROOM
TEMPERATURE

1¹/3 CUPS SUGAR

2 CUPS ALMOND FLOUR

1¹/4 CUPS ALL-PURPOSE FLOUR

1¹/2 TEASPOONS BAKING
POWDER

2 TEASPOONS EXTRA-VIRGIN
OLIVE OIL

¹/2 TEASPOON FINE TABLE SALT

1 CUP MILK, COLD

Preheat the oven to 325°F and line an 8 × 12-inch cake pan with
parchment paper, with a 2-inch overhang on the sides for easy removal.

In the bowl of a stand mixer fitted with the paddle, cream the butter and
sugar until totally integrated and fluffy.

Sift the almond flour, all-purpose flour, and baking powder together into a
separate bowl. Add the flour mixture to the creamed butter and sugar and
mix on a low setting until it all comes together. Add the olive oil and salt
and mix a little more.

Finally, add the cold milk. Continue to mix the batter until it changes
color, to a light yellow.

Pour the batter into the prepared pan, smooth it, and bake for about
50 minutes. Check for doneness by sticking a wooden skewer into it; if it's
not wet, the cake is done. Remove from the pan and cool the cake on a rack
for 2 hours, until it's room temperature.

Chill the cake in the fridge for 2 hours, and then you can cut it into cubes
or whatever shape you like.

PACCHERI CON SUGO DI SEPPIE IN UMIDO CON LARDO E PISELLI

PACCHERI WITH A STEW OF PEAS AND CUTTLEFISH, WITH LARDO AND HERBED BREAD CRUMBS

serves 4 as a main course, or 6 as a starter

2 POUNDS CUTTLEFISH (IF YOU CANNOT FIND CUTTLEFISH, LARGE—NOT BABY—SQUID CAN BE SUBSTITUTED)

SALT AND FRESHLY GROUND PEPPER

2 TABLESPOONS EXTRA-VIRGIN OLIVE OIL, PLUS MORE AS NEEDED

1 GARLIC CLOVE

1 PEPERONCINO CHILI (BROKEN INTO A FEW PIECES, BY HAND)

1/4 CUP SMALL-DICED ONION

1/4 CUP SMALL-DICED CARROT

1/4 CUP SMALL-DICED CELERY

3/4 CUP WHITE WINE

2 PIECES OF LEMON ZEST, THE SIZE OF YOUR THUMB

2 BAY LEAVES

1 (14-OUNCE) CAN SAN MARZANO TOMATOES, CRUSHED BY HAND, HARD BITS DISCARDED

1/2 TEASPOON SMOKED SPANISH PAPRIKA

1 CUP PEAS, FRESH IN SEASON, OR FROZEN

2 SPRIGS OF FRESH MINT, CHOPPED

1 POUND DRIED PACCHERI PASTA

3 OUNCES LARDO DI COLONNATA, OR THE BEST LARDO YOU CAN FIND, THINLY SLICED

HERBED BREAD CRUMBS *(recipe follows)*, TO FINISH

As we traversed Campania in the spring, peas were in season, and the market was full of only a few kinds of seafood—cuttlefish, anchovies, and the odd bream or snapper or sea bass pulled up from the boats.

When he saw them, Paolo was reminded of a classic Roman trattoria dish, seppie con piselli—cuttlefish and peas. He said, "It's a seafood stew, rustic and simple. Between Rome and Naples they fish for a lot of cuttlefish, especially around the island of Ponza, where I used to sail as a kid. In many places, the cuttlefish is often cooked a little too long, as are the peas, which turn to mush. I wanted to change this, and make it into a pasta, with elements of texture. Something a bit more sophisticated."

There are two very important garnishes for this pasta: thin slices of lardo (the cured, aged back fat of the pig) and herbed bread crumbs. Lardo is sweeter and more delicate than guanciale, and when you blanket thin ribbons of it over hot plates of pasta, it melts, adding delicate body to the dish. Over that lardo we added some of these magical bread crumbs—crispy, full of texture, and with a garlicky, herbal twang. The two become one—a fatty, crispy prelude to the sweet peas, tender cuttlefish, and pasta beneath.

Clean the cuttlefish, first by pulling its body from its tentacles, then removing the quill from within the body; it looks like a piece of clear plastic. Now, open up the body and slice it into rectangles, each about 2 inches by 1 inch. Lightly season the cuttlefish with salt and pepper.

Heat a large saucepan or Dutch oven with the 2 tablespoons of olive oil over medium heat until it's hot and the surface shimmers, and then add the garlic clove, chili pieces, and cuttlefish and cook for 3 minutes, stirring occasionally. Remove the garlic before it burns, and discard.

(recipe continues)

Add the onion, carrot, and celery and cook together over low heat until they release their juices and soften, about 10 minutes. While you sweat the vegetables, add a pinch of salt and some pepper. Turn the heat up to high, and when the pan gets very hot and the fish and vegetables begin to brown, deglaze with the white wine, shaking the pan and stirring things a bit, until the wine reduces by half. Add the lemon zest, bay leaves, crushed tomatoes, and smoked paprika.

Cook at a low simmer until the cuttlefish is very tender, about 30 to 40 minutes. Add salt and pepper to taste, take it off heat, and let it rest. Remove the bay leaves.

Set a pot of well-salted water to boil over high heat for the pasta. Put the peas in a strainer and blanch them in the boiling water for 10 seconds, then shock them in a small ice bath. Drain the peas, and marinate them in a small bowl with chopped mint, a little salt and pepper, and a splash of olive oil.

Cook the paccheri in the boiling water until it's al dente, about 12 minutes. Drain the pasta and toss with the cuttlefish stew and about three-quarters of the peas in a deep sauté pan or a shallow nonstick wok over medium-high heat, until hot and combined.

Divide among plates. Finish each plate by draping lardo over the pasta, like a blanket, and then adding your crispy herbed bread crumbs and the remaining peas. Drizzle with olive oil and serve.

HERBED BREAD CRUMBS

makes ½ cup

2 TABLESPOONS OLIVE OIL

1 LARGE GARLIC CLOVE, GRATED OR FINELY CHOPPED

½ CUP BREAD CRUMBS

1 TABLESPOON FINELY CHOPPED FRESH PARSLEY

1 TABLESPOON FINELY CHOPPED FRESH ROSEMARY

In a small pan, heat the olive oil over medium heat, and quickly sauté the garlic, stirring so as not to burn it, for a minute. Add the bread crumbs, and then the parsley and rosemary, and toast the bread crumbs, stirring until they are richly browned and crisp. Make sure to remove them from the pan once ready or they will continue to cook, and will likely burn.

SCOMBRO ALLA GRIGLIA

GRILLED MACKEREL

serves 4 as a main course

2 (1-POUND) MACKEREL, CLEANED AND GUTTED BY THE FISHMONGER

SALT AND PEPPER

EXTRA-VIRGIN OLIVE OIL

MISTICANZA SALAD (*page 298*)

LEMON WEDGES

As we picked our way southward from Rome to Anzio, and then to Naples and the Amalfi Coast, we stopped in many seafood markets. The best time to eat fish is when the seas are colder, and the fish fatter. But it was springtime, and the fishmongers we met were selling mostly shellfish and squid, and lamenting the lack of a good spring catch.

The scombro, or mackerel, is in ample supply, unlike many other Mediterranean fish. It's plentiful everywhere in the Pacific and Atlantic. And cheap. And very easy to grill because of its wonderful fat content; you just grill the fish until it's warm on the bone, and the skin begins to puff and sizzle. Oily fish can stand up to smoke, and even to herbs like rosemary.

After it's grilled, place the fish on a platter, skin-side up, and artfully pile it with your salad of bitter herbs and lemon. This is such a simple but elegant thing to eat.

Set a gas grill on high, or light a fire in the fireplace or in a wood fire grill—preferably with smaller sticks or grapevines, wood that is brittle and dry and will burn fast. You don't need too much fuel—the fish is thin and cooks quickly.

Butterfly the fish, opening it up from the tail through the head. Open the fish up and gently flatten it with your hands. Then, generously salt and pepper the fish inside and out. Brush it with some olive oil.

If you can, use an oiled fish basket, as blue fish such as these tend to stick to grills.

Scatter the coals from your fire—in a hearth or in the grill—and let the grill get very hot. Place the fish just 2 to 3 inches above the hot coals. Cook belly-side down for about 3 minutes, then flip it over and crisp the skin for another 2 minutes. It's done when the skin starts to bubble and it spits fat in your fire. Test the inside of the backbone (go in from the skin side) with a small knife or pin. If it's hot to the touch (I touch the knife to my lip) the fish is cooked through.

Dress with piles of the salad, and serve with wedges of lemon.

Tomatoes, Grown in the Shade of Volcanoes

Tomatoes are like people. Sometimes, they're agreeable. Often, they're sour or bland. They can be beautiful, or insipid, or honestly, sometimes both. They all look better in summer; but the roughest looking ones are often the most rewarding.

In the never-ending summer of Southeast Asia, though, this isn't true. Our tomatoes are sad, pale things; the particular alchemy of rain, earth, and sun in Thailand doesn't create good tomatoes.

About a year after opening Appia, we began work on a pizza project. Paolo studied in Naples and developed our dough recipe, and we opened the first certified, Neapolitan-style pizzeria in the region—but we needed *great* tomatoes.

As we drove south, along the Appia, there was a man we needed to meet in Corbara, a cradle of great tomatoes. Facing Mount Vesuvius to the north, and the Gulf of Naples to the west, Corbara is planted heavily with heirloom varietals that flourish in the volcanic earth. The pumice, remnants of lava that once buried nearby Pompeii, is floury and black. The soil looks like powdered asphalt. Corbara is an edgy little enclave that lies above the valley between the bitten-off dome of Vesuvius, the flat sprawl of Naples, and the slim line of touristy Amalfi towns. This rare combination of sun, shade, volcanic soil, and a Mediterranean wind called the *tramontana*, creates a perfect microclimate for growing tomatoes. The organic plots where we source our tomatoes are shaded by cherry and fat-leafed fig trees. Beans, eggplants, and zucchini also dot the small farms, between the tomato rows.

"The sailors in the Amalfi would wait for this wind, the tramontana," explained a farmer called Pietro. Pietro looked a lot like an aging Bruce Willis, if Bruce Willis spent his time grilling lamb and sopping up the juices with chunks of bread, and eating apricots and drinking fizzy white wine in Campania. His smile was big; his ample belly threatened to split his dirt-stained shirt.

Pietro's fruit trees trembled above us, as the wind swept up the slopes of Monti Lattari, cooling the fields on its way over the Amalfi peninsula, and then northward. We ate cherries and spat out the pits, and Pietro's buyer, Antonio Amato, looked satisfied as we walked through the fields.

The tomatoes wouldn't arrive for another two to three months. But we were here to better understand the terroir—the earth and climate that produces this fruit—and secure a small order of Amato's tomatoes, which are difficult to acquire.

Pietro produces only about three tons of tomatoes each year. Amato sources his tomatoes from several farmers, and helps them manage the agriculture, pushes for quality, and pays them a fair price. "What we do in a year, in terms of production, an industrial producer in Italy does in a single day."

Everything in this tomato-growing collective is farmed and harvested by hand. We finished our tour at another farmer's house, with Pietro, and drank espresso and ate more apricots and cherries. They invited us for dinner, but it was late, and we needed to navigate the mountains and cook supper for our families. We wish we could have taken some tomatoes with us, though.

INSALATA TONNO E POMODORI

TOMATO SALAD WITH TUNA BELLY

serves 4 to 6 as a starter

1 RED ONION

1 HEAPING TABLESPOON SALTED (NOT PICKLED) CAPERS

10 GREEN OLIVES, PITS REMOVED, HALVED

12 OUNCES FRESH TOMATOES, AS RIPE AS POSSIBLE, VARIETIES YOU LIKE

SALT AND PEPPER

EXTRA-VIRGIN OLIVE OIL

1 (6.7-OUNCE) CAN OF BEST-QUALITY TUNA OR TUNA BELLY PACKED IN OLIVE OIL, DRAINED

20 YOUNG CELERY LEAVES (THE SMALL, TENDER ONES)

5 SPRIGS FRESH ITALIAN PARSLEY, LEAVES PICKED FROM STEMS

1 TABLESPOON CHOPPED FRESH DILL

1 TABLESPOON CHOPPED FRESH CHIVES

1 TABLESPOON JULIENNED FRESH MINT

1 TABLESPOON RED WINE VINEGAR

It's summer in Italy, or anywhere, really. Dinnertime is approaching. You want something simple and delicious. And so you go outside and pick tomatoes in the garden, or head to a farmer's market or a good grocery. The addition of beautiful tuna—especially the belly, packed in olive oil—makes your quest for ease and freshness, with a savory undertone, complete.

This is a delicious, easy sort of salad: oil-packed tuna, olives, red onion, capers, extra-virgin olive oil, and fresh tomatoes. It's savory, salty, fresh, sweet, and tart, with many textures. The addition of mint and other herbs adds complexity.

You lightly treat the ingredients separately (it doesn't take long, and you'll master it quickly) and then arrange them on a plate. It's a friendly, plated gathering, rather than a rough tumble through a wooden bowl.

Slice the red onion into thin rounds. Soak in fresh, cold water for 10 minutes, while you prepare the salad.

Wash the salt from the capers, and dry them in a paper towel. Pit and slice the olives.

Slice the tomatoes and season them with salt, pepper, and a splash of olive oil. Remove the onions from the water, add to the tomatoes, and marinate for 10 minutes.

Remove the tuna from the oil and flake it as it is wont to do. Keep the oil for drizzling on the salad.

Compose the tomatoes first on the plate, then the tuna, then ribbons of onion, capers that you open up with your fingers, olives, and celery leaves, and then the herbs.

Salt and pepper the salad to taste, and then drizzle with the vinegar and a little more olive oil, or the reserved tuna oil.

UNA CAPRESE IN PUGLIA

APPIA'S CAPRESE SALAD

serves 4 as part of an antipasti course

2 LONG JAPANESE OR THAI EGGPLANTS

1 MEDIUM BEEFSTEAK OR 2 PLUM TOMATOES

EXTRA-VIRGIN OLIVE OIL

SALT AND PEPPER

PINCH OF DRIED OREGANO

1 SMALL SHALLOT, FINELY CHOPPED

4 FRESH MINT LEAVES, JULIENNED, PLUS MORE FOR GARNISH

3 FRESH BASIL LEAVES, JULIENNED

1 SLICE OF SOURDOUGH BREAD

1 GARLIC CLOVE, PEELED

1 SMALL BALL (4 TO 5 OUNCES) BURRATA, DRAINED

PESTO CETARESE *(see page 174)*, IF YOU HAVE SOME ON HAND (OPTIONAL)

FLAKY SEA SALT (WE LIKE MALDON)

COLATURA DI ALICI (ITALIAN FISH SAUCE) OR A GOOD SOUTHEAST ASIAN FISH SAUCE

As Paolo and I traveled down the Appia, the tomatoes weren't quite at their ripest, but when we got to Puglia and sampled the runny burrata of Andria, and the bitter eggplants that also grew there, an idea for a dish began to take shape. "I wanted to create a salad that followed the concept of Appia—to make a salad that touched all the stops of the road, all the way down to Puglia, and one that we could make year round," Paolo explains. This caprese incorporates ingredients from our journey south: the burrata of Andria, charred eggplants, a few precious drops of Cetara's fish sauce, mint, and roasted tomatoes, which can be made rich and concentrated any time of the year. If you have fresh, sweet, in-season tomatoes, use them as is. But if you don't, we suggest this method to concentrate the flavors.

This is quite a salad, though nothing beats the original caprese, of tomato, basil, and buffalo mozzarella, if the stars and seasons align.

Preheat your oven to 350°F.

Over an open flame, burn the eggplants until the skin becomes charred on all sides. You can do this on a grill, or on the burners of your stove, or even under a broiler. The key is that the skin gets smoky and black.

Put the charred eggplants in a stainless-steel bowl and cover with plastic wrap. They will steam, and the skin will release from the flesh, and they'll be easy to peel in about 20 minutes. Retain the juice, because it is full of smokiness that wants to return to the eggplants.

Meanwhile, quarter your tomato (or tomatoes, depending on size). If your tomatoes are not at their very best, toss them in olive oil with some salt, pepper, and dried oregano, and roast them on a baking sheet for 20 minutes, until they are semi-dried, but not browned or burned. (If your tomatoes are at peak deliciousness, marinate but skip the roasting.)

While the tomatoes are roasting, peel your eggplants and cut into 2-inch pieces. Season them with salt, pepper, chopped shallot, olive oil, and julienned mint and basil.

Remove the tomatoes from the oven, and allow to cool. They should have lost about one-third of their liquid.

When the tomatoes are cool, toast the bread in a pan or grill with some olive oil, rub it with the clove of garlic, then slice the bread into four triangular pieces.

Arrange on a plate by placing the eggplant down first, then the tomato, and a scoop of runny burrata on top of that. Lean the bread on the stack. Repeat. Top with a light drizzle of pesto, if using, and small mint leaves. Then drizzle with olive oil and sprinkle with Maldon salt. Finish with a few drops of colatura di alici.

RAGÙ NAPOLETANO CON POLENTA

A RAGÙ OF SAUSAGE AND SPARERIBS OVER CREAMY POLENTA

serves 6 as a main course

1½ POUNDS PORK SPARERIBS (BABY BACK RIBS), CUT IN 2-INCH SEGMENTS

SALT AND PEPPER

3 TABLESPOONS OLIVE OIL

6 ITALIAN PORK SAUSAGES (ABOUT 1½ TO 2 POUNDS), IN THE CASING

1½ CUPS LARGE-DICED ONION

3 LARGE STICKS CELERY, CUT IN 1-INCH PIECES

1 CUP WHITE WINE

1 (28-OUNCE) CAN SAN MARZANO TOMATOES, CRUSHED BY HAND, TOUGH BITS DISCARDED

5 WHOLE BLACK PEPPERCORNS

3 DRIED BAY LEAVES (OR 3 FRESH LAUREL LEAVES, IF YOU CAN FIND THEM)

1 DRIED ITALIAN CHILI (PEPERONCINO)

PINCH OF SMOKED PAPRIKA

CREAMY POLENTA (*recipe follows*)

GRATED PECORINO

It's not all seafood in Campania. There are pizzas of course, and baby lamb, and fried things from the sea and the land. And there's plenty of pork.

Ragù Napoletano is a Sunday sort of food. When I was growing up, it was the foundation for what my Italian American friends served after Mass. In Paolo's family, especially in the winter, his mother would cook this dish, with sausage and spareribs, and serve it on top of creamy, rib-sticking polenta, smeared across a large wooden slab. Everyone at the table would pick from this inviting pile of tomato, pork, polenta, and pecorino. We recommend serving it in this style if you can find a clean, weathered slab of wood (a large cutting board is good, too).

This recipe is a slow, easy tomato braise, and after time it develops a subtle roundness. You don't want the tomato to dominate, but rather, after cooking slowly, the acid will begin to combine with the fat and collagen, and become one with the meat. Don't rush this process; it takes time. Instead of the bright acidity of tomato sauce, the stew should take on creaminess; the color will fade to orange, and the flavors will mellow and meld.

Pat the ribs dry and season them well with salt and pepper.

Heat the olive oil in a heavy-bottomed pot or large Dutch oven over medium-high heat until it begins to shimmer.

Brown the ribs in the olive oil, turning to color them all over. You want them well-browned—past "golden." Remove the ribs to a plate.

Add the sausages to the pot and brown them nicely.

Add the onion and celery, and sweat them with some salt, and cook, stirring, until the onion becomes translucent, about 10 minutes. As the vegetables cook, use a wooden spatula to start to scrape up the browned bits in the pot.

Add the wine to deglaze the pan. Scrape the bottom of the pan, and let the liquid reduce by half.

(recipe continues)

Add the crushed tomatoes, peppercorns, bay or laurel leaves, dried chili, and smoked paprika, and bring to a simmer. Return the pork to the pot. Lower the heat to a gentle simmer, and cook for 2 hours, covered. Add water if the stew becomes too dry (it should be thicker than soup, but not stodgy, like a beef stew). When the sauce changes from a deep red to a softer, orangish hue, and the meats are tender, you're just about there.

Remove the bay leaves. Taste and season with salt and pepper. Serve over creamy polenta and finish with lots of grated pecorino.

CREAMY POLENTA

serves 6

2 CUPS WHOLE MILK, OR MORE IF NEEDED

1 CUP INSTANT POLENTA

SALT AND PEPPER

4 TABLESPOONS (1/2 STICK) UNSALTED BUTTER, CUT INTO CHUNKS

1 OUNCE GRATED PARMESAN

1 OUNCE GRATED PECORINO

1 TABLESPOON EXTRA-VIRGIN OLIVE OIL

Bring the milk and 2 cups water to a boil in a large saucepan over high heat. Turn the heat down to medium.

Slowly pour in the polenta, whisking as you do so. Cook, stirring the polenta frequently, so it won't stick, or cling and burn. It will thicken quickly as it cooks. You're looking for a consistency like mashed potatoes. If it seems too dry, add more milk or water.

After 3 to 5 minutes, instant polenta should be cooked, though the slow-cooking variety takes about 45 minutes. (We suggest using the instant one.)

When the polenta is no longer crunchy, season with salt and pepper and stir in the butter, Parmesan, pecorino, and olive oil. Serve the polenta beneath your ragù.

CONIGLIO ALL'ISCHITANA

RABBIT STEW WITH OLIVES, CAPERS, AND TOMATOES

serves 4 as a main course

1/4 CUP EXTRA-VIRGIN OLIVE OIL

1 GARLIC CLOVE

1 MEDIUM WHITE ONION, CUT IN THICK WEDGES

1 TABLESPOON SALTED CAPERS, RINSED (THOUGH PICKLED ONES ARE A GOOD SUBSTITUTE)

1/2 CUP GOOD GREEN AND/OR BLACK OLIVES, WHOLE, WITH OR WITHOUT PITS (JUST MAKE SURE THEY'RE NOT THE FLAVORLESS, CANNED VARIETY OF BLACK OLIVES. PLEASE.)

1 SALTED ANCHOVY FILLET, CHOPPED

2 POUNDS RABBIT (1/2 OF A LARGE ONE), CUT INTO 8 PIECES (see page 87)

SALT AND PEPPER

1 1/4 CUPS WHITE WINE

2 STEMS FRESH ITALIAN SWEET BASIL

DRIED OREGANO FLOWERS OR REGULAR DRIED OREGANO, TO TASTE

1/2 POUND RIPE, FRESH CHERRY TOMATOES, HALVED

Before we headed south to Bari, and then on down to Matera, we backtracked to Naples for lunch with a pizzaiolo, Maestro Guglielmo Vuolo. After a light lunch of five pizzas that were so good we decided we'd try to bring the pizzaiolo to Bangkok, we stopped beside the sea for coffee and gelato. As we passed the port, I caught a fleeting glimpse of the islands of Procida and Ischia in the distance. "The rabbit of Ischia," Paolo muttered as we drove by, "it's so delicious. Remind me to cook it. It needs to go in the book." And so here it is, braised with tomatoes and olives. He was right.

Heat the olive oil in a large Dutch oven over medium-high heat and add the garlic, onion, capers, and olives while the oil is warming up. After about 5 minutes, when the onion is translucent, add the anchovy fillet and let it dissolve.

Pat the rabbit pieces dry with paper towels and season well with salt and pepper. Push the onion mixture to the side of the pot to make space for the rabbit. Lay the rabbit pieces in and brown them in the oil, flipping after 3 minutes or so, or after the rabbit has developed some nice color, and then brown on the other side.

Deglaze with the white wine and add 1 stem of basil and some dried oregano. (Start with a large pinch and see if you like the aroma.)

Add the tomatoes, cover, and simmer at low heat, for 30 minutes, until the flavors have melded but are still fresh. Taste for tenderness, and season with salt and pepper. If the rabbit is not yet tender, continue to simmer gently, for up to another 30 minutes. (You want a sauce that is bright; but rabbits are finicky things to cook, and you want a rabbit that is tender, too.)

Finish with torn basil from the remaining basil stem, and serve.

Bari: The End of the Appian Way

At one point on our journey, we picked up another passenger at the train station: our baker in Bangkok, an Australian named Michael Conkey. Conkey bakes some of the finest bread in Southeast Asia. The final leg of our trip down the Appia led us across the country, from west to east, to the breadbasket of Puglia. Puglia is famous for semolina flour, which the Pugliese fold into breads and make into pasta. Across the interior of Puglia, fields of durum wheat, the variety used to make that flour, flutter in the wind. Durum is a wheat high in protein, perfect for making the eggless pastas so popular in the region. Those fields are dotted with ancient olive trees and patches of vegetables and grapes.

We went there to source the best olive oils and semolina we could find, and to eat seafood on the edge of the Adriatic Sea. But as we drove into Bari, things didn't look promising. The industrial sprawl of Bari looked grim. Our hotel, empty save for two children playing in the lobby, wasn't much better.

But after a short walk, we entered the old part of Bari. There's a towering white marble cathedral, and warrens of medieval streets that lead to tiny wine bars and restaurants. And then we stumbled upon Al Pescatore, a family-run restaurant since 1968, owned by fishermen with boats that bobbed in the harbor outside. It was incredible.

At Pescatore we were brought antipasti— oysters and clams and *cozze pelose*, a sort of hairy mussel served raw that is sweet, briny, and bitter all at once. A strange spectrum of taste. A fist-size ball of fior di latte mozzarella and a basket of fresh ricotta followed, along with fat, sweet scampi on ice. There was raw tuna and fried baby squid. We washed all this down with a cold bottle of minutolo, a fresh, aromatic wine reminiscent of gewürztraminer.

We then ate spaghetti with tiny clams, and another pasta with langoustine and a hint of fresh tomato and parsley. They were delicious, but the memory of that spread of antipasti— with crudo, a tartare, raw prawns, hairy mussels, and oysters—remained. It was fresh and light and lively; the chef didn't interfere with the flavors of the Adriatic but, rather, teased them out with oil, salt, and acidity. And so we've taken inspiration from that spread to create one of our own.

A PROPER PLATE OF SEAFOOD ANTIPASTI

serves 8

This is a delicate platter of lightly marinated and dressed raw fish, with a finish of savory, tender seafood meatballs. Given the simplicity here, it goes without saying that the fish has to be of the best quality you can find. The seafood meatballs are panfried and finished with a light tomato sauce. Along with the crudo, some mozzarella, and bread, this is a wonderful spread of seafood antipasti.

CRUDO OF SEA BASS WITH MANDARINS

6 OUNCES SKINLESS SEA BASS FILLET (BREAM WILL WORK AS WELL)

2 MANDARIN ORANGES

FRESH THYME LEAVES, TO TASTE

EXTRA-VIRGIN OLIVE OIL

SALT AND PEPPER

Make sure the fish is free of bones, then slice it into 8 pieces, like sashimi.

Peel 1 mandarin, removing any white bits, and cut it into 8 wedges. Marinate these in a small bowl with a pinch of thyme leaves, a drizzle of olive oil, and salt and pepper.

Juice the other mandarin, and make a quick dressing with the juice, and olive oil, salt, and pepper to taste.

Arrange the fish on a long plate, piece by piece, and top with the dressing. Marinate for 10 minutes.

Garnish with the mandarin wedges on top, and serve.

CRUDO OF YELLOWFIN TUNA
WITH STRACCIATELLA AND BREAD CRUMBS

6 OUNCES FRESH YELLOWFIN
TUNA

2 TABLESPOONS GOOD,
TRADITIONAL BALSAMIC
VINEGAR

2 TABLESPOONS EXTRA-VIRGIN
OLIVE OIL

SALT AND PEPPER

1 TABLESPOON FINELY CHOPPED
FRESH CHIVES

HERBED BREAD CRUMBS (see
page 198)

1 TABLESPOON STRACCIATELLA
CHEESE

Cut the tuna into I-inch cubes and marinate it in a small bowl with the balsamic, olive oil, and salt and pepper to taste for I5 minutes.

Serve in a bowl, topped with the chives, a few generous pinches of herbed bread crumbs, and a few shreds of stracciatella.

CRUDO OF GROUPER
WITH PISTACHIO VINAIGRETTE

6 OUNCES SKINLESS GROUPER
FILLET

1 TABLESPOON CHAMPAGNE
VINEGAR

2 TABLESPOONS OLIVE OIL

1 SMALL SHALLOT, FINELY
CHOPPED

2 OUNCES PISTACHIOS,
TOASTED AND CHOPPED

SALT AND PEPPER

A COUPLE OF LEAVES OF FRESH
OREGANO, FINELY JULIENNED

Make sure the grouper fillet has no bones, then slice it into 8 pieces, like sashimi. Lay it on a flat plate.

In a small bowl, make a dressing by whisking together the vinegar, olive oil, and shallot. Add the pistachios, and season with salt and pepper. After I minute, spoon the dressing over the fish, then sprinkle with the oregano.

POLPETTE DI MARE
SEAFOOD MEATBALLS, WITH GARLIC AND HERBS

4 OUNCES SHRIMP, DEVEINED

4 OUNCES CALAMARI

4 OUNCES FRESH WHITE FISH

A SMALL HANDFUL OF FENNEL FRONDS, MINCED

4 GARLIC CLOVES, VERY FINELY CHOPPED

1/2 CUP HERBED BREAD CRUMBS (*page 198*)

1 EGG YOLK, BEATEN

1 TEASPOON COLATURA DI ALICI (ITALIAN FISH SAUCE) OR GOOD SOUTHEAST ASIAN FISH SAUCE

SALT AND PEPPER

1/4 CUP EXTRA-VIRGIN OLIVE OIL

UNSEASONED BREAD CRUMBS, FOR BREADING

2 TABLESPOONS MINCED SHALLOT OR RED ONION

1/4 CUP WHITE WINE

1/2 CUP ROUGHLY CRUSHED CANNED SAN MARZANO TOMATOES

Finely chop the shrimp, calamari, and fish. You need to mince them very well so that the proteins will bind together like a hamburger does. Using your hands, combine the minced seafood with the fennel fronds, garlic, herbed bread crumbs, egg yolk, and colatura in a mixing bowl, and season well with salt and pepper. As you're mixing, work it slightly so that the mixture holds together, but don't overdo it. It should be just slightly tacky.

Take a small spoonful of the mixture and fry it in a saucepan, in olive oil. Does it taste correct, in terms of saltiness and herbs? Because now is the only chance you'll have to change it. If you'd like to adjust the seasoning, do so now.

Roll the meatballs in your hands, about the size of golf balls. Then roll the meatballs in unseasoned bread crumbs to coat.

Heat the olive oil in a large frying pan over medium-high heat. Add the minced shallot and cook for 1 minute. Add the meatballs and fry until they're golden brown on each side, then deglaze the pan with the white wine. Add the tomatoes and simmer for 5 minutes to create a sauce. Season the sauce to taste with salt and pepper.

Serve with a good sourdough and nice olives, please. When you eat this simply, everything matters.

ORECCHIETTE CON CIME DI RAPA

ORECCHIETTE WITH BROCCOLI RABE

serves 6 as a starter

1 POUND FRESH APPIA'S (ALMOST) EGGLESS PASTA DOUGH (see page 84) OR 3/4 POUND DRIED ORECCHIETTE

SEMOLINA FLOUR, AS NEEDED

SALT AND PEPPER

1 POUND BROCCOLI RABE, LEAVES AND STEMS SEPARATED

1/4 CUP EXTRA-VIRGIN OLIVE OIL, PLUS MORE FOR FINISHING

2 GARLIC CLOVES, CRUSHED WITH THE FLAT SIDE OF A KNIFE

2 OR 3 SMALL PEPERONCINO CHILIES, OR CHILI FLAKES TO TASTE

1 CUP WHITE WINE

GRATED RICOTTA SALATA DI PECORA CHEESE OR PECORINO, FOR FINISHING

"Puglia is the capital of pasta!" Paolo exclaimed, as we drove across its durum wheat fields. "But not egg pasta like in Rome. Here the pasta is made simply with flour and water. Orecchiette is a pasta that has an incredible texture—and this texture just grabs on to sauce. Cavatelli is also from Puglia; there is so much durum wheat grown there, and they've mastered this dough in so many shapes. Their approach to pasta is very different to the rest of Italy. It's really rustic, the shapes are very diverse, and there is so much craftsmanship involved."

Orecchiette is a wonderful pasta, aesthetically. It resembles an ear (hence the name, which means "little ears") and when made by hand, you stretch little disks of dough until they become both concave and wrinkly. It traps most any sauce in its grip, though simpler, quicker sauces work better with this absorbent pasta.

In the city of Bari, there is a group of old ladies who, famously, make orecchiette for the old part of town. And this is how they do it.

FIRST, MAKE YOUR PASTA DOUGH. Wrap it in plastic wrap and let it rest in the fridge for an hour or up to a day.

Flour your work surface and a tray with semolina flour.

On the floured work surface, roll out a rope of pasta about ½ inch thick. Now, take the rope and lay it out in front of you, leading away from you with the end pointed toward you. Take a slightly serrated butter knife, or even better, a cheap, flexible steak knife. Cut a ½-inch piece off the bottom of the dough. As you cut, apply downward pressure on the dough piece, dragging it toward you, and lifting the blade slightly so that the dough flattens, and curls around the knife in a small cup. This takes practice. Once you get the hang of it, you'll be making them quickly.

Place the formed orecchiette on the floured tray, and dry them for at least an hour or up to 2 or 3 days.

NOW FOR YOUR SAUCE. Bring a large pot of well-salted water to a boil. Blanch the broccoli rabe stems and shoots in the boiling water for 1 minute and then add the leaves, and cook for another 1 minute. This will remove some—but not all!—of the bitterness. It's supposed to be sharp. Strain out the broccoli rabe, reserving the water for cooking your pasta.

(recipe continues)

Place the blanched broccoli rabe in a strainer and squeeze out most of the water by slowly pressing on it with an open palm.

Now, pour your olive oil in a large sauté pan, over medium-high heat. As the oil begins to shimmer, add the garlic.

Sauté the blanched broccoli rabe in the olive oil, with salt, pepper, and peperoncino or chili flakes to taste. Add the white wine and reduce over high heat for 1 minute, then add ¼ cup water, and simmer over low heat, covered with a heavy lid, for 15 minutes to break down the broccoli rabe. You want to braise it until tender, as is the custom for many bitter vegetables in Italy. Check to see if you need to add splashes of water to keep the pan from drying out.

Meanwhile, return your large pot of salted water to a boil. Boil the pasta in this water until tender, 3 to 5 minutes. Drain, and add the pasta to the braised broccoli rabe sauce and sauté for a minute. Add a splash more olive oil if need be, and season with salt, pepper, and chili to taste. The sauce should taste spicy, bitter, sweet, and green. Finish with grated pecorino or, more appropriately, ricotta salata di pecora (salted sheep ricotta).

THE END OF THE ROAD

The last leg of this trip was in search of burrata, mozzarella, and bread. We stopped by the roadside to try the famous Pane di Altamura, a bread made only with the local semolina flours from around Altamura. Meanwhile, in the back of our Peugeot van, Conkey somehow mixed a sourdough inside a plastic bag with starter he'd brought from Bangkok and Altamura's semolina flour. A hot car does wonders for a sourdough.

We continued across the wheat fields of Puglia, gently rolling and interrupted by gnarled olive trees, some of which are centuries old. Nearing the end of the Appia Antica, it passes through several ancient posts, before its terminus in Brindisi. We headed south, and then back westward. In the distance, a dark, gray rise emerged. It was Matera—a city of caves—one of the last posts on the southern end of the old Via Appia.

We checked into an Airbnb, a well-appointed home that also happened to be a cave. Matera is a natural amphitheater; the entrances of cave dwellings, in a rocky crescent, look out into a steep canyon that is protected by a sharp ridge opposite. It is powerfully fortified. Incredibly beautiful. And mildly terrifying.

The Sassi, as this rocky part of town is called, is hard for the eyes, and the mind, to absorb. The sheer suffering it took to build this place is palpable, the sophistication of the cave architecture is impressive, and the synergy between man-made dwellings and naturally occurring geography is puzzling. We spent a day wandering and stopped in a restaurant, Baccanti, for lunch. The food was simple. Matera is not known for its food.

That night, we gathered all the things we'd bought from our long road trip through the ancient roads to Rome—salamis made of goat meat; rounds of aged pecorino from Lazio; gobs of creamy burrata; Corbara tomatoes packed in seawater; anchovies; Conkey's bread and bread that we'd bought in town; olives; and pickles. Paolo whipped up a frittata from the rest of our fresh leftovers. We drove across the canyon, as the sun started to creep toward the church tower opposite us. And as we sat, we were besieged by clouds of mosquitoes that thrive in the humid caves dotting the canyon.

We had a lighter, and mountain scrub of thyme and juniper surrounded us—and so, like countless humans had done before, we built a small pyre to drive away the insects. The smoke from the shrubs was incense-like. And the food tasted like the earth from which it sprung—herbal, salty, sweet. We brushed off the dirt from our bread loaves and pushed fat slices of salami and cheese between pieces of it and drank wine from the bottle, letting it drip down our chins.

Just behind where we'd been sitting, I entered an ancient cave that had once served as a church—its altar a pile of stone, its walls stained from woodsmoke. Paolo, Michael, and Jason roared like troglodytes from across the valley. We added more fuel to the fire, howled at the rising moon, and drank another bottle of wine.

Four

BACK TO ROME:
TESTACCIO,
AND THE FARM

S IX TRIPS, spanning five years, chasing history, and dinner. And
then it was over, as we reached the end of the Appia near Brindisi.
From there, we sped back west, to spend our last night in Matera,
a city of caves carved over centuries into the steep stone walls of a canyon.
We drank and told stories, many of which you've read in these pages. Soon,
snores echoed through the cave. The next day, groggy from long days on
the road and too much wine, we packed and headed north. We would take
the roads back to Rome, and then a plane back to Bangkok.

But first, we stopped in Rome, back to the neighborhood of Testaccio,
for a few more meals. We also needed to look at a place, outside the city. . . .

Atop a crumbling building in Testaccio—the neighborhood that once
housed Rome's old meatpacking district—there is a statue of a naked
angel, struggling with a bull. Wildflowers break through the brickwork
around the statue. Monte Testaccio, the ancient mountain of discarded
pottery, rises above the working class neighborhood. Car repair shops
poke out of it, as cave dwellings once did in the days of the Empire. This
hill marks the port where provisions that fed Rome were offloaded from
the Tiber River, in clay amphorae. Beside Monte Testaccio lies the old
mattatoio, or slaughterhouse—a place that for eighty-five years had supplied
a more modern Rome with meat. There are also bars. A new market, with
beautiful produce. And a few thousand nooks in which to wedge a Fiat.

Testaccio is where Paolo took me for my first meal in Rome. He took
me here because it's impossible to separate the old trade of butchery—using
every inch of the animal, and in manifold ways—from the Roman kitchen.
Pasta may always land on the dinner table first, but soon after arrive waves
of tripe stewed with tomato, or the rolled spleen of a pig, or tongue, or
sweetbreads panfried with chops of baby lamb.

That slaughterhouse, built in the last decade of the 19th century, now
houses an art museum and a school of architecture. There is a shop selling
natural wines and organic produce where hens used to peck. Students
blithely drink coffee where pigs were led to slaughter. One morning, as I
walked through its corridors, a piano played beautifully, like an apology.

But the bones of the old abattoir remain.

The tackle for raising the carcasses of cows still hangs there, as do chutes that drove animals to their end. Great iron hooks are strewn across marble floors, and stone tubs that once filled with blood now gather garbage. The archways above the grand buildings are labeled in crisp, Fascist fonts: There is the Vitellara, where veal was processed, and the Tripparia where the stomachs of cattle were scrubbed and readied for Roman-style tripe. Sheep were killed in the Machello Ovino, and larger beasts in the Stalle Pel Bestiame Domito.

Every city has slaughterhouses, but few slaughterhouses have worked their way into a cuisine quite like Rome's. Just outside the walls lie some of the city's most celebrated trattorias; they serve hearty pastas and roasted meats, but train much of their attention on what Romans call the *quinto quarto*—the "fifth quarter."

"Other Italians say that we Romans eat shit," Paolo told me once, as we dug into dinner at Da Enzo, a trattoria in nearby Trestevere. And, in a sense, it's true. "Basically, it's said that the animal is about one-quarter guts. The—how do you say—noblemen were given the best cuts. The rest went to the *clero* [the clergy]. Then the rest of the meat went to whomever could afford it—the other rich classes and the army. The people who processed the meat, and the rest of the working class, got the guts. Look, Italy was kind of a shithole then, a developing country, for hundreds of years. Warring states, suffering, poverty. It's only in the last seventy years, after the wars, that we've come to appreciate this food of poverty."

Italians have a way of romanticizing the food of peasants—the *cucina povera*, they call it. The food of hardship in Italy has a strong undercurrent of nostalgia because Italians, like most of us, eventually came to glorify their unglamorous past. But there's also a proud thread woven into that fabric—of how talented, resourceful Roman cooks demonstrated that a great meal could be created out of something so humble. That the poor could eat as well as the pope. This isn't foie gras, or caviar, or oysters; it's blood and guts made glorious.

Which brings us back to Testaccio. The slaughterhouse there functioned both as a marketplace for meat and a kind of public workspace. Paolo's father came here as a young man, from Le Marche in the east, to butcher pigs and bring them back to his local *norcineria*—a place that cures hams and salamis—and later, he aged them himself in Norcia. Butchers and apprentices from across the city and the surrounding countryside would travel to Testaccio, purchase a carcass, and transport it to age in the cool mountains, or to sell back at their shops. In part as payment for their work, the workers would then keep the innards: the "pluck" of the lamb, the stomach and tendons of cows, sweetbreads, brains, kidneys, tails, cheeks, spleens. The meat would be sold to folks across the river. And the offal would be eaten in small restaurants in Testaccio, or taken home to cook.

Some of the dishes that emerged here might surprise. The tendon salad (*insalata di nervetti*), a dish of braised beef tendon, olive oil, and chili reminded me more of China than Italy the first time I tried it, with its emphasis on textural contrast over flavor. Before I went to Ristorante Augustarello for the *coratella*, the only other place I'd ever eaten a springy bit of lung was in Sichuan. But few of the dishes are truly challenging to eat for newcomers. Organ meats are cleaned and often soaked to remove the iron that tends to characterize their flavor. They're stewed for long periods of time, baptized with lemon, or

sautéed with rosemary, garlic, white wine, and olive oil. The dishes of the fifth quarter play with texture, but employ familiar tastes like tomatoes, chili, red wine, and cheese.

Perhaps the most explicit dish in the repertoire, *pajata*, is a perfect example of the delicious economy of Roman cooking. Intestines of veal or a milk-fed baby lamb are tied after slaughter, to preserve the milk within. They're then sautéed with onion and stewed in a tomato sauce. What results is not alien at all—it's addictive. A tender, meaty tomato sauce, bound by a rich, deep creaminess that tastes like marinara folded with a fresh, soft cheese, with a subtle funk.

In this chapter, we're going to explain to you how to cook classic Roman pastas, artichokes, and especially dishes using offal—the repertoire of dishes that first led us on this quest. It shouldn't be intimidating; the meats we'll be cooking are more forgiving than, say, chicken or fish. The process starts by locating a good butcher. You must be flexible, as we are in the restaurant, and cook what's available—offal is perishable and not exactly popular despite its deliciousness, so call ahead first and ask for what you'd like. When baby lambs are slaughtered in spring, we make coratella at Appia. If there's tripe at the market, that goes in the pot instead. Offal needs to be very fresh, and cleaned quickly and thoroughly, to be at its best. If you strike up a relationship with a good Mediterranean, Latin, or Asian butcher, they might even be able to provide you with clean tripe, trimmed oxtails, or the skinned head of a lamb. People who cut meat for a living appreciate those who care for the off-cuts, and everyone benefits: You get cheap, delicious meat; they throw less away.

Before we returned to Bangkok, Paolo and I took one more road out of Rome. But this one wasn't ancient. We raced down the highway, past the outskirts of the city, and got off at the Castel Romano exit. There is an outlet mall there, and American fast food restaurants, and gas stations. It is not the Italy one dreams about.

But we drove past the mall, up past Cinecittà World, a film studio and theme park, and there was a tiny road at the back of the parking lot. A sex worker sat in a lawn chair at the top of the road—a common yet ever jarring sight in the Roman countryside—and winked at us as we drove past.

We took the tiny road, and crested the hill. This road was planted with century-old shade pines, their roots pushed up the blacktop in great mounds; we had to crawl, it was so bumpy. The sea was in front. There was a medieval hunting preserve, and three farms—communes built during Mussolini's reign—on either side. We pulled up to one, and rang the doorbell. A sheepdog snarled at us, until an old man arrived, opening the creaky gates to a forgotten farm called La Santola.

We bought that farm, at the end of our trip. And now, slowly, we're pulling the brush from old hedgerows, and planting artichokes, and trying to raise a flock of sheep and a herd of goats. Soon—in fact, perhaps when this book is published—you'll be able eat there. Because our travels, and our shared love of this food, led us back to lay down roots where we'd started.

And so we'll end with a few recipes from our farm, a place where we've just started to cook, and where each and every one of the recipes you see here was made, photographed, and devoured by Paolo, Jason, and me. In a tiny farmhouse kitchen with no electricity, but with a hearth, and a gas stove, and a dream that it will someday be something much greater.

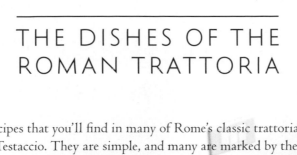

THE DISHES OF THE
ROMAN TRATTORIA

These are recipes that you'll find in many of Rome's classic trattorias, especially the ones of Testaccio. They are simple, and many are marked by the trade of butchers, and the remains of their craft—the quinto quarto. Three of the four pasta dishes most associated with Rome are here (the fourth, Amatriciana, we encountered in Amatrice), as well as an ode to Rome's love of artichokes.

TRIPPA ALLA ROMANA
ROMAN-STYLE STEWED TRIPE

serves 4 as a starter

1/4 CUP EXTRA-VIRGIN OLIVE OIL

1/3 CUP FINELY DICED ONION

1/3 CUP FINELY DICED CELERY

1/3 CUP FINELY DICED CARROT

2 BAY LEAVES

PEEL OF 1/2 LEMON, CUT INTO TWO PIECES

PINCH OF DRIED MINT

PINCH OF CHILI FLAKES

1 POUND HONEYCOMB TRIPE, CLEANED BY THE BUTCHER (see note)

1/3 CUP WHITE WINE

10 OUNCES CANNED SAN MARZANO TOMATOES, CRUSHED BY HAND OR PUREED

SALT AND PEPPER

ABOUT 1 CUP VEGETABLE STOCK OR WATER

LOTS OF FRESHLY GRATED PECORINO, FOR FINISHING

10 LEAVES OF FRESH MINT, JULIENNED (IF YOU FIND MENTUCCIA [LESSER CALAMINT], A VARIETY OF MINT THAT HAS A HINT OF OREGANO FLAVOR, IT IS PERFECT FOR THIS DISH)

CRUSTY SOURDOUGH BREAD, FOR SERVING

Note

When purchasing tripe, be sure it is very white, with no discoloration or bile, and smells only gently funky, like passing a farm with the windows down.

If there is one dish that can make Romans weep, long for their mother, or turn up their nose and argue long into the night, it's tripe. Whenever Romans come to Appia and see tripe on our menu, they smile. It's a mandatory offal dish from this part of Italy. Roman-style tripe is made from washed white honeycomb, rumen, or omasum tripe, from three of the cow's four stomachs.

Our recipe is very straightforward and within the reach of any cook: You sweat onions, celery, and carrot, then add tripe, white wine, tomato, and bay leaves to create a sauce. It's slowly stewed, in this case with dried mint, and finished with fresh mint and pecorino cheese. A perfect tripe should be tender and buttery in texture, luxurious in the mouth, with the assertive snap of sharp pecorino cheese, a shade of spice, and the lift of mint. This should always be served with bread.

Add the olive oil to a large saucepan over medium heat. When the surface of the oil shimmers, add the onion, celery, carrot, bay leaves, and lemon peel. Cook until the onion is translucent, about 10 minutes, stirring so as not to brown the vegetables.

Add the dried mint, chili, and the tripe, and cook, stirring, for another 5 minutes, until the tripe tightens up and the aroma of mint arrives. Add the white wine to deglaze and simmer for 2 minutes to remove the alcohol. The fat from the tripe will make the liquid a little milky in color. Add the tomatoes and bring to a simmer. Season lightly with salt.

Cover and simmer, over low heat, for about 45 minutes, or until the tripe is tender and buttery, but not overly soft. Be careful that the heat is low, and that it doesn't burn—tripe likes to haunt the bottom of pots. This is where your water or vegetable stock comes in—add some if the mixture becomes too dry during cooking. It should be a thick but runny sauce, much like a ragù, and not a wet paste that simply coats the tripe.

When the tripe is tender, add salt and pepper to taste. Finish with pecorino.

To serve, scoop servings into nice bowls, and top with more grated pecorino and julienned mint leaves. Serve with the sourdough bread.

LINGUA DI VITELLO

CALF'S TONGUE, WITH TWO SAUCES

serves 8 as a starter

1 WHOLE (2-TO-3-POUND) VEAL OR BEEF TONGUE

1 CELERY STALK, LARGE DICE

1 LARGE CARROT, LARGE DICE

1 LARGE ONION, LARGE DICE

2 BAY LEAVES

½ CUP WHITE WINE VINEGAR

1 BUNCH OF FRESH ITALIAN PARSLEY, STEMS ONLY (USE THE LEAVES IN THE SALSA)

SALT, AND COARSE, FLAKY SALT FOR FINISHING

SALSA VERDE *(recipe follows)*

SPICY TOMATO SAUCE *(recipe follows)*

Note

If you'd like, you can also grill the cooked tongue over charcoal or fry in a pan with some olive oil until crispy. It's nice just poached, or crisped. Your choice.

This is an extremely forgiving dish. A tongue is mostly muscle; it's not actually offal, and it doesn't taste like it. In fact, tongue is beefy—beefier than most of the prime cuts of steak. It's easy to procure from most butchers, and it becomes tender in a slow simmer. In this version, it is cooked with carrots, onion, and celery. Slice it thick and serve it warm with a simple *salsa verde*—an herbal sauce made with olive oil, parsley, garlic, and salt. We've also added a spicy tomato sauce, the way this dish was prepared in Paolo's home. "I like the texture of the tongue—the slight chewiness," Paolo says. "My mother would cook this dish very soft, but I like the tongue with a bit of snap. It was always a heated conversation at our dinner table, when I became a cook." Of course, you can choose your preferred doneness—cook it a little less for more bounce, or more for a softer texture.

Place the tongue in a large pot and cover it with water. Add the celery, carrot, onion, bay leaves, vinegar, and parsley stems, and enough salt so that the liquid tastes nicely seasoned. Bring it to a simmer over medium-high heat, turn the heat down to maintain a gentle simmer, cover, and cook, submerged, for 1½ to 2 hours, until you reach your desired tenderness. Add water if necessary to keep the tongue submerged.

When the tongue is very tender (you can test by cutting off a small piece), remove it from the water and let it cool just until you can handle it.

Using a paring knife, cut the thick membrane right down the middle of the tongue, and under it, then peel it off. Cut the spongy tissue off the lower, rear section of the tongue and discard. Slice the tongue into ½-inch-thick slices. Serve warm, with flakes of coarse salt and the sauces either spooned on top or on the side.

SALSA VERDE

makes about 1 cup

2 GARLIC CLOVES

2 SMALL SHALLOTS

1 SALTED ANCHOVY FILLET

1 HARD-BOILED EGG WHITE
(YOLK RESERVED FOR
ANOTHER USE)

½ BUNCH OF FRESH ITALIAN
PARSLEY LEAVES, CHOPPED

¼ CUP CHOPPED FRESH MINT

¼ CUP CHOPPED FRESH
ITALIAN BASIL

2 TABLESPOONS RED WINE
VINEGAR

¼ CUP EXTRA-VIRGIN
OLIVE OIL

SALT AND PEPPER

The salsa verde is easy to make in a food processor, or you can do it the old-fashioned way, in a marble mortar and pestle. If you do it that way, chop all ingredients, and then smash them in the mortar in the order of their hardness—which is the order the ingredients are listed in. Otherwise, throw all the ingredients into a food processor or blender, and blend to a paste. You're after a pesto-like texture. Taste for salt and acidity from the vinegar and adjust.

SPICY TOMATO SAUCE

makes about 1 cup

2 TABLESPOONS EXTRA-VIRGIN
OLIVE OIL

¼ CUP DICED SHALLOT

½ GARLIC CLOVE

HEARTY PINCH OF DRIED CHILI
FLAKES

6 OUNCES FRESH TOMATOES,
CHOPPED

1 TEASPOON RED WINE VINEGAR

PINCH OF CHOPPED FRESH
PARSLEY

10 LEAVES FRESH MENTUCCIA
(LESSER CALAMINT) OR MINT,
CHOPPED

SALT AND PEPPER

1 TEASPOON SUGAR

The spicy tomato sauce is cooked, but only just. Begin by heating the olive oil in a medium sauté pan over medium-low heat and add the shallots and garlic. Sauté for 5 minutes, until softened but not brown. Add the chili flakes, then the tomatoes, vinegar, parsley, mint, a pinch of salt and pepper, and sugar. Cook for 5 minutes—just to bring the flavors together, but keeping them bright and fresh—and season to taste with salt and pepper.

TAGLIOLINI CON ANIMELLI E PISELLI
PASTA WITH VEAL SWEETBREADS AND BABY PEAS

serves 4 as a main course, or 6 as a starter

Sweetbreads

1 CUP WHITE WINE

2 BAY LEAVES

1 MEDIUM CARROT, LARGE DICE

1 CELERY STALK, LARGE DICE

1/2 MEDIUM ONION, LARGE DICE

12 OUNCES SWEETBREADS
(LAMB OR VEAL)

ALL-PURPOSE FLOUR, FOR
DUSTING

SALT AND PEPPER

Pasta

SALT AND PEPPER

3/4 CUP BABY PEAS (FROZEN
ARE FINE; DEFROST THEM)

1/3 CUP UNSALTED BUTTER

3 TABLESPOONS WHITE WINE

3 1/2 OUNCES BEEF DEMI-GLACE
OR STOCK

1 POUND FRESH TAGLIOLINI
(STOREBOUGHT, OR MADE
FROM ONE OF THE DOUGHS *on
pages 83–84*)

2/3 CUP FINELY GRATED
PARMESAN, OR 3 TABLESPOONS
PARMESAN FONDUE (*see
page 57*)

2 TABLESPOONS GREMOLATA
(*page 46*)

Note
If you have leftover Parmesan
fondue from the Tortelli alla
Amerigo (page 57), a few
spoonfuls of it in the pasta,
just before you serve it, will
be beautiful.

"One night I was in a restaurant in San Lorenzo, at a place called Pommidoro," Paolo says. "I tasted the animelle all' cacciatora (veal sweetbreads cooked in white wine and rosemary), and I decided I wanted to do a pasta with those ingredients. So after playing around a bit, I came up with this dish—which is lighter than simple sweetbreads, and pairs perfectly with mentuccia, Parmesan, and peas. It's become one of my favorites."

Sweetbreads are the thymus glands of veal or baby lamb. They have a delicate texture and they're very mild in flavor, without any of the iron that one might expect in liver or kidney. Veal sweetbreads are a bit sweeter and even more delicate, but far larger; lamb sweetbreads, predictably, are just a tinge gamy. Both are delicious.

Tagliolini is a thin, soft egg pasta. In a delicate dish like this one, it acts as a conduit for a gentle sauce. You want the noodles to taste completely of this dish: of Parmesan, and of umami from the demi-glace, with the slight tinge of rosemary and citrus, of sweet green peas, and brown butter. The taste should be spun right through the noodles, as if the dough was made with the wonderful things sizzling in your pan. Tagliolini is essential for this dish; try to use it or another very delicate fresh pasta.

FOR THE SWEETBREADS: Bring 2 quarts of water, the white wine, bay leaves, carrot, celery, and onion to a boil in a large saucepan over high heat. This is your bouillon. Add the sweetbreads, bring back to a boil and boil for 1 minute, then turn off the heat and cover. For veal, let sit for 30 minutes; for lamb, 15 minutes is fine.

Drain the sweetbreads and, when just cool enough to handle, use your fingers to peel off the membrane, and all other veins or dark material. Cut the cleaned sweetbreads into 1- to 1½-inch chunks. Pat them dry with paper towels. Dust the sweetbreads with a thin coating of flour, and salt and pepper their exterior.

FOR THE PASTA: Bring a pot of well-salted water to boil over high heat. Preheat your oven to warm and heat some serving plates inside it. Because tagliolini is delicate, it will cool quickly and stick to a cold plate.

(recipe continues)

Blanch the peas in the boiling water if they're fresh, for just 30 seconds. (Omit blanching if they are frozen.) Remove the peas from the water, and keep the water boiling for the pasta.

Heat a large sauté pan or nonstick wok over medium-high heat. Add the butter, and when it's bubbling and starting to foam, add your sweetbreads. Cook them on all sides until they're golden brown, and a little bit crispy, about 3 minutes per side. Add the peas, white wine, and demi-glace to the pan. Be careful, it might spit back up at you. Cook, shaking the pan or stirring with a spoon to emulsify the butter and liquid into a smooth sauce. Turn off the heat.

Drop the pasta in the boiling water and cook for 60 to 90 seconds, until just cooked. Save a cup or so of the pasta water and then drain the pasta.

Turn the heat under the pan with the sauce to high. Add the pasta, with a half cup of the pasta water. Cook, and add salt and pepper to taste. You'll want to agitate the pasta by stirring it aggressively, or flipping it over itself, in the pan.

Finish with lots of Parmesan and gremolata, making sure that your pasta is perfectly seasoned, rich, bright, deep, and delicious. Serve it on the hot plates from your oven, with some more cheese. This pasta needs to be eaten quickly, while it's hot.

STRACCIATELLA ALLA ROMANA
CHICKEN BROTH WITH EGG AND CHEESE

serves 4 as a light dinner, with bread and salad

2¹/₂ POUNDS CHICKEN CARCASSES, FROM THE BUTCHER OR FROM LEFTOVER ROAST CHICKEN

1 MEDIUM CARROT, CUT INTO 1-INCH PIECES

1 MEDIUM WHITE ONION, HALVED

2 LARGE CELERY STALKS, CUT INTO 1-INCH PIECES

BULB OF GARLIC, SKIN ON, HALVED

10 WHOLE BLACK PEPPERCORNS

2 BAY LEAVES

6 EGGS

6 OUNCES FINELY GRATED PARMESAN

FINELY GRATED ZEST OF ¹/₂ LEMON

SALT AND FRESHLY GROUND PEPPER

GOOD EXTRA VIRGIN OLIVE OIL, FOR FINISHING

I remember having a sublime version of this dish at Perilli, an old-school trattoria in Testaccio. It was lunch, and after a week of eating in Rome, I was starting to swell. So I ordered a bowl of soup and some *chicoria* on the side. The surly waiter said, "That's it?" and muttered something unpleasant as he wandered into the kitchen. The soup he served me, with a rich stock, swimming with eggs and Parmesan, more than made up for his scorn.

Stracciatella means, approximately, "to stretch." It describes the process that happens as you whisk egg into the hot soup. You may have seen this before in egg drop soup, except here you also whisk finely grated Parmesan and a bit of lemon zest through the egg mixture.

Preheat the oven to 400°F. Place the chicken carcasses on a roasting pan and roast until browned, about 30 minutes.

Remove the carcasses to a heavy-bottomed pot. Splash some water, if necessary, to dissolve any of the browned bits on the roasting pan, scrape, and add that to the pot as well. Then, add 2 quarts of water, the carrot, onion, celery, garlic, peppercorns, and bay leaves. Bring to a simmer over high heat, skimming off the scum that rises to the surface. Cover and turn the heat down to maintain a gentle simmer. Note how high the water is in the pot.

Cook for 2 hours, replacing the water as it reduces. You want to finish with 2 quarts of stock, so check every once in a while, and replenish the water as it evaporates.

When your stock is ready, strain out and discard all the solids, and return the stock to the pot. Cook it over medium heat to maintain a gentle simmer while you prepare the egg mixture.

In a mixing bowl, beat the eggs together with the Parmesan and lemon zest, and allow to sit for 5 minutes.

Turn off the heat, and stir the stock in one direction, while slowly pouring all the eggs and cheese into the stock. These will break into strands. Taste for salt and cheesiness. It should be assertive yet gentle. Add salt or cheese as desired.

Serve in large, shallow bowls with ground pepper and a drizzle of good olive oil on top.

FETTUCCINE ALLE RIGAGLIE DI POLLO
FETTUCCINE WITH CHICKEN GIBLET RAGÙ

serves 4 as a main course, or 6 as a starter

1 POUND CHICKEN OFFAL—A MIX OF LIVERS, GIZZARDS, AND HEARTS (WE USE ABOUT 60% LIVERS AND 40% GIZZARDS AND HEARTS.)

1/4 CUP OLIVE OIL, PLUS MORE IF NEEDED

SALT AND PEPPER

2 GARLIC CLOVES, CRUSHED WITH THE SIDE OF A KNIFE

1 SMALL PEPERONCINO CHILI

1 BAY LEAF

FRESH ROSEMARY SPRIG

FRESH THYME LEAVES, TO TASTE

1/3 CUP FINELY DICED ONION

1/2 CUP WHITE WINE

3/4 CUP CHICKEN OR VEGETABLE STOCK, PLUS MORE IF NEEDED

1 POUND FRESH FETTUCCINE (STOREBOUGHT, OR MADE FROM ONE OF THE DOUGHS *on pages 83-84*)

PLENTY OF GRATED CHEESE (RICOTTA SALATA, PECORINO, OR PARMESAN)

FINELY GRATED ZEST OF 1/4 LEMON

This is a wonderful recipe. It's a very brown ragù—a dance in the dirt, full of iron. But it also has the flavors of a cozy gravy, of roasted birds on cold winter days. Meanwhile, it's a grand gesture of thrift and deliciousness. When we cooked this pasta it came to about one dollar per portion.

The insides of a chicken are so neglected, but with some care, and patience, one of the best pastas you'll ever taste will take shape with its "nasty bits."

With a sharp paring knife, remove any visible fat, arteries, or membranes from the offal, as best as you can. Pat it dry with paper towels.

Add most of the olive oil to a large sauté pan over medium heat. When the surface begins to shimmer, fry the offal in the olive oil, spreading it out in one layer, and season with salt. If the offal gives off water, cook until the pan starts to sizzle again; you are looking for it to brown. Then flip, and brown the other side.

Add the crushed garlic cloves, another whirl of olive oil, the chili, bay leaf, rosemary, and thyme. Add the onion, lower the heat, and cook until the onion is very soft and begins to melt, about 7 minutes.

Add the white wine to deglaze and scrape all the flavor from the bottom of the pot, reduce the wine by half, and add the chicken stock. Simmer gently, covered, for about 20 minutes, then let it rest for at least 10 minutes and as long as a few hours, for the flavors to meld. Remove the bay leaf and taste for salt and pepper.

Meanwhile, bring a pot of salted water to a boil. Add the fettuccine to the boiling water and cook until tender, 2 to 3 minutes. Drain the pasta, and toss it with your ragù over medium heat. Loosen it with some olive oil and stock if necessary. Season with salt and pepper, and finish with grated cheese and lemon zest.

RIGATONI CON LA PAJATA
RIGATONI WITH VEAL INTESTINES

serves 4 as a main course, or 6 as a starter

EXTRA-VIRGIN OLIVE OIL

1/2 POUND PAJATA (see note)

1/3 CUP JULIENNED ONION

1 PEPERONCINO OR A PINCH OF CHILI FLAKES

1 GARLIC CLOVE

1/2 CUP WHITE WINE

1 (14-OUNCE) CAN SAN MARZANO TOMATOES, CRUSHED BY HAND

SALT AND FRESHLY GROUND BLACK PEPPER

3/4 POUND DRIED RIGATONI

COARSELY GRATED PECORINO

Note

Pajata is not an easy ingredient to obtain. It must be ordered very fresh, from a butcher who knows what it is, and it must be harvested from an animal the day before you cook it. Or, ideally, that morning. It's highly perishable. See if the butcher will provide you with some outer casing from the small intestine as well. The idea of pajata is to conserve the milk inside the intestine—this is what gives the sauce such a rich flavor and creamy texture. If the butcher doesn't provide the casing, you can simply tie the intestine in knots. If you do have extra gut, cut the intestine into 6-inch strips. Make a loop of the intestine, and then tie the two open ends tightly at the top, like a ring. This is a slow process. But be patient. It's worth the effort.

My brain did a somersault with that first spoon of sauce. It was rich and creamy and deep. I was eating pajata, a dish stewed with tomato and the small intestine of a calf still holding its milk. It was meaningful, and almost mournful; you could taste the countryside within that dish, and the passage of milk from mother to calf. It was flavor in a way I hadn't experienced before.

Pajata is a dish that haunts me and so—though it might be difficult to source the necessary ingredients—I had to include it. I ate it for the first time in the ruins of Monte Testaccio, at a bustling trattoria with Paolo. And it changed me. I liked offal, but never loved it—until I tasted pajata with its creamy, cheesy tomato sauce and tender bits of meat. It's a perfect example of purity, and how mother nature can season a dish. A good pasta with pajata makes me wonder why this ingredient ever gets thrown away.

Add enough olive oil to slick a large, heavy-bottomed saucepan over medium heat. When it's hot and the oil's surface begins to shimmer, gently sauté the pajata, along with the onions, chili, and garlic, over medium-low heat. The idea is to sort of sweat it in the oil, rather than brown it. Cook it on both sides as you gently slide the onions around it. It will shrink about 40 percent and some curds will release—this is a good thing.

After the pajata shrinks, and is just starting to lightly brown, deglaze with the white wine. Reduce the wine by half.

Add the tomatoes and some salt and pepper. Simmer for 20 to 30 minutes, until the flavor has deepened and the sauce is thick enough to coat pasta. Taste, season with more salt and pepper if needed, and turn off the heat.

Bring a large pot of well-salted water to a boil, and cook the rigatoni until it's al dente. When the pasta is nearly done, return the sauce to high heat. Drain the pasta and toss it with the pajata sauce, taking care not to break all the intestines you so carefully tied.

Top with lots of grated pecorino and black pepper. Eat with gusto.

CODA ALLA VACCINARA
OXTAIL STEW

serves 4 as a main course

3 POUNDS OXTAIL, CUT INTO SECTIONS AT THE JOINT

SALT AND PEPPER

3 TABLESPOONS EXTRA-VIRGIN OLIVE OIL

1 MEDIUM CARROT, 1/2-INCH DICE

1 MEDIUM ONION, QUARTERED

3 STALKS OF CELERY, 1/2-INCH DICE

1 CUP WHITE WINE

1 (14-OUNCE) CAN WHOLE SAN MARZANO TOMATOES, CRUSHED BY HAND

1 THICK STRIP OF LEMON ZEST, ABOUT THE WIDTH OF TWO FINGERS

2 DRIED BAY LEAVES

1 STEM OF FRESH ROSEMARY

RED CHILI FLAKES

3 CUPS VEGETABLE OR CHICKEN STOCK

GREMOLATA *(page 46)*, FOR FINISHING

Note

You can take your leftovers, remove the meat from the bones, and reserve it with the rich sauce. It makes a wonderful pasta sauce. Or you can mix that meat with eggs, bread crumbs, and grated cheese and form it into meatballs. Brown the meatballs and then simmer them in tomato sauce.

"Oxtail is something I grew up with," Paolo says. "It's a rich secondary cut with a strong beefiness. It's a piece of meat I prefer over primary cuts. Because of the long cooking time, there's an alchemy of gelatin and vegetables and meat where they become a single thing. Also, for a family, it's one preparation that can become two courses . . . you can make pasta the following day or *polpette*. Meatballs made with braised oxtails are amazing."

Oxtail is a cheaper cousin of the short rib—packed with gelatinous goodness, it develops over time into a lavish stew. Slowly cooked with onions, carrots, wine, and (sometimes, and traditionally) chocolate, it should be nearly fall-off-the-bone tender, without quite getting there. We don't use chocolate in our recipe, though you could add some unsweetened chocolate if you'd like; it adds a richness and mysterious background flavor. This dish is also incredible when taken off the bone and made into a pasta sauce that clings to the noodles, or is served over grains like polenta or farro.

"I prefer to use white wine in this recipe," Paolo explains. "I like the dryness of white wine, and it doesn't mask the flavor of the beef, like, say, in beef bourguignon, where red wine is very prominent."

Pat the oxtails dry with paper towels, then season them well all over with salt and pepper. Heat the olive oil in a wide, heavy-bottomed braising pot over medium heat until it begins to shimmer, and then fry the oxtails on each side until they're nicely browned; this can take up to 15 minutes total, turning every few minutes.

Add the carrot, onion, and celery, reduce the heat to low and cook—stirring so they pick up the browned bits—until the vegetables are soft, 10 minutes. Raise the heat to high, and deglaze with the wine, scraping the pot to get the rest of the browned bits. Add the tomatoes, lemon zest, bay leaves, and rosemary. Add chili flakes as desired.

Add the stock and a teaspoon of salt. Bring the liquid up to a simmer, cover, and cook over low heat for 3 hours, or until the meat begins to part with the bones and is tender and very soft. Make sure you check it occasionally—you do not want anything to cling to the pot and burn; add water as necessary to keep the braise liquid, though you will want it to reduce to a rich sauce by the end of the cooking.

Remove the bay leaves and season again with salt and pepper if needed. Drizzle with gremolata to serve.

On Pasta, and Restraint

In the (very) old days, aristocratic Romans relied heavily on strong flavors—cumin, ginger, star anise, honey, and garum (their fish sauce). Today, the essential dishes in the Roman canon display a simplicity that is almost ascetic. The keenest tool you can use, when cooking this sort of food, is a very measured restraint. Resist the urge to add flavors; instead, try to isolate and purify the ones already at hand. There is one central philosophy: Develop complexity from purity; flavor from feeling; addition from subtraction.

Let me explain.

Like most Americans, I grew up eating what I understood to be Italian food. Overcooked spaghetti with tomato sauce spooned on top; chicken parm; watery ricotta lasagna; store-bought meatballs. My mother is a very good cook, and she recreated certain dishes like *aglio olio peperoncino* on our dinner table in Pennsylvania. But she had never been to Italy. And at that time, in the 1980s, red-sauce joints reigned. And they lacked restraint.

I think this is true of most Italian food outside of Italy. As we cook there's often a lot of time to tinker; to add rather than isolate. And so we throw in some chili or sugar or more salt or mushrooms or wine to create a certain roundness that pleases the palate. Instead of simply grilling a fish and serving it with lemon, sauces and garnishes make their way to the plate. A puddle of Gorgonzola cream suddenly appears on a piece of beef. A balsamic reduction gets drizzled across a lamb chop. This is decidedly not how things are done in Italy.

Like the Japanese, Italians tend to favor a singular, or perhaps a mere coupling of, flavor. Have a look at *cacio e pepe*, perhaps Rome's most popular pasta: pasta, pasta water, pecorino, black pepper. That's it. The water and the cheese make the sauce for the pasta, the spice of the pepper cuts the richness of the sauce, the pasta (usually tonarelli, a dense, square, spaghetti-like noodle that is made fresh) is there for supple texture and the taste of grain.

A great cacio e pepe wants nothing more. It is complete—a perfect song.

On our trip to Rome in 2013, Paolo's mother, Pia, cooked a pasta that will forever live in my memory. The day before, Paolo's brother, Stefano, had wandered around the hills near the Via Appia, foraging for wild asparagus. It was early May. Wild asparagus grows beside a very distinctive plant, which is what foragers search for when they're rooting through tall patches of wild grass, and Stefano found many of them. Wild asparagus are gnarled, undignified-looking things; they appear alien beside the clean, streamlined shape of our supermarket shoots. But they are also powerful—nutty, grassy, sweet, and deep. It is as if this vegetal stubble had sucked up all that was around it, the aroma of thistle flowers and fennel and wild rocket and weeds, and encapsulated it all in its thin stalks.

It made a sauce nearly all by itself.

I had just stepped off a fifteen-hour flight from Bangkok to Rome, and into Pia's charming little kitchen in Falcognana. As I laid out the itinerary for the trip Paolo and I were about to take, and poured a glass of white wine, she began to cook lunch silently, effortlessly, as she has nearly every day for the past fifty-five years.

In fifteen minutes, lunch was ready. There was a bowl of *trofie*—a delicate fresh pasta, made only with flour and water and gently rolled between the fingers to form little, wizened strands—coated with the light green sheen of wild asparagus and olive oil. We grated some pecorino on top and the table fell silent.

That pasta haunts me for many reasons. I asked Pia how she had made the sauce: "Did you melt some guanciale, and then add onion and the asparagus? Is there stock in there too?"

She smiled and shook her head. "The sauce is made of olive oil, water, and wild asparagus." (Paolo disagrees, and thinks she added some guanciale. However, he wasn't present, and I didn't see any.)

"That's all, Jarrett," she said, amused by my extravagance.

There is nothing more humbling than eating an Italian mother's cooking. Especially when it contains three ingredients. And particularly when it manages to taste richer and deeper and more purposeful than that which you might produce with twice as many things, in a professional kitchen.

This is the basic rule of creating Italian pasta—let the sauce speak, but not too loudly. Cook with purpose. Showcase the taste of the few ingredients you're using, rather than building flavors on top of one another, like layers of clothing. Use great ingredients, and trust in them.

TONNARELLI CACIO E PEPE
PASTA WITH PECORINO AND BLACK PEPPER

serves 4 as a main course, or 6 as a starter

SALT AND LOTS OF FRESHLY GROUND BLACK PEPPER

6 OUNCES GRATED AGED PECORINO (THE BEST YOU CAN FIND), PLUS MORE TO FINISH

1½ TO 2 OUNCES GRATED GRANA PADANO OR PARMIGIANO-REGGIANO

1 POUND FRESH TONNARELLI PASTA

Cacio e pepe means, literally, cheese and pepper. It's made by emulsifying starchy pasta water with pecorino cheese, and then adding lots of freshly ground pepper. Every restaurant does it differently; sometimes the sauce is thin, almost watery, other times it's custard-like, more like American mac and cheese. It should be fruity and spicy with the pepper and pungent with pecorino.

Cacio e pepe can be made in minutes, but I think about it another way: The best aged pecorino takes months, even years to mature. It's only quick to make because the cheesemaker has done all the work for you. Tonnarelli is a traditional pasta shape from Lazio, very similar to the square-cut spaghetti alla chitarra. So you can also make it with a chitarra. Or use spaghetti. Rules are for restaurants, not dinners at home.

Bring a large, well-salted pot of water to a rolling boil over high heat. Put both cheeses and some black pepper in a warm stainless-steel bowl.

Boil the pasta until al dente. Scoop out and keep about a cup of the cooking water. Drain the pasta.

Add the pasta to the warm bowl with the cheese and pepper and, using a fork and spoon, toss it aggressively. Stir it in circles, and then toss it again. Add a splash of pasta cooking water if you need it to be creamy. This dish is about feel and taste—you're creating a sauce from just two things and that requires adjustment and some instinct. When that goal is achieved, plate the pasta, and top with fresh pepper and more grated pecorino cheese.

PASTA CARBONARA

PASTA WITH GUANCIALE, PECORINO, AND EGGS

serves 4 as a main course, or 6 as a starter

6 OUNCES GUANCIALE

SALT AND FRESHLY GROUND
BLACK PEPPER

2 WHOLE EGGS PLUS 4 YOLKS

1/2 CUP FINELY GRATED
PARMESAN

1/2 CUP FINELY GRATED
PECORINO ROMANO

3/4 POUND DRIED PASTA—WE
LIKE A THICK, TUBULAR PASTA
LIKE CALAMARATA OR RIGATONI

We arrived in Italy on April 6th to shoot the recipes for this book. As we drove from the airport to the farm, past the Appia Antica and the beautiful ruins that ring the outskirts of Ostia, a radio host was pledging her love for carbonara. People talk about food in Italy a lot, so I thought nothing of it.

That evening, when we sat around the television, the local news featured four chefs, and their different takes on carbonara. Guanciale sizzled in a skillet in the background as a chef waxed lyrical about shapes of pasta. Another chef said one must never use egg whites, while the third let out a groan and rolled his eyes. It turns out we had arrived on La Giornata della Carbonara—literally, Carbonara Day.

How wonderful.

That night we ate carbonara at a trattoria in Ostia called Buzzicona. "It's carbonara day!" the waiter explained, with a wink. Four plates were ordered, and quickly dispatched. It was delicious—Buzzicona is a very good restaurant and carbonara is a very good pasta. Two million more eggs were sold than normal in Italy that day, according to the local news.

Carbonara belongs to Rome, where it was perfected. And in Rome, it is almost unspeakable to change a formula—one which has been tampered with the world over—with blasphemous additions like cream, bacon, onions, and (gasp) mushrooms.

Start with a rough-looking dried pasta. Buy a very good piece of aged pecorino cheese and some Parmigiano-Reggiano. You will need fresh chicken eggs (though duck eggs work very well, too). Guanciale is crucial, but if you simply cannot find it, unsmoked pancetta is a good substitute. Finally, you'll need freshly ground black pepper and a little hot water. That's about it; if you follow our steps carefully, you'll have a perfectly emulsified, rich, intense pasta just like the one we ate at Buzzicona.

Begin by cutting your guanciale. Remove the skin (but reserve it—it's great for adding some heft to a stock). Cut the guanciale into lardons slightly smaller than your pinky finger.

Bring a pot of well-salted water to a boil.

(recipe continues)

Fry the guanciale in a large frying pan over medium or medium-low heat, as you would bacon. Cook it until it's crisp on the edges and rendered, turning it every few minutes to cook evenly, about 7 minutes. When it is brown but not burned, turn off the heat.

Place the eggs and yolks into a mixing bowl, and whisk about three-quarters of each kind of cheese into the eggs, and lots of pepper.

Boil the pasta until al dente. Reserve a cup of the pasta water, and remove the pasta from the water using a strainer. Keep your pot of water boiling.

In a stainless-steel mixing bowl, add the pasta, and the egg and cheese mixture, and stir vigorously. Also add most of the crispy guanciale, and half of its fat.

Now, protecting your hand with a dish towel, place the mixing bowl over your pot of boiling water and continue to stir, uniting the pork fat, eggs, and cheese into a rich, custard-like sauce. Don't let the bowl touch the water. The steam will warm the eggs and cook them gently; you want them to thicken but not curdle into scrambled eggs. Taste for salt (we rarely add salt to this dish as there's usually plenty in the cured pork and cheese, but taste and adjust).

Serve on warm plates, with the rest of the guanciale, the remaining cheese, and a bit more pepper.

GNOCCHI ALLA GRICIA
GNOCCHI WITH GUANCIALE AND PECORINO

serves 4 as a main course, or 6 as a starter,
with leftover gnocchi

SALT AND FRESHLY GROUND
BLACK PEPPER

10 OUNCES GUANCIALE

1½ POUNDS PREPARED
GNOCCHI *(recipe follows)*

2 OUNCES GRATED PECORINO
(PREFERABLY GRATED FINELY
ON A BOX GRATER), PLUS MORE
TO FINISH

"There are so many versions of alla gricia, a dish that is one of Rome's four essential pastas, along with carbonara, amatriciana, and cacio e pepe," Paolo explains. Most simply, you can think of gricia as a cacio e pepe with the addition of guanciale . . . or as a carbonara without the eggs. "You can modify it in many ways, too. Some places might use fresh pasta rather than dried, and one variation, with fresh artichokes, is also extremely delicious. But here, I wanted to do something different, and share with you my recipe for gnocchi, which can also be made for any of the ragù recipes in this book—especially the Ragù Napoletano (page 213). For the gricia you'll want to save all the fat and be generous with the cheese and pepper; that's the sauce in and of itself."

Gnocchi freezes well, and is a bit of a chore to make, so we've included a recipe here that will yield about 4 pounds. For this recipe, use 1½ pounds of gnocchi (a little less than half) and freeze the rest, in a container or wrapped in plastic.

Bring a large pot of well-salted water to a boil.

Remove the skin from the guanciale, and then cut the meat into lardons half the length and thickness of your pinky finger. Cook the guanciale in a deep frying pan over medium-low heat until rendered crispy, and set aside.

Boil your gnocchi in two batches. Cook them until they float to the top, 2 to 3 minutes. Use a skimmer or slotted spoon to remove the cooked gnocchi to a plate. Reserve a cup of the cooking water.

Now, raise the heat in the frying pan to medium, and drop the gnocchi in the guanciale and fat and lightly sauté, adding a little of the water from the pasta pot along with the pecorino and plenty of pepper. Gently stir, until a sauce develops. Do not overly agitate the gnocchi or they will break.

Serve on plates with more cheese, and lots of pepper.

(recipe continues)

GNOCCHI

*makes about 4 pounds,
enough to serve 10 as a main course
or 15 as a starter*

3 POUNDS RUSSET POTATOES
(see note)

2 CUPS ALL-PURPOSE FLOUR,
PLUS MORE FOR KNEADING

2 EGG YOLKS, BEATEN

3/4 CUP GRATED PARMESAN
CHEESE

Note

Choose medium-sized
potatoes, about 1/2 pound
each. The older the better,
for a higher starch content, as
long as the potatoes are firm
and not sprouting.

Preheat the oven to 250°F. Wash, prick with a fork, and then roast the potatoes on a sheet pan until they are soft to the touch, and yield easily to a small knife, about 90 minutes. Flip them over once so they don't begin to caramelize.

Remove the potatoes from the oven, and allow them to cool just until you can handle them. Split them open, and scoop out the flesh from the skins (which you'll discard) into a bowl. Pass the potatoes through a vegetable mill or a ricer into a large bowl. Let the potatoes cool to warm.

Add half of the flour, the egg yolks, and the Parmesan cheese, and lightly mix the dough together. If you can get a good, stable dough with this amount of flour, that's perfect. If it's too wet, add more flour until the dough binds and becomes one.

On a lightly floured surface, knead your potato dough for just 1 or 2 minutes, until it is smooth but light and soft, much more so than pasta dough. Do not overwork it or your gnocchi will be tough. Tear off a piece of dough that fits in your fist, or slice off a slab about 2 inches thick from your "loaf" of dough, and gently roll this into a rope that is about the thickness of your thumb.

Cut the dough into 3/4-inch pieces, and lightly indent the tops by pressing on them with the curved part of the bottom tines of a fork. Lightly flour the gnocchi, and use within a few hours or freeze. (If you're cooking from frozen, it's best to let them defrost first.)

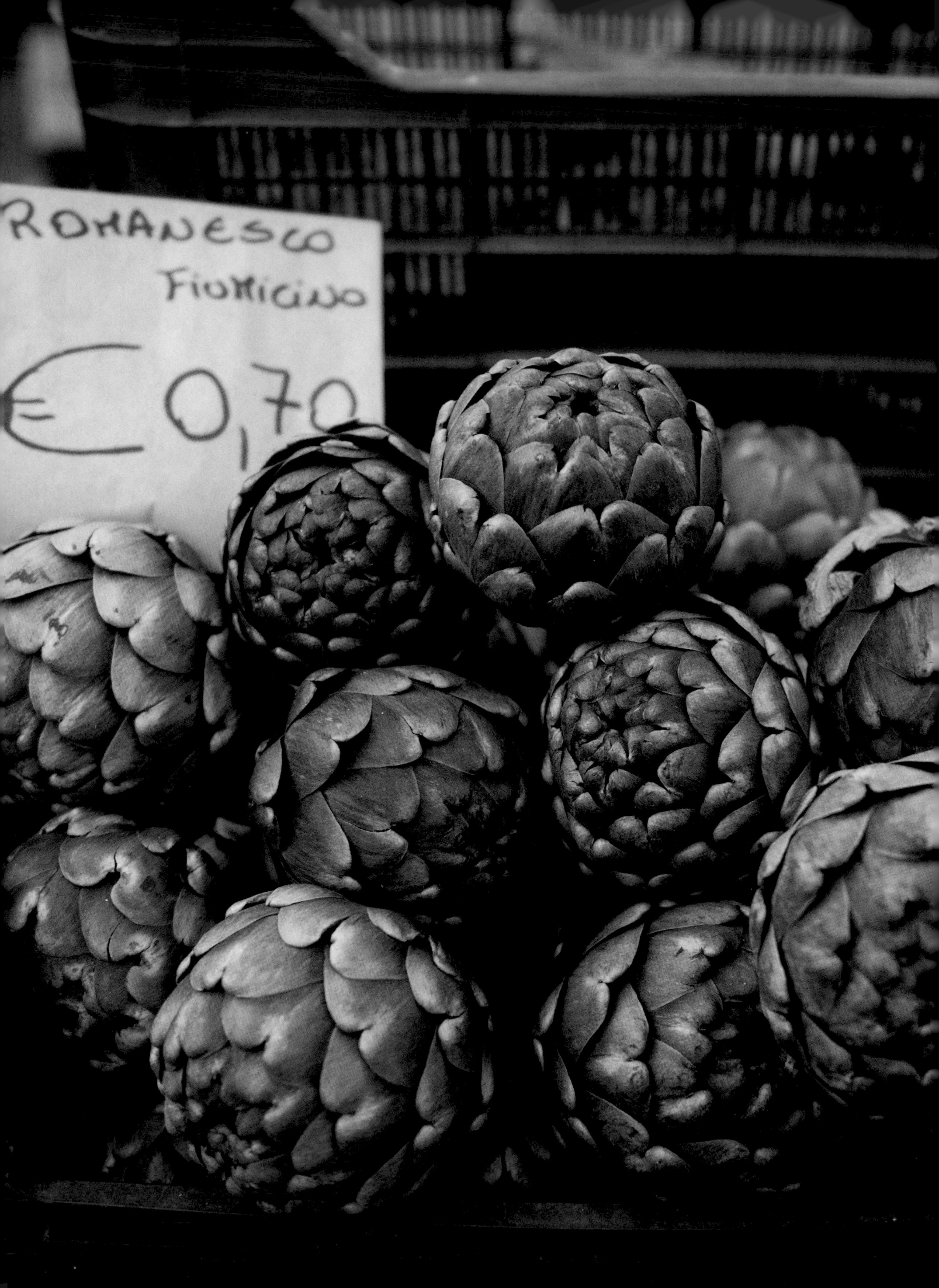
ROMANESCO
FIUMICINO
€ 0,70

On Artichokes

In December and January, artichokes begin to arrive in markets in Rome from Sicily and Sardinia. They're small, and the Sardinian ones are particularly spiny and difficult to clean. But when the mammole artichokes arrive at the end of February, from the seaside town of Ladispoli, the city holds its collective breath. These are the best of the best.

"There are two seasons we really get excited about in Rome—fall, with the arrival of the mushrooms, but especially spring, with the artichokes. There's a kind of euphoria," Paolo explains. "The market is suddenly full of color. Peas, artichokes, the vignarola . . . the days get longer, and the food fresher. But mostly, yes, it's the artichokes. They're my favorite vegetable. You can braise them, you can sear them, you can fry them, you can roast them. Romans, we are in love with artichokes."

While we chased the food of Rome through the countryside, there were a few dishes that seemed quintessentially Roman. And those were of the slaughterhouse—the quinto quarto—and, especially, the artichoke dishes you'll find here.

Cleaning artichokes is a meditative thing. At home on Sundays, at Paolo's mother's round table, we would slowly clean artichokes, *puntarelle*, and the *cicoria* which she foraged from the Appia Antica park behind her home. On afternoons, the family would sit around the table, preparing them for dinner. Turn the page to see how it's done.

CLEANING ARTICHOKES

First, you need to figure out what you're going to do with the artichokes, because that affects how you prepare them. With this method, you can deep-fry them for Carciofi alla Giudea (page 284), or stuff them for Carciofi alla Romana (page 283).

You get a bucket of cold water, and halve and squeeze two lemons into the water. Add ice to the water if you have it on hand, especially if it's warm outside.

Take a small, very sharp paring knife, and, if the artichokes come with a long stem, cut off the bottom, leaving 3 to 4 inches of stem, and peel the stem. You can/should keep the stem you cut off, because it's delicious in a frittata or in pasta or whatever you like. Peel those too and add them to the water.

Cut off the top third of the artichoke to create a flat surface and expose the heart. If it's a mammole artichoke, it will have no beard inside; if it is a globe or another variety (likely, if you are in the United States), you will need to scoop out all the fuzz inside with a melon baller or a spoon. If the leaves are thick and tough at the base, remove those by working inward and upward. As soon as you get to the leaves that are bright green and tender, you're good.

Soak the prepared artichokes in the lemon water until you finish cleaning all your artichokes, and then for 20 minutes more.

INSALATA DI CARCIOFI CRUDO
A SALAD OF RAW ARTICHOKES

serves 4 as a starter

1 LEMON

3 LARGE ARTICHOKES

3 TABLESPOONS EXTRA-VIRGIN OLIVE OIL

1 GARLIC CLOVE, FINELY CHOPPED

FRESH MINT LEAVES, JULIENNED, PLUS WHOLE MINT LEAVES TO FINISH

SALT AND PEPPER

PARMESAN, TO FINISH

Artichokes need not be cooked. In fact, they're perfectly delicious, sweet, and mild when thinly sliced and simply dressed with lemon and olive oil. Romans have a great fondness for bitterness—and the tannic acidity one finds in a red wine also shines through in this salad. Artichokes oxidize nearly as fast as one can cut them, so make sure to have cold lemon water ready for soaking. Finish with freshly shaved Parmesan and mint.

Juice half a lemon and reserve the juice. Fill a large bowl with ice water, squeeze the remaining lemon half into it, and add the lemon peel to the water. This is for soaking your artichokes.

Cut the artichokes in half from top to bottom, and remove any furry bits from the heart with a teaspoon or melon baller. Then slice the artichokes in a fine, thin julienne, much like you would cabbage for coleslaw. Soak the raw artichokes in the lemon water for 20 minutes or up to 1 hour.

Add the olive oil, garlic, reserved lemon juice, julienned mint, and salt and pepper to a stainless-steel bowl and mix with a fork. Taste for salt and balance of oil and acidity.

Strain the artichokes from the water, squeeze them gently to remove excess water, and add them to your dressing, gently massaging the artichokes with your hands in the bowl. Taste again and season with salt and pepper if necessary.

Serve with fresh mint leaves, and plenty of freshly shaved Parmesan.

FRITTATA ALLA CARCIOFI
A FRITTATA WITH ARTICHOKES

serves 4 as an antipasto

2 MEDIUM ARTICHOKES

8 LARGE EGGS

SALT AND PEPPER

1 CUP FINELY GRATED
PARMESAN, PLUS SOME
COARSELY GRATED FOR
GARNISH

EXTRA-VIRGIN OLIVE OIL

1/2 MEDIUM WHITE ONION,
JULIENNED

SPLASH OF WHITE WINE

5 FRESH MINT LEAVES,
JULIENNED, PLUS A FEW SMALL
LEAVES FOR GARNISH

On the lip of a cliff in Matera, at the end of our journey down the Appian Way, we ate a massive frittata that contained bits and pieces of everything we'd bought on the trip. Sheep sausage. Cheeses. Tropea onions. Green tomatoes. Peppers. Bread. It was marvelous. There is no better place to hide your leftovers than in a gentle pool of eggs and cheese and olive oil.

A frittata is also so versatile. It can serve as the star in a delicious breakfast or brunch, but also works as an antipasto—sliced and served warm or at room temperature—or as a main course.

At one point, we had beautiful artichokes that were starting to head southward, and so we cooked the frittata you see here for lunch. This is a classic Easter dish in Rome. It's wonderful as is, but you can make it even better with the addition of some leftover porchetta (see page 28), cooked or raw ham, or even roast chicken. This is a foundation to build upon. A resurrection of sorts.

Preheat the oven to 400°F.

Halve the artichokes lengthwise. Remove the leaves and pull out the "choke"—the hairy-looking part just above the heart with a teaspoon. Halve the halves to quarter the heart, and then slice these and the stem.

Crack and beat your eggs in a bowl, only lightly, for about 30 seconds. Put a few generous pinches of salt, pepper, and the finely grated Parmesan in the eggs and let them commingle for a few minutes.

Get a 10-inch nonstick or well-seasoned skillet hot over medium heat. Slick the pan generously with olive oil, and sauté the artichokes until golden brown on both sides. Season with salt and pepper. Then add the onions and a pinch of salt, and sauté until softened. Deglaze with a small splash of white wine, and when it's almost gone, add the julienned mint.

Remove the vegetables from the skillet. Pour 3 tablespoons olive oil into the pan, and wait until it's shimmering hot. Add half the eggs, and wait until the edges are set. Add half of the artichoke and onion mixture, delicately, atop your eggs. Let it cook for a minute or two. Add the rest of the eggs, and the rest of the artichokes. Then bake the frittata for about 8 minutes, or until it's just cooked through and set.

Slide it out of the pan, or flip the pan over with a plate underneath it if it refuses to budge, and top with coarsely grated cheese and mint leaves.

CARCIOFI ALLA ROMANA
ROMAN-STYLE ARTICHOKES

serves 6 as a starter, or 3 as a main course

1/2 POUND GROUND PORK

SALT AND PEPPER

1 GARLIC CLOVE, FINELY CHOPPED

1 OR 2 EGGS

1/3 CUP BREAD CRUMBS OR PANKO

1 TABLESPOON FINELY CHOPPED FRESH ITALIAN PARSLEY

1 TEASPOON FINELY CHOPPED FRESH MINT, PLUS JULIENNED MINT LEAVES FOR GARNISH

6 ARTICHOKES, CLEANED, STEMS PEELED, CHOKES REMOVED (see page 276)

2 TABLESPOONS EXTRA-VIRGIN OLIVE OIL

1 MEDIUM SHALLOT, OR 1/2 MEDIUM ONION, JULIENNED

1/2 CUP DRY WHITE WINE, OR AS NEEDED

1/2 CUP CHICKEN OR VEGETABLE STOCK, OR AS NEEDED

This is comforting, satisfying Roman soul food. The dish takes many forms—in some trattorias the artichokes are just braised in white wine with mint. But Paolo's mother would fill them with a simple stuffing of ground pork, salt, pepper, and mint. Paolo explains, "We were a pork family; we used pork in our house for everything—my father was a *norcino*." The artichokes cloak the savory sausage with a delicate sweetness after a simple braise in white wine. They are first sautéed meat side down; that is, with the stems of the artichokes pointing up toward the lid of the pot. Once the meat is browned, we add white wine, and the dish is left to simmer for a little while.

In a mixing bowl, season the pork well with salt and pepper and stir in the garlic. Let rest for 1 hour.

Add 1 egg, the bread crumbs, parsley, and chopped mint, and mix together. If it appears very dry, add another egg. Stuff the artichokes with the meat mixture to the top.

In a wide, heavy-bottomed pot, heat the olive oil over medium heat until it begins to shimmer. Fry all the artichokes in the oil, meat side down, for 5 to 10 minutes, or until the filling is browned nicely. Remove the artichokes to a plate. Add the shallot or onion to the pot, and when it's translucent, add the wine and the stock. Return the artichokes to the pot, meat side down. Your artichokes should be cooking in about 1 inch of liquid; add a bit more wine and stock if need be.

Put the lid on. Cook the artichokes for about 30 minutes; check once in a while, and if the liquid has nearly evaporated, top off with a little water. But you want to finish with a nice, reduced sauce, so don't add too much water toward the end.

When the artichokes are still firm enough to handle but very tender, remove from heat. Taste the sauce for seasoning and add salt and pepper to taste. Let the artichokes rest in the pot for 30 minutes.

Serve warm, garnished with julienned mint, in shallow bowls with sauce poured around for sopping.

CARCIOFI ALLA GIUDEA

JEWISH-STYLE ARTICHOKES

serves 4 as a starter

NEUTRAL VEGETABLE OIL LIKE SUNFLOWER OR RICE BRAN OIL, FOR DEEP-FRYING

4 MAMMOLE ARTICHOKES, OR OTHER FRESH LARGE ARTICHOKES, CLEANED, STEMS PEELED, CHOKES REMOVED AND SOAKED IN LEMON WATER (*see page 276*)

FLAKY SEA SALT (WE PREFER MALDON)

RED WINE VINEGAR

Note

These are delicious but will make your wine taste very weird. So serve them with something white, and fresh, and cold!

Once a specialty of restaurants inside Rome's Jewish Ghetto—where the city's small population of Jews had a tremendous influence on its cuisine—"Jewish artichokes" are now a staple on menus during the season. It is important that the artichokes' thick, chewy outer leaves are removed, because the end result of this recipe is extraordinarily simple: You eat the whole, crispy, deep-fried flower. This requires a lengthy process of cleaning, soaking in water acidulated with lemons, and then frying twice (once at a relatively low temperature, to cook it through, and then again at a higher temperature, to crisp it). After the second frying, the artichoke's petals will open up, as a morning flower does to the sun. "I never made this at home—the first time I did this was at Appia. This is a dish people usually eat in restaurants, and so when I opened a Roman trattoria, I made it. And quickly, it became something we were known for," Paolo says.

Fill a heavy-bottomed pot with enough oil to cover an entire artichoke. Bring your oil to 250°F over medium heat. Remove the artichokes from their water, shake them well, and pat dry with paper towels, lest they send up sprays of hot oil when they go in the fryer. Fry the artichokes for about 10 minutes, or until you can easily slip a toothpick into the base of the flower, and through its heart. Remove them from the oil and drain on paper towels. Let them rest for at least 10 minutes; if you want, they will keep at this stage for 3 days in the fridge.

Now bring the oil to 350°F over medium-high heat (if you need to add a bit more oil to cover the artichokes, do so). Fry the artichokes, 1 or 2 at a time, giving yourself plenty of space to let them fry. Flatten the artichokes, flower side down, with tongs, so that they open up. Then turn them over so the stems cook a bit. Remove when they're golden brown, the leaves are crispy, and the hearts are soft. This should take about 5 minutes. Again, drain on paper towels.

Dress with flaky salt and a few drips of red wine vinegar (sparingly, for just a hint of acid). Then, eat the whole thing.

THE FARM:
THINGS WE COOKED BECAUSE WE HAD TO

When Paolo and I finally completed the first draft of this book, after years of traveling and writing and eating, we purchased a farm just outside of Rome, in Castel Romano. It sits on a bumpy road lined on both sides by majestic pines. The sea is not too far off. It's still a wild place, and I think we'll work quite a while on it before it's ready for people to stay there. No one, save for a single shepherd, had lived there for thirty years.

We wanted to finish the book, and cook all its recipes, in the farmhouse. But the old, dusty kitchen was empty. So for a few days we set out to create a cooking studio. The morning and afternoon light streamed in through big windows, and there was a hearth where a fire hadn't been lit in decades. We started to sweep, and mop, and strip off years of neglect.

We went to a restaurant supply store to purchase a stove from a restaurant that had closed for one reason or another. The stove ran severely hot—just the pilot alone was enough to cook ragù and other dishes. It needed adjusting, but we were in a hurry.

We wandered through the barn and found a beautiful piece of marble, and set it atop a solid table that we also found outside, in the stable. This is where we would shoot many of the photos you see here. Then, using steel rebar and a welder, Paolo and his brother, Stefano, built a long steel rack for hanging pots. I found some old boards outside near the sheep stable, and sanded them down. After that, I rubbed the wood with olive oil and let it dry in the sun. Then I built shelves for spices and equipment, with a drill and some anchor screws, and after four days of hard work we were ready to go.

Most of the recipes here are resolutely rustic—it's the sort of food that we like to cook, and to eat. I think there's more than a bit of that farmhouse kitchen in these recipes, too. Without all the trappings of our restaurant's kitchen, we were forced to cook more like home cooks. Sometimes, for a stew, I would build up the fire, and then set a pot on a grate across coals that I scattered in front of the hearth. Other times, Paolo would hang a piece of meat in the fireplace, on hooks, to brown before braising in a pot.

I will miss our month of cooking in that kitchen. The measured way of waking, cleaning, and cutting; of lighting fires and peeling and chopping; then shooting, and finally eating. We were creating real Italian food. Real food, period.

Each day during the photo shoot was a slow, steady race for good light. When the sheep's bells clanged as they trudged up from the pasture, with our two dogs and our shepherd, Giallo, leading them along, the sun would be setting behind the pines, sinking toward the sea. And then there was nothing for us to do but pack up, drive downhill to our rented home, on the outskirts of Ostia, to drink a beer and sleep. One thing was certain, the sun would rise early, and our cooking would follow its path the following day.

While we set out to simply use the farmhouse kitchen to cook and photograph the recipes in this book, the kind of cooking we did on the farm inspired its own collection of new recipes—recipes informed by our travels, and by the farm and inn and restaurant we dream of building here one day. We'll share those recipes with you now, though, before you arrive.

GRILLED BEEF OR LAMB HEARTS

serves 8 as a main course

1 BEEF HEART OR 5 LAMB
HEARTS (3 TO 4 POUNDS
TOTAL)

OLIVE OIL

SPLASH OF RED WINE VINEGAR

SALT AND PEPPER

1 LEMON, QUARTERED

GREMOLATA (TRIPLE OR
QUADRUPLE THE RECIPE
ON PAGE 46), FOR SERVING
(OPTIONAL)

Hearts are hugely overlooked as an ingredient. They have a deep meatiness and a springy texture, and unlike liver or kidneys, they don't have a strong iron taste. A heart—whether from a bird or a beast—should never be cooked more than medium. All it needs is salt and lemon, though it will be wonderful with a drizzle of herbal gremolata. Like other simply grilled meats, this is best served with a salad and some sourdough with butter or a good, green olive oil.

Hearts require a bit of trimming. Like most organs, it's cloaked in a layer of fat; remove this (and save it for rendering and use it to fry things). Slice off the arteries that will be sticking out. Cut the hearts in half, and remove any coagulated blood by rinsing them under water. Feel your way around the muscle and use a sharp paring knife to cut out any tough, fibrous tissue in the interior. Remove any silver skin. If you're using beef, slice the cleaned heart into 3- to 4-inch-wide pieces; lamb hearts can be cleaned and simply cut in half. Pat it all dry, then coat the pieces with olive oil and a splash of vinegar and season well with salt and pepper, and marinate for 20 minutes.

Light a fire in your grill, or set it to medium-high heat. You want to cook the hearts with a good sear, and this takes a brisk fire.

Grill the hearts until medium-rare (130°F), turning often to brown both sides. The time on the grill depends on the thickness of the meat—poke it with your finger to test the doneness (it should stiffen but yield to the touch), or, better, use a thermometer. Remove from the grill and wrap in foil. Let them rest for 5 minutes. Slice into ½-inch-thick slices and season with salt and pepper. Serve with lemon and gremolata, if desired.

TESTARELLE D'ABBACCHIO ARROSTO
ROASTED LAMB'S HEAD

serves 4 as a main course, with salad and bread

4 LAMB HEADS, SPLIT
LENGTHWISE (YOUR BUTCHER
SHOULD DO THIS FOR YOU)

GLUG OF OLIVE OIL (TO COAT)

SALT AND PEPPER

4 GARLIC CLOVES, SMASHED

5 BAY LEAVES

4 SPRIGS OF FRESH ROSEMARY,
LEAVES REMOVED AND
CHOPPED

ZEST OF 1 LEMON

SALSA VERDE, FOR SERVING
(DOUBLE THE RECIPE on
page 247)

BREAD AND SALAD, FOR
SERVING

"This is a recipe you don't find in restaurants anymore. It's a farm dish, a thing people only involved in agriculture would eat. My mother wouldn't even cook it," Paolo explains. "But my grandmother Betta lived in our house, and she made this dish. She had about a hundred rabbits and fifty or sixty pigeons, in an old house down the street from the one we lived in. There was also a Ping-Pong table, and a couple of lambs. My village is a suburb now, but thirty years ago, when I was a child, this is how we ate. I cooked this dish in the same pan that my grandmother Betta used to cook it in."

In the spring, most of the male sheep are slaughtered. In Italy, we're not allowed to process our own meat, so it's sold to butchers who take the animals away. However, we do harvest a few for ourselves. And this bit—the head—is something we really relish eating.

If you see tongues and cheeks on restaurant menus, know that they're there because they're delicious, and, until recently, rather cheap. *Testarelle* is a celebration of those lovely things and all the other wonderful little bits on a lamb's head that would otherwise go unused: tender suggestions of meat on the back of the neck and the brim of the head. Rich, pillowy brains. We roasted ours in our farm's eighty-year-old bread oven, after the fire from baking the sourdough had died down.

If you've got some offal-loving friends, invite them over, and place this on the center of the table. Make a good salsa verde for the head (see page 247), and put some bitter leaves and onions in a bowl with oil and vinegar as a foil. Misticanza (page 298) is perfect. Bread and butter wouldn't hurt. Pick away. Deliciousness will ensue.

Rub the heads with olive oil, salt, the garlic, herbs, and lemon zest in a roasting tray. Let them marinate for an hour, or until they reach room temperature. Preheat the oven (or a gas grill) to 425°F. Set the heads in the roasting pan, brain side down, and cover with foil.

Roast for 30 minutes. Remove the foil, lower the temperature to 350°F, and flip each head over so the face is down, and the brains up. Roast for another 10 minutes, or until everything has caramelized to golden brown. Remove the heads from the oven and let rest for 10 minutes. Discard the bay leaves. Serve with salsa verde, bread, and a simple salad.

FEGATO DI MAIALE

PIG LIVER WRAPPED IN LARDO WITH HERBS

serves 6 as a starter

1½ POUNDS PORK LIVER

SALT AND PEPPER, PLUS FLAKY
SEA SALT FOR FINISHING

2 TEASPOONS CHOPPED GARLIC

GRATED ZEST OF 1 LEMON, THE
REMAINING FRUIT CUT INTO
WEDGES FOR SERVING

EXTRA-VIRGIN OLIVE OIL

1-POUND BALL OF CAUL FAT,
SOAKED IN WARM WATER, SO
THAT IT'S PLIABLE AND SOFT

4 OUNCES LARDO, SLICED
VERY THIN

12 BAY LEAVES

This dish is perfect for barbecues, and pre-prepared ones are a common sight in the ornate cases of good Italian butcher shops. The pork liver is wrapped in caul fat and herbs. Caul fat acts much like a sausage casing, albeit one that adds richness and succulence, and allows you to sneak some lard and a bouquet of aromatics inside. Guanciale or pancetta or even bacon would be a fine substitute if you cannot find caul fat (but omit the lardo, in that case). Serve with flaky sea salt and slices of lemon—the acidity makes it even more delicious. If you'd like to soften the taste of the liver, marinate it in cold milk (or water with a bit of white wine vinegar) for an hour before skewering and grilling.

Soak 24 wooden skewers in water for about 30 minutes.

Meanwhile, trim the pork liver of any visible fat, veins, and, if it's there, the membrane. Cut the liver into 2-ounce pieces, roughly the size of a small, thick sausage. You should have about 10 to 12 pieces.

In a mixing bowl, season the liver with salt and pepper, garlic, the lemon zest, and a splash of olive oil.

Open the caul fat on a long table and cut it into as many 10-inch squares as needed to wrap each piece of liver at least twice.

Cover each piece of liver with a slice of lardo, a pinch of salt, a bit of pepper, and a bay leaf. Wrap it tightly with 2 layers of caul fat, like a sausage. Using skewers, pin the "sausages" as if you were sticking a toothpick through them, to keep the caul fat from unraveling. For cooking, you may find it easiest to skewer a few liver bundles on each skewer, leaving some room between the bundles so they cook evenly. You want to use two skewers, spaced a few inches apart from each other so the bundles don't spin when you flip them.

Light a fire in your grill, or set the grill to medium heat. Grill the liver bundles for about 10 minutes, turning frequently to brown evenly, until they're cooked medium-well. Season again with flaky salt and pepper, and serve with the lemon wedges. Be sure to tell your guests to not eat the bay leaves.

MISTICANZA

A SALAD OF WILD, FORAGED HERBS IN AN ANCHOVY DRESSING

serves 4 as a starter, or as a foil for grilled meats

1/2 CUP LIGHTLY PACKED FRESH MINT LEAVES, PICKED FROM STEMS

1/2 CUP LIGHTLY PACKED FRESH DILL, PICKED FROM THE THICK STEMS

1/2 CUP LIGHTLY PACKED FRESH ITALIAN PARSLEY LEAVES, COARSELY CHOPPED

2 CUPS LIGHTLY PACKED WILD ARUGULA

1 CUP CHOPPED BEET LEAVES OR ANOTHER BITTER GREEN

2 SALTED ANCHOVY FILLETS

1 GARLIC CLOVE

2 TABLESPOONS EXTRA-VIRGIN OLIVE OIL

2 TABLESPOONS RED WINE VINEGAR

1 TEASPOON COLATURA DI ALICI (ITALIAN FISH SAUCE) OR GOOD SOUTHEAST ASIAN FISH SAUCE

2 OUNCES ASPARAGUS, PEELED, CUT INTO THIN MATCHSTICKS

SALT AND PEPPER

Valeria Rocca arrived at the farm with a bag slung over her shoulder. It reminded me of the bags that monks carry in Buddhist temples in Asia. When I shook her hand, a feline head poked out of this purse, and startled me. Another Siamese cat followed behind, on foot. Her earrings were silver statuettes of trees. Valeria practices shiatsu massage and tai chi, and also specializes in Ayurvedic medicine. She is the only vegetarian I've met in Rome. And she knows, importantly, what one can and cannot eat in the fields of Lazio.

We invited her to our farm because she is fascinated with edible wild plants. Paolo and I can identify many things—arugula, fennel, rosemary, sage, thyme—yet there are so many edible herbs that we don't know. And because much of the land is wild, we wanted to see what we could eat from the fields.

"My whole life, I've been interested in herbs," Valeria said, as we stumbled through the thick grass. "As I walk through a pasture, I try to remember the things that you can eat; to capture the image of that plant, and the taste of it, in my mind." She left one cat behind, to play with a baby goat and the sheepdogs that treat cats kindly. The nervous cat came with us, in her bag.

Valeria spent many years in India, and her appreciation for herbs stems from this experience. As we picked through the brush, she identified wild mustard, which looked like broccoli rabe. "It's cleansing," she explained, "and very good for your kidneys, especially if you eat it uncooked." We went on to forage *borragine* (borage), a furry, flowering plant that has a distinct saltiness, and wild chervil, which leaves one's mouth with an acerbic, immediate bite that lasts a long time. Use this one with caution—it's extremely bitter.

As we walked further we discovered *ministrella*, a cabbage-like vegetable, and plenty of wild asparagus, which grows everywhere at la Santola. There was also *cicoria*, identified by the base of its stems—which are purple, rather than green. *Cardo mariano*, an edible thistle that is used to cure cheese, was also picked, along with nettles, which sting if you fall upon them but are delicious when cooked.

We understand that you might not have acres of greens to walk through, picking at will, to make your salad. But the end result can be the same. Consider flavor. Forget neutral lettuces, and think of something more primal. More bitter. More severe. In a grocery store, I'd buy arugula, mint, chervil, radicchio, kale, dill, Italian

parsley . . . your aim is to create a pungent, tannic, memorable collection of leaves. And then dress it.

That afternoon, we ate a vegetarian lunch. A large salad of wild, bitter, fuzzy, funky greens, and an eggplant Parmesan. It's a meal I'll never forget.

Soak the mint, dill, parsley, arugula, and beet leaves in some water for a bit (repeat if they're wild and very dirty). While that's happening, prepare your dressing.

Finely chop the anchovies and garlic. Use the back of a spoon to smash them together in a small bowl, then add the olive oil, red wine vinegar, and colatura and whisk until it holds together without breaking.

Drain and dry the greens, and toss them and the asparagus with your dressing. Season with salt and pepper. If you have some nice edible flowers attached to your herbs or leaves, decorate with them.

TROFIE CON ASPARAGI SELVATICI
TROFIE WITH WILD ASPARAGUS

serves 4 as a main course, or 6 as a starter

1 POUND APPIA'S (ALMOST) EGGLESS PASTA DOUGH (*page 84*) OR ⅔ POUND DRIED PASTA, A SHORT SHAPE

EXTRA-VIRGIN OLIVE OIL

½ MEDIUM ONION, JULIENNED

1 POUND WILD ASPARAGUS (OR TIPS AND TENDER PARTS OF REGULAR ASPARAGUS), CUT INTO 2-INCH PIECES

½ SMALL ITALIAN PEPERONCINO OR A PINCH OF CHILI FLAKES

4 GARLIC CLOVES, CRUSHED WITH THE SIDE OF A KNIFE

SALT AND PEPPER

3 TABLESPOONS GRATED PECORINO ROMANO

2 TABLESPOONS GRATED PARMESAN

2 TABLESPOONS GRATED RICOTTA SALATA

The first time I ate this pasta, it was cooked by Pia, Paolo's mother. It was so simple, yet so deeply satisfying. It haunted me with its counterintuitive complexity. Wild asparagus is delicious. If you drive in the countryside around Rome in the spring, you'll occasionally see a beat-up car wedged in the shoulder of the road, and a person wandering through the weeds, searching for asparagus.

Wild asparagus grows in tandem with a small bush with feathery, pine-tree-looking needles, in the shade of larger trees, or in thick brush, or in thickets of thorny blackberries, near water. It doesn't like full sun. It's very difficult to see with an untrained eye. But now we know which kind of land it likes to grow on, and so we walk fence lines on the farm in the early evening, crawling around and foraging the sweet, herbal shoots. I like to eat the tenderest shoots raw, as I drop more in my basket.

If you choose to forage, you'll most likely have cuts on your ankles and elbows from the stubborn thorns during your venture through the brush. When you see that signifying pine-like bush, relax your eyes, and search. And the spears will appear. This is truly slow food; you find a source, and then creep, relax, and suddenly see a few, tender stems. Pick, crouch, and continue on. It takes about an hour for me to find enough wild asparagus for dinner. But I'm a novice. A solid bouquet of wild asparagus, about a pound, should be plenty for a good pasta. Make sure, when you forage them, that you snap only the tender tips (maybe eight inches), allowing the rest to grow again, so in time, you'll return to this delicious gift in spring.

If you can't get wild asparagus, you can certainly use the more common farmed kind. I recommend using the thinnest asparagus you might find, as it seems that the flavor is more concentrated in slim, purposeful stalks.

Trofie pasta resembles the gnarled stalks of wild asparagus; if you don't feel like making or buying it, use any short pasta shape.

If you're making the pasta, begin by rolling an inch-thick rope of the pasta dough. If you're a righty, hold that dough in your left hand. With your right hand, snap off a small piece of it and place it under your ring finger. Using barely any pressure, press the dough down on your board and push your hand away from you, rolling the dough into a strand. When the dough reaches the meaty side of the palm of your hand, drag your hand

down and to the left, in a diagonal motion, with slight pressure. The idea is that the pasta will escape from the right side of your hand, while the pressure will make it curl out like a beautiful spindle of dough. (Honestly, if this is hard to picture, you can search for a video on the internet.)

In a large sauté pan, heat enough olive oil to generously coat the pan over medium heat. Add your onion and cook, stirring occasionally. When it is soft and translucent, after about 10 minutes, add the asparagus, chili, and garlic. Add enough water to just cover, bring it to a simmer, and let it braise. Add a few splashes of water, if needed, to cook the asparagus until quite soft. We are braising vegetables here—crispness is not a virtue. Push on the stalks with the back of your spoon, unwinding the fibers, creating a green blanket of sauce. Season with salt, pepper, and a little cheese.

Bring a pot of salted pasta water to boil, and cook the trofie for 4 to 6 minutes (or according to your package directions). The texture should be elastic, and there should be no uncooked flour at the center of the pasta, when you bite it in half.

When the pasta is finished, drain it and toss it in your pan of melted asparagus, and season with salt and pepper. Finish with pecorino, Parmesan, and salted ricotta.

PAPPARDELLE AL RAGÙ D'ANATRA

PAPPARDELLE WITH DUCK RAGÙ, ANCIENT ROMAN SPICES, AND FAVA BEANS

serves 4 as a main course, or 6 as a starter

1½ POUNDS DUCK BREASTS, WITH THEIR FAT

2 TABLESPOONS EXTRA-VIRGIN OLIVE OIL, PLUS MORE TO FINISH

½ SMALL CINNAMON STICK

1 PIECE OF STAR ANISE

2 WHOLE CLOVES

¼ TEASPOON POWDERED GINGER

1 TEASPOON PAPRIKA

ZEST OF ½ LEMON, CUT IN TWO BIG PIECES

2 BAY LEAVES

⅓ CUP FINELY DICED CELERY

⅓ CUP FINELY DICED WHITE ONION

⅓ CUP FINELY DICED CARROT

1 CUP WHITE WINE

1 QUART DUCK OR CHICKEN STOCK

SALT AND PEPPER

5 OUNCES FAVA BEANS, PREFERABLY FRESH

1 POUND FRESH PAPPARDELLE (STOREBOUGHT OR MADE WITH A DOUGH on pages 83–84)

3 SPRIGS OF FRESH THYME, LEAVES ONLY

SMOKED RICOTTA SALATA OR PARMESAN, FOR FINISHING

"Growing up, my uncle Renato Callisi was a *guardia caccia*, the warden of a famous hunting preserve called Riserva di Caccia Fogliano," Paolo tells me. "It was 50 kilometers south of Rome, on a saltwater lake that is just beside the sea. On fall weekends, wealthy Roman men would head there to shoot the thousands of ducks that would stop on their migration south. And during this time in my life, we used to eat a lot of duck. In fact, it was my job to clean them after the hunt, boiling them, plucking the feathers, and breaking down the birds. Though ducks aren't all that common on Roman menus, they were for me and my family to eat." Paolo and I plan to raise them at our farm, for the restaurant.

The spices in this recipe are a reflection of ancient Rome's fascination with what they termed the Orient. With the opening of the trade routes to Asia and North Africa, aristocratic Roman food changed dramatically, incorporating new spices. We developed this recipe while still living in Bangkok, where warming spices like ginger and star anise work so well with the meaty nature of duck, so it all kind of makes sense.

The dish returns to Rome with the addition of fresh fava beans. The pasta below is at its absolute best when it's topped with smoked salted ricotta (*ricotta salata affumicato*), but feel free to grate some Parmesan on it too.

Lay the duck breasts on a chopping board, and chop the duck with a cleaver or mince with a very sharp knife, or run through a grinder (we prefer hand-mincing for texture's sake). Please mince all of the fat along with the duck.

Place a large, heavy-bottomed pot over medium-high heat, and add the olive oil and minced duck. Add the cinnamon, star anise, cloves, ginger, paprika, lemon zest, and bay leaves, and cook, stirring frequently, until the fat separates from the meat, the water has all evaporated, and the duck meat begins to sizzle and fry in its own fat. It needs to caramelize deeply, and when it does, add the celery, onion, and carrot. Turn the heat to medium-low and cook the vegetables slowly, stirring often, for about 15 minutes, until they become very soft and caramelized.

(recipe continues)

Add the white wine to the pot, and let it reduce by half. Then add the duck or chicken stock, and a few nice pinches of salt. (It should taste seasoned—but underseasoned—as the salt will concentrate as it reduces.) Bring the liquid to a boil over medium-high heat, turn it down to a gentle simmer, cover the pot, and cook for 2 hours or until it becomes a thick, unified sauce and the meat is very tender.

Bring a large pot of well-salted water to a boil over high heat.

Quickly blanch your fava beans, dropping them in the boiling water for just a few seconds to shake their rawness off. Scoop them out with a strainer and reserve.

Cook the pasta in the same pot of boiling water until it's al dente. Reserve ½ cup of starchy pasta water and then drain the pasta.

In a large sauté pan or nonstick wok over medium-high heat, add the pasta, a splash of olive oil, enough ragù to generously coat the pasta, the fava beans, and the thyme leaves. Cook for a minute, stirring, and adjust with salt and pepper. Remove the bay leaves, cinnamon sticks, star anise, and cloves if you see them, as they can make for a surprising bite.

Finish with finely grated smoked ricotta salata or parmesan, and serve hot, with a bit of olive oil drizzled atop each plate.

PAPPARDELLE AL RAGÙ DI PICCIONE E QUAGLIE

PAPPARDELLE WITH A RAGÙ OF PIGEON AND QUAIL

serves 4 as a main course, or 6 as a starter

6 TO 8 SMALL QUAIL

1 LARGE OR 2 SMALL PIGEONS

Stock

1 SMALL ONION, UNPEELED

GENEROUS SPLASH OF
OLIVE OIL

1/3 CUP LARGE-DICED CARROT,
UNPEELED

1/3 CUP LARGE-DICED CELERY

1 TEASPOON WHOLE BLACK
PEPPERCORNS

Ragù

1 TABLESPOON EXTRA-VIRGIN
OLIVE OIL

2/3 CUP FINELY DICED FRESH
PORCINI MUSHROOMS, IF IN
SEASON

SALT AND PEPPER

1/3 CUP FINELY DICED CARROT

1/3 CUP FINELY DICED ONION

1/3 CUP FINELY DICED CELERY

1/2 CUP WHITE WINE

2 JUNIPER BERRIES

2 BAY LEAVES

1 CLOVE

1 POUND FRESH PAPPARDELLE
(STOREBOUGHT OR MADE WITH
A DOUGH *on pages 83-84*)

GRATED LEMON ZEST, FOR
GARNISH

JULIENNED FRESH PARSLEY
OR FRESH THYME LEAVES, FOR
GARNISH

When Giallo, from Mali, was a teenager, he walked across the Sahara and through Libya during the war. He was shot at during his journey, but eventually he made his way to one of the overcrowded boats that cross the Mediterranean, and then to Lampedusa, and then Corleone. He finally made it to Rome, and to our farm, where he lives and works.

Giallo only eats what he kills and grows himself. One day, he brought us some pigeons he'd hit with his slingshot in our attic.

Pigeons are dark and gamy and delicious. Quail is a bit lighter, sweeter, and more accessible, but a little fussy to strip from the bone. Here is a dish that we made because there's more to birds than just chicken and duck—and because we have a bit of a pigeon problem on the upper floors of our unfinished farmhouse.

Debone the quail and pigeons by first removing the breast meat: Run a small, very sharp knife along the breastbone, then down under the wing, tracing the outline of the breast muscle, returning to where you started. Remove both breasts, making sure to scrape all the meat from the bones (the meat will be chopped, so it doesn't need to be uniform, or pretty). Then sever the small tendons at the bottom of the legs, running your knife around the bone, with pressure, just above where they meet the feet, and run your blade up the leg to the thigh. Pull the leg meat from the bone, if you'll pardon the metaphor, like taking off a tight pair of jeans.

MAKE THE STOCK: Put the carcasses of the birds in a medium stock pot with the small onion. Add a bit of olive oil, and pan-roast them over medium heat, turning occasionally, until nicely browned, about 10 minutes. Add the large-diced carrot and celery and the peppercorns. (If they're still lying around, add some carrot tops and celery leaves to the stock as well.) Add 6 cups of water, bring to a simmer, and cook gently, skimming the stock of foam as it appears. Let the stock simmer as you continue the prep for the recipe; the stock will be ready when you're ready to use it.

Mince the pigeon and quail meat with a cleaver, until it is nearly but not quite as fine as hamburger. Or, slice with a sharp knife like tartare. Or, throw it through a grinder. You get the point—chop it up.

(recipe continues)

MAKE THE RAGÙ: Heat the olive oil in a large sauté pan over medium-high heat. Brown the mushrooms, if using, then add the bird mince, spreading it out and leaving it alone to cook. Season with a pinch of salt and pepper. Like with other ragùs, we need to get all the moisture out of the meat, and then release the fat, and then let it brown. This takes time and attention.

When the meat begins to brown and it clings to the pan, add the finely diced carrot, onion, and celery, and aggressively scrape the bottom of the pot until the browned bits break loose.

Add the white wine and cook it off, until dry. Add the stock from the bones, 2 juniper berries, bay leaves, and the clove. Bring it to a boil, then lower the heat to a gentle simmer and cook the ragù, covered, for 2 hours, until the meat is very tender, and the liquid and the meat have become one dark, unified sauce. Taste and adjust the seasoning with salt and pepper. Remove the bay leaves.

PREPARE THE PASTA: Bring a large pot of well-salted water to a boil over high heat. Add the pappardelle and cook until just done. Drain and toss the pasta with the ragù, finishing with a few gratings of fresh lemon zest and a garnish of parsley or thyme.

If you chase down these birds, and follow our instructions, you'll be rewarded in a way that only wild game provides. I wouldn't add cheese; the meat speaks for itself.

Volpetti

Now that we've come to the end of our story, I keep thinking of how it began. In the beginning, before there was even a story to tell, or a restaurant to open, Paolo took me to a small shop near where his father once lived in Testaccio. He introduced me to a short, joyfully nervous man called Claudio Volpetti, who promptly slipped an anchovy—which he told me cost four euros—into my mouth.

Four euros is a lot to pay for an anchovy.

But not when its salty promise was slipping off the tip of Claudio's knife, as the tiny man reached up, beaming with pleasure, draping it onto my tongue. (That knife, incidentally, had been whittled out of pig bone, from one of his hams.) Before he retired, Claudio was one of Rome's most famed purveyors of food products. And, in a country where food is valued over almost anything, that's saying something.

A whirl around Claudio's shop, Volpetti, was what sent us out of Rome to begin with, in a quest to meet the people who make the things Paolo and I wanted to eat and import to Bangkok. His romanticism pulled us into this long trip, and it all happened one afternoon, while the shop was closed, and then dragged long into the night.

After that anchovy, there was a mess of runny burrata over which Claudio recklessly grated bottarga, speckling the glass deli case with flecks of orange roe. That was his way: He insisted that you eat. Maybe you groan with pleasure. Or sigh, quietly. I scratched my head above my temple, like a mathematician trying to solve a problem. The stuff Claudio sold does things to you. His delivery, part magician and part tactician, didn't hurt either.

Claudio's smile grew wider as a bottle of Brunello came down off the shelf and into small glasses, and his enthusiasm rose again as he sliced soft, sweet sheets of Culatello to eat. He draped the slices on his forearms, because it looks ridiculous (he, himself, is a ham) and because he wanted the meat to warm up to room temperature. Culatello is Italy's most expensive style of ham, aged in the bladder of hogs and baptized in red wine, before resting for three years or more in a cool, damp cellar.

While we're on the topic of hams, Claudio had forty-one kinds of prosciutto crudo—cured from raw pork, never cooked—opened and ready for slicing in his shop. "The central philosophy here is quality," he said, his arms draped in pink slices of pig.

One Monday afternoon, Paolo, our photographer Jason, Claudio, and I gathered in Claudio's shop to eat. This was while I was still falling in love with the food of Rome, and I remember it because this afternoon helped cement that love. The shop closed each day from 2:30 to 4:30. As we sat and stared into the cheese case, I noticed passersby outside doing the same—ogling the two hundred varieties that Claudio described as his "mosaic."

Then, like a child, he grabbed a wheel of ten-year-old Bitto, from Lombardy. The cheese is concave, he explained, from a long ride down mountains on the side of a donkey. He showed me which part of my mouth I should use to taste it by opening his mouth wide and pointing to the rear of his tongue. Then he hung two sausages from his belt—two shrunken, leathery meatballs—and broke out into laughter. "They're called *coglione di mulo* [donkey's balls]!" We ate the donkey's cheese and the balls together. It was a delicious schtick.

Later, Claudio led us into his narrow prep kitchen, past staff in white jackets who silently wrapped sausages in paper, and parcels of cheese with hemp twine. He motioned toward a small staircase, and whistled through his teeth.

Paolo doesn't fit as neatly in the narrow corridors of Claudio's basement, nor do I. But we climbed down the ladder-like stairs. We rubbed up against huge wheels of Parmigiano-Reggiano—each weighing almost ninety pounds. Pressure and time develop moist crystals inside them, like diamonds. His selection of Parmesan outshines anyone else's.

There are also hams there—hams from Norcia, hams from Parma, salami from Naples, spicy 'nduja, and that mystifyingly delicious Culatello. The air in the cellar smells deeply of a fine fermentation—a bouquet of salt, nuts, and yeast. It's almost like the smell of soft, buttery leather in a new car you could never afford. You wish this magic little place was yours. You feel a short stab of sadness that it isn't.

"The smell . . . it's like a young woman," Claudio creepily said to me, raising his Roman nose, breathing deep. I'm sure that's not true, but I understood his intention.

Later, Claudio, Paolo, and I climbed back up the stairs and continued to eat: a small spoonful of syrupy balsamic from Modena that has the perfect fruit and acid balance of the best botrytis wines; farm cheeses that rang with rot and barnyard, packed in hay; unfiltered olive oils whose tannins curled the tongue and burned your throat. There was colatura di alici, the fish sauce made from fermented anchovy, which we ate atop more mozzarella. That drop of fish sauce sent us, a year later, to find the best ones, in Cetara.

Claudio's shop was both a throwback to the old-fashioned delis that Romans used to stop by on their way home and a huge step forward in terms of sourcing and selection. There are few places that packed this many wonderful products into such a small space, so gracefully. In fact, I can't think of any.

But Claudio was getting old, just as it became harder to compete in modern Rome. Butcher shops, delis, and grocers were neighborhood affairs, places to stop on the way home from work, or after dropping the kids at school, while considering dinner. To cook a great Italian meal, you might wander into Volpetti for some Parmesan, fresh pasta, and olive oil. Then, to a local butcher for fresh meat, and finally, to a grocer for plum tomatoes, an onion, parsley, some garlic.

But in Rome they're consolidating, just like everywhere else. A few minutes away, giant "artisanal" retailer Eataly had opened a Rome location, with unprecedented buying power, cheaper prices, and, according to some, free rent. And while consumers now are trained to consider the artisanal nature of products, shouldn't we treat the art of the product selection, and the passion of those who devote their lives to selling it, the same way?

The afternoon we spent with Claudio stands out in my mind because it was an incredible introduction to Italian products; one that cemented my love for this food, and the abject devotion of its followers.

We drank another bottle of wine with Claudio and considered heading back to Paolo's house. But then his brother, Stefano, called to say he was heading into town. Claudio, who at sixty-seven years old didn't seem to miss an opportunity for a night out, decided to join us.

And so we headed out into the street, tipsy with wine. We walked behind Claudio, who had a bent back and a childlike gait, the pied piper of food products. We walked past relics of ancient Rome, and he stopped to drink from a fountain on the roadside. He gracefully balanced on his front left foot, knee bent, back hunched, his right heel pointed at the night sky. He pressed his thumb on one side of the fountain and water shot from the ancient spout right into his mouth.

I tried it, and got wet.

ACKNOWLEDGMENTS

FROM JARRETT:

This book is for my mother, Jane, who taught me how to appreciate good food; and for my father, Jim, who made me understand the importance of hard work. And for my wife, Candice, who painted the beautiful maps in these pages, and so gracefully managed my frequent trips to Italy, while building a family and a restaurant, together.

I wouldn't have been able to write this book without the friendship, advice, and generosity of my coauthor, Paolo. You are a brother to me. And to Pia, the best home cook I've ever known, and Stefano, for everything you've done at La Santola. You've all treated me like family, from the start.

To Jason Lang, for your patience and your gift. (Now get back in the van. One more stop!)

To Francis Lam, for believing in two guys with an Italian restaurant in Bangkok.

To Zack Waldman and Almerindo Portfolio. To Michael Ferchak and Alex Browne, who believed in me when I needed it most.

I'd like to thank my friends and mentors—both in the kitchen and behind a keyboard—for their guidance. To the Shanghai crew, Brad Turley and Eric Johnson and Jason Casey and Kelley Lee, who tolerated my longing to open a restaurant, and who kindly suggested that I shouldn't (perhaps I should have listened). To David Thompson, my dear and crazy friend, for taking me under your tattered wing and inspiring me both as a writer and as a cook. To

Andy Ricker, whose words help spring me from my first restaurant. To Rick and Dianne Bayless, for your generosity and advice. To Dylan and Bo, Chalee and Prin, and Tim, and the rest of the proud community of chefs in Bangkok. To the Black Sheep fam in Hong Kong.

To Jim and Deb Fallows, for your kindness and guidance as I navigated the world as a young writer (I'm still coming for my sandals!). To Anthony Bourdain, for opening my eyes to all the possibilities of traveling through food. To Corby Kummer and Ed Behr. To Mark Kitto, for my first writing gig, and Michael Cole. To Trefor Moss, my former editor and lifelong friend, and Adam Williams and Charlene Dy and the whole 8 Days crew. We made food writing in a cloud of kerosene smoke fun.

To Michael White, Jean-Georges (and Danny!), Ken Hom, Leela, and everyone else that so kindly supported this book.

To Dado and Steve.

Finally, I'd like to thank everyone who appears in these pages. Italy has been kind and gracious, occasionally infuriating, and always fascinating. There's plenty more to come, I suppose.

FROM PAOLO:

To Pia, my mother. I love you so much. You gave me everything.

And also to my father, who introduced me to so many amazing things to eat, and the mentality of hard work.

To Stefano Vitaletti, my brother, ready to lend a helping

hand at any time. Your support in helping us find so many interesting people made this book possible.

To Jarrett. You are awesome to deal with an asshole like me.

To Jason. We started in Parking Toys and ended up on the Via Appia. Much love.

I also can't forget the people who shaped my life throughout my career:

To Graziano Bonacina, my first real head chef, who introduced me to the old-fashioned romance of the kitchen.

To Domenico e Leonardo di Clemente, who mentored me during the most amazing two years, and taught me another world of techniques that would change my mind about food.

To Martin Knaubert, the "German Tanker," for showing me how to lead a team.

To Marco Bax, who taught me so much and didn't let me give up.

To Riya Sawamiwas (Jean), who loved what we were doing and supported us to the max, and to the opening team at Appia, who helped bring a dream to life.

To the Bangkok crew who has always been supportive and helpful: Dylan and Bo, Tim, Daniel, Billy, Brian, and the rest of the chefs and hooligans who were there for us from the beginning.

And last but not least, to my beautiful wife, June, who has allowed me to spend fifteen hours a day in the restaurant and continues to love and support me while raising our two amazing creatures, Giulio and Giorgio.

INDEX